UFOS:
KEY TO INNER PERFECTION

by

Bryce Burleigh Bond

Additional Material:

Timmothy Green Beckley, Marc Brinkerhoff and Shawn Robbins

LET THERE BE LIGHT

Intuitive art by Carol Ann Rodriquez

UFOS: Key To Inner Perfection
by
Bryce Burleigh Bond

Published by Timothy Green Beckley

This edition Copyright 2015 by Bryce Burleigh Bond and Timothy Green Beckley dba Inner Light/Global Communications

All rights reserved. No part of these manuscripts may be copied or reproduced by any mechanical or digital methods and no excerpts or quotes may be used in any other book or manuscript without permission in writing by the Publisher, Global Communications/Inner Light/Conspiracy Journal, except by a reviewer who may quote brief passages in a review.

Revised Edition

Published in the United States of America By
Inner Light Publications
Box 753 · New Brunswick, NJ 08903

Staff Members
Timothy G. Beckley, Publisher and Editor
Carol Ann Rodriguez, Assistant to the Publisher, Artist
Sean Casteel, General Associate Editor
Tim R. Swartz, Graphics and Editorial Consultant
William Kern, Editorial and Art Consultant

Sign Up On The Web For Our Free Weekly Newsletter
and Mail Order Version of Conspiracy Journal
and Bizarre Bazaar
www.ConspiracyJournal.com

**Order Hot Line: 1-732-602-3407
PayPal: MrUFO8@hotmail.com**

CONTENTS

Introduction: Bryce Bond, The 007 of UFO Experiencers
—Timothy Green Beckley v

Bryce Bond—Onboard A Physical UFO And His Alien Encounter Of The Third Kind
—Marc Brinkerhoff xi

My Close Encounters With President Jimmy Carter And Bryce Bond
—Shawn Robbins xvii

UFOs: A Personal Encounter—Bryce Bond 1

Higher Techniques To Inner Perfection—Bryce Bond

Acknowledgments 82
Preface 82
Self-Discovery 86
Self 90
Unconditional Love Is The Highest Form Of Service 98
Needs And Wants 99
What Goes Around, Comes Around 100
The Bird That Flies Highest Sees Furthest 104
Heaven And Hell 106
Seven Year Cycles In A Human's Life 109
The Magus 117
The God Within 118
Your Thoughts Create Your Conditions 120
Relatedness 124
Community 140
We Never Get More Than We Can Handle 145
Seeker Beware 150
Our Earth, Our World 157
The Earth Is A Living Entity 160
Time 163
Life Is An Endless Series of Events 167
Past, Present, Future 172
Developing Psychic Energy—Sonic Breathing 176
Autosuggestion: Valuable Techniques 184
How To Meditate 187
We Can All Be Perfect 190
About The Authors 197

Timothy Green Beckley, Editor and Publisher

BRYCE BOND – THE 007 OF UFO EXPERIENCERS

By Timothy Green Beckley

In the beginning, Bryce Bond and I had a very casual relationship, if you could even call it that.

It was the mid-60s – around 1966 I think – and I was helping noted UFO researcher James W. Moseley to promote his regular flying saucer club meetings that he held at one of several midtown Manhattan Hotels, mainly the Woodstock and the Diplomat. These were not high class joints in those days, and Times Square was pretty unseemly in general during this period. But, hey, you could rent a lecture hall that held 200 people for like $50. Try to get it for under a thousand bucks today! And if your guest speaker had appeared on the Long John Nebel show the night before and L. J. himself promised to show up, for $125 more you could squeeze as many people as possible into a larger banquet room and toss out your 350 folding chairs till there was standing room only. Not that you were going to make any money, regardless how you cooked the door, as admission was either 50 cents or a sawbuck back in those days. It was typical to split the money with the speaker who had to make his way on to the next town by rail or bus.

Anyway, Bryce was hosting a nightly pop music show called Moondile out of WTFM, a radio station somewhere on the outskirts of the City. Bryce was not a big fan of rock and roll or blues and limited himself to spinning low-key jazz and Frank Sinatra hits. But I guess he had enough interest in the UFO subject that he would announce our "Saucer News" club meetings ("Saucer News" was the name of the magazine J. W. M. was publishing at the time and of which I eventually became Managing Editor) as a public service notice free of charge since we were obviously a nonprofit group. (But have saucers ever made anyone money?). Just recently I found out from a longtime friend of both Bryce and myself that Mr. Bond had been a "closet UFO experiencer" since an early age.

During one of our brief conversations held while Old Blue Eyes could be heard crooning away in the background – the melody going out over the air to God knows how many desperate souls who enjoyed this kind of pop music (I say this being a big fan of rock and roll, unlike my friend Bryce) – Bryce said that he was going to England on vacation to get away from work for a while. He wanted to know if I had any suggestions as to what he might do "off the beaten track" while visiting jolly ole England.

I had just published a book called "UFO PROPHECY" by a Briton named Arthur Shuttlewood. It was a remarkable – almost sensationalistic – volume about the ongoing wave of UFO sightings over the tiny hamlet of Warminster, located on Salisbury Plain a stone's throw from the megalithic Stonehenge. The Warminster phenomena, first dubbed "The Thing," kicked in on Christmas Eve 1964 as a loud hum like the sound made by a "million bees" and filled the evening sky, tossing a woman to the ground and pinning her there as she was on the way to church services. The sightings of lights and ships began on a regular basis shortly thereafter and attracted hordes of observers to such locations as Cradle and Starr Hills on the skirts of town.

In the book, Shuttlewood, editor of the daily "Warminster Journal," revealed how his town had gone from a placid spot on the countryside to a locale where you could go almost any night and have a personal sighting – or encounter – with a UFO. All you had to do was go to one or two observations points – Cradle Hill or Starr Hill. Maybe bring along a small telescope or a pair of binoculars and perhaps a torch light in case you felt comfortable in trying to communicate with the craft by signaling to it as it hovers up in the heavens, almost hidden among the stars, but decisively brighter and somewhat pulsating. You will, I am told, almost immediately know the difference.

I quickly dashed off a letter of introduction and sent it air mail to Arthur Shuttlewood in advance of Bryce's departure from the States.

The next thing I heard was that the two gentlemen had gotten along rather famously and that Bond had become, in essence, Shuttlewood's sky-watching buddy. Word came back to me from several sources that Bryce had not only seen a UFO but that he had felt the psychic energies given off by standing inside a crop circle (one of the early ones at that) and that he had had several unexplainable experiences which are detailed throughout the pages of this book. And, although he does not speak of it directly in the typed manuscript he gave me, I did find out from a mutual associate that Bryce had undergone his own encounter with the crew of a landed space pod who took him for a brief sojourn in their craft and brought him back safely. Apparently this was all part of several "missing time" episodes that took place while he was staying in Warminster. As Shuttlewood tells it, he and his fellow sky-watchers insisted that their comrade had been gone for hours while to Bond it seemed like a much shorter period of time had expired.

Now such an experience might shake up almost everyone else but our intrepid newsman and radio host. Far from being shaken up by his otherworldly adventure, Bryce was elated. He says he felt high on life and had to do whatever he could to change his calling in life. He no longer felt like he had an affinity for Frank Sinatra tunes. He knew that he had to do whatever he could to make the Earth a better place in which to live, regardless of whether or not his peers in the entertainment business might make fun of him for discussing such matters as if they were actually true.

Almost the minute he arrived back at WTFM, he marched into the Program Director's office and said he was quitting his job, that he could no longer do something so, to him, superficial. He had to be free to help others and save humanity. Well, OK, perhaps I am going a bit overboard, but I do know that when I saw Bryce next he was no longer the hip DJ but had committed himself to a "higher purpose." He began lecturing at my NY School of Occult Arts and Sciences (one of the first of many-to-come metaphysical groups in the U.S.), became an instructor for Silva Mind Control and a well-known faith healer in the area.

UFOs had changed his life as they have done for many other individuals – both positively and negatively. Sometime later, Bryce began working on a book he called "Keys to Inner Perfection" which he asked me to publish and which I did. There was nothing really significant about UFOs in the book but I felt that what Bryce had to say was important enough to print a small edition of 2,000 copies. He did discuss one near-death-experience which I found both compelling and chilling. Over the ensuing years, Bryce's experience would be given much attention by reviewers discussing his book. In any case, I figured that Bryce had such a good media personality that he would be able to help sell many copies by appearing on radio and TV in the metropolitan area.

Unfortunately, Bryce Bond never lived to see his book published. He passed away less than a month before the cartons arrived at our warehouse from the printer. I was always sad about this fact as I knew Bryce had put his heart and soul into preparing this publication.

"Keys to Inner Perfection" sold moderately well over the next several decades. We were recently down to just one copy on the shelf, not because we had sold all two thousand copies, but because our storage area, which was a freight car parked on a back lot near the train yard, was destroyed little by little by weather and, frankly, even rodents that chewed into the cartons of boxes.

I was, of course, determined not to sell our only copy even though we had an order for it. I decided to return the customer's money and tell them that we were going to scan the book and reissue it. I sent it off to our graphics department headed by the Adman himself, Wm. Kern.

There was no rush on this, I told BK. Something told me the book was missing something. Initially, I decided I would add a couple of pages of my own ramblings about my meetings with Mr. Bond. Then, as "luck" would have it, I was going through one of my forty file cabinet drawers and came across this black binder. I opened up the dusty volume and found a partially-edited, typewritten manuscript by none other than Bryce Bond on his experiences in the U.K.

I vaguely remembered that Bryce had given me this book around the time he had submitted the "Keys to Inner Perfection" manuscript and asked me to publish it at a later date if I could. The years passed, the pages became almost brittle and changed color from white to a brownish-yellow.

Looking over the manuscript, I realized this was the missing "Key" to the puzzle and that the book by Bryce would now take on a greater importance beyond being just a backlist title of little consequence. Thus the book you are now either holding in your hands or reading as an e-book. After doing some research, it became apparent that UFOs had impacted Bryce's life more than he had let on. There were even elements of his experiences which he had never let out of the bag. But now, with the help of Marc Brinkerhoff's and Shawn Robbins' recollections, we are able to put this jigsaw puzzle together.

Frankly, I can't help but believe that somehow Bryce was behind all this. As he looked down from some lofty place in space or a heavenly realm, I am sure he wanted others to discover the glory of his transformation experiences so that they might experience their own.

I think Bryce put me up to doing this because his complete story was never really told.

I had no real intentions of reprinting "Keys to Inner Perfection," but someone ordered a copy after all these years and I was down to my last copy and didn't want to part with it.

A few days later, I came across Bryce's UFO manuscript, which I had in the bottom of one of my many file cabinets – one of 40 file drawers – and realized the work needed to be updated and a "final" version published.

Graphite Drawing of Bond's contact with the alien beings—by Marc Brinkerhoff

Marc Brinkerhoff, Artist, Psychic, Contactee

BRYCE BOND – ONBOARD A PHYSICAL UFO AND HIS ALIEN ENCOUNTER OF THE THIRD KIND

By Marc Brinkerhoff

The picture)facing page) that accompanies this personal tribute is a graphite illustration that I did under my close friend Bryce Bond's guidance and direction in 1987. It depicts his physical onboard spaceship encounter with spiritually advanced alien beings. The UFO encounter happened in the area called Cradle Hill in Warminster, Wiltshire, England, in 1974. He had several UFO experiences on subsequent nights at that same location. He was at first very hesitant to discuss his closer-than-life-encounter with a group of extraterrestrials in what for over a decade remained a virtual UFO hotspot where a person could see a UFO on almost any given occasion.

Bryce Bond was visiting Arthur Shuttlewood, who was showing a group of people the area where the UFO sightings were frequently occurring. Arthur lived in Warminster on Portnoy Street. The time was around 2:00 PM on a week day. Arthur took them down a dirt road on a farm where the owners knew Arthur and allowed people to go in the back field with him. Arthur was discussing the "Invisible Walker" with the group, explaining how in certain areas you can hear the footsteps of someone very big walking and see the grass get pushed down, but there would be no physical person there. He described how the footsteps will go past a person and stop a short distance away. No one was ever hurt by the "Invisible Walker," just amazed and bewildered. Bryce had experienced the "Invisible Walker" a couple of times in Warminster, and so did I when I was out in the Starr Hill Valley fields. They often saw "nothing" – maybe a vague outline of a tall being against a hedge or fence. But they could hear the footsteps shuffling around on gravel and stone pavement as well as lumbering through the hedge rows.

While Arthur was talking to the people, he encouraged them to go off to sky-watch a little and commune with the energies and meditate. So, Bryce took off down a little dirt tractor path that led to another field. He said he ducked through a fence and went into a field with long, golden, 18-inch-tall grass or possibly hay. He walked about 20 to 30 feet in and stopped and stood for a while, just looking at the sky for UFOs. He sent out telepathic thoughts of peace and love to the universe. After a while, he noticed that he didn't hear the people in Shuttlewood's group talking anymore and thought they had all just settled down to meditate a bit.

Bryce said it was a beautiful day with the sun shining and some clouds moving slowly in the sky. He was standing in the field and had closed his eyes to send out a prayer when he noticed an unusual energy building up around his aura. He thought it was very peaceful and had a loving vibration, as if he was being caressed by Angels.

Suddenly he smelled the intense and intoxicating beautiful scent of Lily of the Valley flowers with a mixture of honey! He felt very calm and almost euphoric with the smell and the energy surrounding him. He began to feel a tingling pressure in his temples and surrounding his head; he also heard a strange whirring sound above him. He tried to look up and turn around and he couldn't. He was held still in place by a gentle pressure. He opened his eyes and could see forming around him a perfect circle in the grass as it was being pressed gently down in a clockwise direction. Then the energy changed in front of his eyes, a bit blurry for a few seconds. Then he could see, in the energy superimposed around him with the grass still moving, the interior of a spaceship and some translucent people! In a few more seconds he was standing in a physical spaceship and was confronted with a beautiful space woman with large blue eyes, dark hair, and dressed in a form-fitting, medium-blue space suit. In front of Bryce stood a smiling benevolent alien being who was about seven feet tall. He had kind, large, amber-green eyes, no hair, a short and somewhat flattened nose, very small ears and long slender fingers. He was wearing a dark blue-gray spacesuit with a reflective belt and a shimmering silver white cape. Both of the aliens spoke to Bryce telepathically and asked him some questions, like "How are you feeling? Are you thirsty?" and said "We have been watching you for some time." Then he had telepathic information transferred into his thoughts and mind regarding energy and healing. He said the alien with the cape was a wise teacher or master and he felt humbled in front of him. He remembered that for a second he thought of how beautiful the woman was and he felt that she heard his thoughts and looked down and smiled. He told me that he then felt embarrassed to have thought that because he knew she was very advanced spiritually and he was acting like a lustful man in his mind. The space woman sent him a thought of "It's ok, let it go." Then she directed him to look out the porthole windows. Bryce said he could see our planet Earth in the distance with the stars. He also recalled how beautiful and blue the planet was from space.

After what seemed like almost 15 minutes or so, Bryce was told they were bringing him back, and that someday maybe they would meet again. He thanked them all for the experience and said "God bless you all." The aliens smiled at him and said "Good-bye and bless you too." Bryce told me he suddenly began feeling the tingling energy throughout his body with the smell of flowers surrounding him! Then in seconds he was standing back in the golden grass again, but the sky was now a bit darker. He was standing in the center of a perfect crop circle!

Soon he felt the energy shifting around him and he began to hear the sound of a slight wind in his ears and birds chirping in the distance. Arthur was yelling, "Bryce! Bryce! Where are you! Bryce!!!" "I'm here Arthur! In the field!" Bryce answered, as he now could finally move his feet, and he sprinted in seconds through the field, under the fence and up the dirt path towards Arthur. "Where have you been? We've been searching for hours!" Bryce replied, "I was on a spaceship! Come see the circle I was standing in Arthur!"

Bryce and Arthur, as well as some of the group, walked towards the field. Then Arthur, upon seeing the crop circle, exclaimed, "Oh, my! We searched around the area and you were not here! Bryce, you had disappeared!" Bryce was amazed. They had searched for him and he was missing – what a story this will make, he thought! Bryce asked, "Arthur? What time is it, because my watch has stopped?" Arthur said, "Bryce, it is close to 5:00 PM, and you have been missing for a few hours." Bryce exclaimed, "Wow! That's incredible, because it felt like 10 to 15 minutes to me." With a look of pure delight and awe, Arthur said, "They took you man, they took you for a ride. Let's go talk about it over some tea now, mate!" So, Bryce and Arthur walked with the rest of the group out to the dirt road and drove back to the town of Warminster to share tea. Later they discussed the amazing encounter Bryce had as well as the UFO sightings all the people had that day. Bryce mentioned how having that experience changed him forever, as well as the small group of people who were witnesses.

As for Arthur Shuttlewood? Well, he knew that what Bryce had experienced was very real and he was happy for him. Arthur knew the Space People were trying to enlighten mankind on Earth and came in peace. Bryce said, "It was one more story for the book." Bryce told me that during the experience he had no fear and felt unconditional love and immense joy while in the space beings presence.

Bryce Bond never got to write his UFO information and encounters book. So, I am writing his story here as he told it to me back in 1978, and again in 1987, when I drew the picture for him of his onboard UFO encounter.

WORDS ABOUT BRYCE'S PASSING – AS STRANGE AS HIS LIFE

In Memory of Bryce Burleigh Bond. (12/21/1928 to 1/12/1992)

Bryce hosted his own national TV shows 'UFO Update' and 'Dimensions in Parapsychology with Bryce Bond.' He was an Inspirational Speaker/Interviewer/Teacher/Lecturer, Professional Photographer, Writer, UFO Contactee, UFO Investigator, Metaphysician, Coordinator and Leader of Spiritual Journeys to other countries. He was also at one time in the U.S. Navy, was a Member of the Spiritual Healers of Great Britain, Author of the book 'Higher Techniques to Inner Perfection' published by Inner Light Publications, Ex-Radio DJ and Talk Show Host, and Record Producer. He always gave Unconditional Love to animals and all the people he met and knew.

On the day of Tuesday, January 7, 1992, Bryce lost consciousness from what was later diagnosed as a brain aneurism. Somehow, and we do not know how (but perhaps through Angelic intervention), Bryce was able to dial 911 to get an ambulance to come to his apartment. The paramedics were able to get into his front door because, somehow, it was open and unlocked. Yet when they came into the apartment, Bryce was found on his apartment floor in his hallway heading towards his door. They could not understand how he could have made a phone call or unlocked a door while heading to it if he was unconscious. That was a mystery.

Now, at the same time, friends were waiting for him at the UN, and, when he didn't show up, they called me at work. I knew Bryce was going to be giving a talk that day but I didn't know what time he was scheduled to speak. He had been preparing to go to the UN, where he was to give a short lecture on metaphysics and healing to a group of people. Our mutual friends knew that everyday Bryce would call me while I was at work, or I would call him around 9:30 to 10:00 AM. I had known Bryce since 1975, and we had talked every day for years and occasionally a few times a day. So, when I didn't get a call from him that morning, I called his number and got the phone just continually ringing. Usually his answering machine would pick up. I felt this was very strange and not like Bryce at all to not have his answering machine on. I told my friend that called me that I had not heard from Bryce and I tried to call him, too. She knew that I could not leave work to go over to his apartment. So, my friend said she would call the police. Not long after she called me back to tell me that he had been taken to the emergency room and was in a hospital now. I did not like the feeling I was getting for Bryce, and later I left work to go over to the hospital with my wife when my day was through.

Bryce was kept on life support for many days. Friends and family came to show their love for him and to say their good-byes at the hospital. We were told that he was being kept alive for his organs, and that he had really been brain-dead since Wednesday, January 8.

I met Bryce out-of-body on January 7th at the hospital. He was young looking at the time and was holding his head and complaining of a headache and not feeling that good. He was a little confused but he recognized me in my tall, blonde-haired "other self" body and we talked. I told him what happened to him and how he was on a lot of medicine keeping his body in a coma-like condition along with a machine that helped him breathe. He looked at me with a look that was so sad. I knew that he knew intuitively that he was in bad shape. We hugged and I helped him cross over as we walked through an energy flux-like doorway through a wall. I took him to get energized on the higher dimension in a spaceship. There we both learned that Bryce could not come back to his body and that the damage to his brain would make him like a vegetable. Bryce had once survived a near death experience in England in 1973 in which he was clinically dead for over 20 minutes. So, this time we thought he could come back through a miracle or something like a spontaneous healing. At the age of just 64, Bryce's time seemed to be cut short here on Earth. I know that he chose to leave and to help others and continue his spiritual work on the other side. With deep sadness in my heart, I would miss my best friend Bryce always. I said my good-bye to him while in the hospital room on January 8th. Since then I have seen him many times while out-of-body over the years, and he is happy, young looking at around 30 years of age. He sometimes works on the spaceship with me. In space his name is Solnahma and he teaches, lectures and helps people discover the beautiful sights on the other dimensions.

Bryce Bond was taken off life support and passed away on January 12, 1992, in New York City.

Shawn Robbins, Psychic

MY CLOSE ENCOUNTERS WITH
PRESIDENT JIMMY CARTER AND BRYCE BOND
By Shawn Robbins

Be patient a few moments while I set the stage to tell you about my friendship with the late Bryce Bond.

My relationship with Bryce actually goes back a few years before I met him, but that shouldn't really matter because premonitions are a common occurrence in my life. For years I have been a professional psychic and a medium, having trained with the famous ghost hunter Hans Holzer. This was before there were any paranormal ghost hunting shows on television and before everyone was an "expert" in the field. Hans would take me to a place that was known to be haunted, and I would pick up on any lingering spirits who did not realize they had passed on. I also taught at Tim Beckley's NY School of Occult Arts And Sciences. This was probably one of the first metaphysical schools in the country, and many soon-to-be-famous paranormal researchers cut their teeth there.

Back in 1973 or 1974 I was lecturing on the paranormal in Louisville, KY. Call it fate, Kismet, or whatever – I had a psychic flash to look up Jimmy Carter, then Governor of Georgia. Yes, he was listed in the phone book at the time and I was nevertheless a bit surprised that he answered my call. In fact, he was quite receptive when I told him I was a psychic and that he would become the next President of the United States. During our phone conversation, Carter told me that he had experienced a UFO sighting. Our call lasted for about five minutes. The details of his sighting are a matter of record.

Apparently, he was standing outside with a group who had attended one of his political fundraisers when all of a sudden they saw a mysterious object in the sky. Others in the same area would report sightings on subsequent days, including the landing of a craft near the town's water tower. A movie is being shot and edited about this event as I write these words. The film is called "The Leary Lights." Here is what the IMDb site has to say about this film:

Carter's UFO: The Truth Behind The Leary Lights tells the never-before-heard story behind President Jimmy Carter's UFO sighting and explores the rash of sightings that continued until 1973. The Leary Lights were seen by dozens of witnesses, including many members of law enforcement. The film also features the first-ever interview with Fred Hart, the last living member of Carter's group who witnessed the UFO event alongside the future President.

I met Bryce Bond years later and we eventually became good friends. We saw and talked with one another quite often. One day I happened to mention to Bryce that I had spoken to President Carter about his UFO sighting. I don't think Bryce and I had ever discussed the subject, certainly not in any detail. But, upon hearing this, Bryce seemed to open up quite a bit on the subject and revealed to me something that I doubt he had revealed to anyone else at that point.

Bryce told me when he was younger he had also seen a UFO and felt that somehow he was in mental contact with the beings onboard this craft.

I didn't think anything about this as, being a believer, it seemed quite normal that he would have a sighting. But as time went on, I began to feel that Bryce was trying to make contact with these beings through me. Many times he would hypnotize me and would ask if I was getting any messages from the unknown. One has to remember that I was trained by Hans Holzer to become a medium, and anyone can check on this because I am in many of Hans' early books. I truly believe Bryce felt he was an outsider in search of who he was, and that his mission was to be a UFO contactee who could communicate with the people. I believe the book you are now reading bears out this concept.

I myself have continued my evolution with the UFOs. Three years ago I was in Puerto Vallarta, Mexico. At 2 A.M. I went out on the balcony for a smoke. I saw what appeared to be two bright cylinders hovering over the mountain tops. They moved fast and in different directions, followed by a third cylindrical object. They were something I had never seen before, and, somewhere in the back of my mind, I can't help but believe Bryce was behind this sighting so that my belief would be cemented for all time. I certainly believe we are not alone!

Shawn Robbins

January 2015

NY NY

Newspapers and Newsletter Journals Revealed The Warminster Mystery

PHOTOGRAPHS FROM CRADLE HILL
John C. Ben

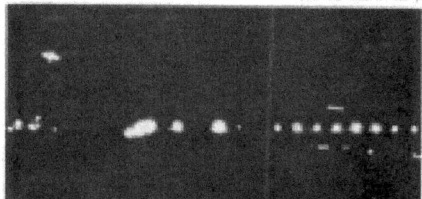

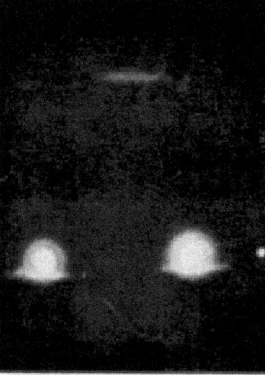

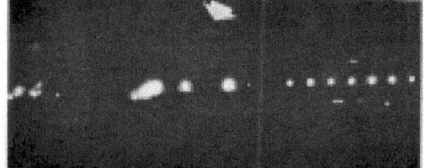

UFOs: Key To Inner Perfection

UFOs: A PERSONAL ENCOUNTER

The True Adventures of a Psychic Researcher,

BRYCE BURLEIGH BOND

by Bryce Bond

INTRODUCTION

"With our rapidly growing understanding of the universe has dawned the profound belief that we are not alone.

"Not long ago at a symposium on this subject, Professor George Wald, Nobel laureate and professor of biology at Harvard, declared, 'I think there is no question that we live in an inhabited universe that has life all over it.' His view was echoed by Professor Richard Berendzen, an astronomer from Boston University: 'The question has become not so much one of if as of where. And of these forms of life are probably far more technically advanced than ourselves.'"

NATIONAL GEOGRAPHIC MAGAZINE, Mat 1974

Article: **THE INCREDIBLE UNIVERSE**, pg. 624

by Kenneth F. Weaver

Often when I introduce myself, "Hello, I'm Bryce Bond," a quizzical eyebrow will go up and someone will ask, "Is your name for real?"

Yes, my name is very much for real, but I do share with the fictional Ian Fleming character, James Bond, not only a name, but an occupation, or shall we say a preoccupation to solve the mysteries of life.

I, too, am an investigator. However, my research deals with the real, you might say super-real aspects of life, often much stranger than fiction.

UFOs: Key To Inner Perfection

I have spent most of my years questioning myself and the world in which I live. Notice that the word quest begins the word questioning. My quest has been to find the answers to mysterious and unknown questions about man and his world. I delve deeply to find these answers. Being a man of action, much like the fictional Bond, I go after my prey. My desire to know has led me to investigate areas of metaphysics, psychic healing, meditation; many areas of the paranormal including psychokinesis, mediumship, spiritualism, teleportation, clairvoyance, as well as intense research into the question of Unidentified Flying Objects. You name it. I've gone out and looked at it, squarely in the face.

I've traveled extensively to interview psychically gifted and spiritually developed individuals in the United States and abroad. These meetings and subsequent experiences have radically changed my view of the world. Of special interest and excitement has been my interviews with highly knowledgeable people involved with the sighting and recording of Unidentified Flying Objects and the higher intelligences who pilot these "craft". The four professionals presented in this book are reliable, stable personalities within their communities, as well as being men of repute in their chosen occupational fields. They have each been separately led through their personal interest and experience to closely and carefully investigate the UFO phenomena. Each has a special point of view, but all conclude that Unidentified Flying Objects do exist in our dimension of space and time.

Arthur Shuttlewood, now deceased, had over twenty-four years experience as a British journalist, making him a professional and trained news observer not prone to fantasies or science fiction. He recorded the actual sighting and contact with over one thousand UFOs. He was the author of several books dealing with the subject: THE WARMINSTER MYSTERY, UFO PROPHECY, and UFOS: KEY TO THE NEW AGE, etc. He was considered to be one of the great UFO authorities in England. Arthur Shuttlewood was a man of high standing in his community. He was a former Grenadier Guardsman, member of the Air Ministry Constabulary and was Warminster Urban Councillor.

Ivan Sanderson, now deceased, was a world-renowned scientific researcher with Masters Degrees in Zoology, Geology, and Botany from Cambridge University in England. He travelled the world over many times in pursuit of answers to the unexplainable. In the latter part of his life he resided in New Jersey where he founded **THE SOCIETY FOR THE INVESTIGATION OF THE UNEXPLAINED** and presided as Trustee and Administrative Director. His wife continues to oversee his work. He was author of many books and articles dealing with the real physical world: **LIVING MAMMALS OF THE WORLD; THE CONTINENT WE LIVE ON; THIS TREASURED LAND**, to name a few; as well as books dealing with unknown phenomena: **UNINVITED VISITORS; "THINGS"; MORE "THINGS"; INVESTI-

UFOs: Key To Inner Perfection

GATING THE UNEXPLAINED. Ivan Sanderson began with a well grounded knowledge of our physical environment, then went on to project his highly disciplined scientific mind far beyond the world of the five senses. His conclusions will amaze you.

Brinsley Le Poer Trench, 8th Earl of Clancarty, (18 Sep, 1911 - 18 May, 1995) was an English researcher, author and international chairman of **CONTACT**, the largest UFO movement in the world with active branches in almost every country. The aim of **CONTACT** is to present evidence of extraterrestrial visitors and to foster better understanding of them. Brinsley Le Poer Trench has investigated many civilizations including ancient Atlantis, Lemuria and Mu, as well as other planetary systems. He is the author of five books dealing with UFOs and beings of higher intelligence: ***THE SKY PEOPLE; MEN AMONG MANKIND; FORGOTTEN HERITAGE; OPERATION EARTH***, and the more recent ***ETERNAL SUBJECT***.

Dr. George King (1919-1997) was a great Metaphysician and founder of ***THE AETHERIUS SOCIETY*** in Britain and The United States. He was a man dedicated to the study of the science of being. Dr. King viewed the UFO question from a different perspective than our other spokesmen, bringing to the enquiry the view of a trained and gifted psychic and healer. He was author of many books: ***THE NINE FREEDOMS***, a book based on truths given to him by the Cosmic Master; ***THE TWELVE BLESSINGS***, a cosmic concept of an extension of the original teachings given Jesus; and a book called ***YOU ARE RESPONSIBLE***. Dr. King was also involved in ***OPERATION SUNBEAM***, which we will discuss anon.

I present this book after years of research and many visits with these renowned men of letters and science. I have not only spoken with these individuals, but I, too, have made face to face contact with UFOs. You will discover as you read on that UFOs and extraterrestrial beings are here among us now!

While the material presented in this book is for real, I submit it for your appraisal. It is still up to you, the reader, to decide if the following is fact or fiction. Join me in my adventures into the unknown. You have nothing to lose but your disbelief.

UFOs: Key To Inner Perfection

Arthur Shuttlewood
Bond's host in the UK.
Newsman, author, lecturer, contactee

UFOs: Key To Inner Perfection

PART 1

ARTHUR SHUTTLEWOOD AND THE WARMINSTER MYSTERY

CHAPTER 1

"I wish to dedicate this serious work, on what must obviously be a still-futuristic subject, to questing souls for the radiance of Truth and Light everywhere, both on this Earth and all the other inhabited regions of the vast Universe. I hope that it makes the right appeal to curious minds unsullied by prejudice or closed to possible enlightenment; and that it may further the knowledge of all who desire to gain even a little universal insight and understanding."

Arthur Shuttlewood; *THE WARMINSTER MYSTERY,* **dedication**

Contact with Arthur Shuttlewood began Saturday night, August 26th, 1972. While in England interviewing healers, psychics and UFO experts, I made an appointment with Arthur to discuss his view of the UFO question.

Bill Dysart, my good friend and English counterpart, drove me from Holdstone Downe, in Ilfracombe, near Bristol Bay where we had witnessed a ceremony conducted by Dr. George King which we'll discuss later.

Bill left me off and continued to London. I arrived late for my appointment with Arthur Shuttlewood which was scheduled for 5 PM. Mrs. Shuttlewood told me that Arthur had waited and then left on an errand but would return by 9 PM. It was then about 8:30 PM. I decided to check later transportation to London and survey the area.

Warminster at this time of night, even for a Saturday, was almost deserted. Only a few people ambled along the very narrow streets. I asked a couple where I could find the railroad station and they pointed the way. As I walked along I had a strange feeling that the tall brick walls of the buildings were watching me. It was as if this strangely quiet town with its overcast sky was setting the mood for what I was about to witness that evening.

UFOs: Key To Inner Perfection

I experienced deja vu, that feeling you often get when you somehow feel you've been somewhere before, though you are certain you have not. I seemed to know my way instinctively once having been directed and felt that all this had taken place already. I was merely reliving an old experience.

I found the station and the man in the baggage room kindly informed me that there were no more trains running that night. The last had left at 8:14 PM, but if I hurried I could catch the 8:45 PM from Salisbury. It was already 8:40 PM. I decided to leave my transportation back to London up to the powers that be.

I headed back to Arthur Shuttlewood's home. Warminster, England is a very special place where many mysterious things happen besides the constant sightings of UFOs. This quiet, clean little town with its quaint narrow archways and flower-lined paths is a place where the unexplained happens with regularity.

Warminster, the oldest part of Wessex, is the most ancient part of Britain. There are great gravitational anomalies and distortion areas around town. Just beyond the lines of Longleet, near Heaven's Gate there's a little village called Maiden Bradley where the water actually flows up hill. There's an inscription on an old water trough, perhaps a changing station in olden times, in the main street of the village where horses, foam-flecked and tired after long journeys could drink freely. There's a verse on the side which tells you that, "Here the rill flows uphill for a mile or more". It can be measured. There is no scientific sort of gauge for denying the fact that this is an absolute gravity anomaly.

All around Warminster, especially around UFO sighting points, Cradle and Starr Hills, for example, are ancient burial barrows that date back to about four thousand to forty-five thousand years ago. They rest between Stonehenge and Glastonbury. The meccas for all sorts of religious thoughts and attitudes in the past were situated between these two points. It is as if strong electromagnetic energies converge at these particular points of earth. There may be lines of power that extend from under the earth's surface and form gravitational interactions; thus, a giant gravitational grid framework is formed. Ancient civilizations seemed to follow certain—as they're now called— "ley lines", or lines of power, which radiate off the network. Perhaps it is this centering of electromagnetic energy which attracts the UFOs. Arthur Shuttlewood was to elaborate on this and other theories later.

I arrived back at the Shuttlewood's home. There was my host, Arthur, a tall, scholarly, neatly dressed Englishman. I explained why I had arrived so late. He understood. I found Arthur to be humorous, gentle, well mannered and intelligent. We shared our interest in journalism and in true investigation of the facts of existence. I learned that this warm, sincere gentleman definitely knows what he is writing about, knows about UFOs, knows the area and its people.

UFOs: Key To Inner Perfection

He told me that we might see something that evening. In a very blasé tone he stated, "It's a good night, Bryce. The low cloud cover seems to be going over a bit. I think you may see a UFO tonight. I believe you are destined to be here now."

We had a cup of tea and talked about how he had gotten involved with UFO investigating.

"It all began with a big bang, literally, around here. So many reputable people heard these sound vibrations on their roofs. Earthquake, earth tremor, seismographic equipment couldn't register them because they weren't coming from earth at all."

All Arthur's comments were stated as clear, precise fact. He continued. "They were coming down, beating sonic booms onto the roofs. As a journalist, I interviewed a number of people who were frightened by these things. It all began Christmas day and that might be quite relevant, in a nonscientific sense, if you know what I mean?"

I followed Arthur's every word, somehow feeling there was a deeper meaning to all he was saying.

"It began in 1964. My first book was called simply, THE WARMINSTER MYSTERY, because it was indeed an enigma, a mystery apparently insoluble. One couldn't solve it because one hadn't got sufficient clues. Then things really started to happen, sightings of various types of aeroform, the apparent non-tangibility of them. Although a few photographs were reproduced faithfully. As time went on, we had sufficient clues which formed a gradually, progressively coherent pattern. This gave us food for deeper thought than the merely superficial layer of thinking that everything we see is from another planet.

"We became more precise in our sightings. You know, Bryce, other dimensional forms and levels of existence do exist in the whole of the universal structure."

Not only Arthur's words, but his voice expressed the deep concern he has for clear thinking and accuracy. As I listened to him talk, my mind raced ahead to what he had said when I first arrived, "I think you may see a UFO tonight!". Was I to be one of the many who had made sightings in this area? Was I truly destined to come here at this time? Many questions filled my mind as I listened to Arthur speak. He continued.

"'**THE WARMINSTER MYSTERY'** listed hundreds of sightings by very reputable people: the head postmaster of the town, the vicar and his family, a hospital matron, a hospital physiotherapist, a chairman of the regional council, housing manager of the council, an ex-grenadier guard Army Major. His car had virtually

UFOs: Key To Inner Perfection

stopped dead in its tracks at forty miles an hour along a point where hundreds of motorists had suffered from shattered windscreens.

"All these things were pretty frightening, but, the point is that progressively having announced, having loudly knocked at the door of consciousness around here, whatever this intelligence was/is it made itself known.

"Though we call this intelligence 'alien', gradually the truth percolated through that this was not a hostile thing at all and we are now convinced of this. Nothing of a negative nature has happened since the original contact.

"'**THE WARMINSTER MYSTERY**' was simply a listing of sightings by reputable people. It was confirmation of evidence and testimony. Now, of course, there is worldwide testimony and gradually we interlock with that. We've got very good friends abroad, too, who share information with us. Even the people behind the Iron Curtain. I must say, the Russians are very interested in all this."

Arthur Shuttlewood really had me excited. By this time, after two cups of tea, I was anxious to get started. It was almost midnight and the hour of truth was quickly arriving. We had planned to go to Cradle Hill to await a sighting. Arthur called a taxi and as if by appointment, as soon as we reached the sidewalk, the taxi arrived. Somehow, I had the feeling that it was planned that way.

For those readers who may not know anything of the Warminster UFO sightings, the following brief explanation may shed some light on the enigma.

Warminster. Mention the name of this small Wiltshire town to any young ufologist, and the chances are you will receive a blank look. To us older students of British UFO research, you will get one or two reactions. Either a mocking smile and dismissive retort, or the subject of your question will elicit a dreamy expression, and then hopefully a long conversation will ensue, with memories of those long gone halcyon days and nights spent on the hills outside the town, scanning the skies for that elusive sighting, or any UFO activity.

Warminster's long and chequered UFO history began on Christmas Day, 1964. Mrs. Marjorie Bye was walking to early morning Mass at Christ Church when as Arthur Shuttlewood reports in The Warminster mystery: "The air was brazenly filled with a menacing sound. Sudden vibrations came overhead, chilling in intensity. They tore the quiet atmosphere to raucous rags and descended upon her savagely... shockwaves pounded at her head, neck and shoulders."

Other such "sonic attacks" which occurred at around same time in different locations around the town were later reported to Shuttlewood, who at the time was the features editor on the local weekly newspaper, **The Warminster Journal.**

Within weeks, the floodgates opened, and the phenomenon was christened

UFOs: Key To Inner Perfection

"The thing", as no-one had actually seen anything that could be attributed to the cause. Most of the townsfolk had never heard of UFOs or "flying saucers" at the time. When interviewed by Shuttlewood, all the witnesses referred to the fledgling phenomena as "Things or "The thing".

Cradle Hill

By June 1965, strange objects were beginning to be seen in the skies around the town. Shuttlewood amassed a sizable file on these sightings, and it was not until September, 1965, when he reported seeing a UFO from his home, that he became a believer in the enigma.

This was a turning point, as Shuttlewood soon became the voice and champion of The Warminster mystery.

The most iconic image of Warminster's UFO activity is a photograph, taken by Gordon Faulkner in 1965. A typical "flying saucer" photograph which is so enlarged that the grain of the emulsion is clearly visible was handed to the Daily Mirror and gained the town a vast amount of publicity when it was printed in the paper on September 10th, 1965. Warminster would never be the same again.

Within weeks, thousands of people converged on the town to see this strange phenomenon for themselves. Such was the concern of the local populace that a public meeting was held in the town over the August bank holiday to allay fears that as the chairman of Warminster council, Elwyn Rees explained "The happenings were a danger to Earth"

Shuttlewood was by now contemplating writing a book on the events in the town. Indeed, as the flyleaf to Brinsley Le Poer Trench's then new book, **The Flying Saucer Story** (Neville Spearman, 1966) attests. The Warminster sighting is advertised, and the book's title was then changed to the more familiar **The Warminster Mystery** prior to being published in 1967 by Neville Spearman.

The BBC were quick to latch on to the events in the town. BBC west filmed a half hour documentary in 1966, entitled "Pie In The Sky". Of all the programmes made about the town, this is by far the most level and fair.

With all the attention that Shuttlewood was giving the enigma at this time, he was the centre of a possibly rather cruel hoax. Shuttlewood claimed, at the end of **The Warminster Mystery** that he had been contacted by the occupants of the craft that were haunting the skies around the town. These "contacts" initially began with telephone calls, without the then usual pips associated with the coin operated call boxes of the time. After a number of these calls, Shuttlewood was then visited by these beings at his home on the town's Portway Road, by the then typical stereotyped manifestation of "Aliens", namely blond, perfect Aryans, reported

UFOs: Key To Inner Perfection

by contactees such as Adamski and Allingham.

The reports of these encounters form the appendix in ***The Warminster Mystery***. Further revelations from the "space people" were revealed in his second book, ***Warnings From Flying Friends***, which was self published by Shuttlewood in 1968.

Sightings, by the early 1970s, however, were beginning to decline. This was partly due to Warminster being old news, and the numbers of skywatchers on the hill dropped due in main to lack of nationwide publicity.

A local UFO buff, Ken Rogers, began publishing his ***The Warminster UFO*** newsletter in August, 1971. Shuttlewood allied himself to Rogers, and it is interesting to note, that among Roger's papers, which were donated to the town's Dewey museum after his death in 1993, there are a number of original diagrams and reports of sightings in the museum's files that found themselves in Shuttlewood's third book on the phenomenon ***UFOs: Key To The New Age***, which was published by Regency Press in 1971. This book, of all the titles written by Shuttlewood, is probably the most contentious of all.

By now, Shuttlewood had become totally immersed in UFO lore. Ken Rogers had a book posthumously published by Coates and Parker (Warminster) entitled ***The Warminster Triangle*** in 1994. Although the book is heavy in UFO content, it also delves into the legends and folklore of the area.

The ***Warminster UFO*** newsletter continued publication as far as I am able to ascertain, well into 1973. Shuttlewood, it seems, took a sabbatical from writing books for a number of years, but still took an active part in skywatches and the local UFO scene.

In the same year, ***The Warminster Mystery*** was published in paperback by Tandem books, an imprint of the Howard and Wyndham publishing group. It was this book, which sparked my own interest in the UFO phenomenon in Warminster, as until that point, the only books I had read were such titles as Brad Steiger's ***Flying Saucers Are Hostile*** and ***Strangers From The Skies***, and other American authors.

Late in 1975, or early 1976 saw a new research centre open in the town. The Fountain Centre, located in Carlton Villa, Portway, was run by Peter and Jane Paget. Along with Jane's mother, Mrs. Margaret Tedder-Shepperd, the Pagets renamed the property Star House with the intention of running not only a research facility in the town, but to offer bed and breakfast to skywatchers who were visiting the town.

Another project they planned was the publication of ***The Fountain Jour-***

UFOs: Key To Inner Perfection

nal, a bimonthly magazine centered around the UFO sightings reported in and around the Warminster area. Shuttlewood joined the editorial team early on, before the publication of issue one.

The Fountain Journal was by today's standards of desktop publishing a quite primitive affair, with a hand drawn calligraphy title page, possibly designed by and drawn by Shuttlewood himself. Photographs were simply cut out from either books or other magazines and simply glued into place on the relevant page. Each page was typewritten, at first on a primitive manual typewriter until issue 9 when Paget managed to obtain a more up to date electric typewriter.

The first three issues, which were edited by the Pagets, Mrs. Tedder-Shepherd and Arthur Shuttlewood, contained much more information on the local UFO scene than later issues. This was in part due to the input of Shuttlewood himself, until he had, I believe a major disagreement with the Pagets, which was also allied to a protracted period of ill - health.

Shuttlewood bowed out, and at around the same time, *The Flying Saucerers*, Shuttlewood's fourth book, was published in paperback by Sphere books in November 1976.

The Pagets then had another disagreement, this time with Mrs. Tedder-Shepherd, who was a co-owner of the centre and had a 50% stake in the property. Mrs. Tedder-Shepherd withdrew her support, leaving the Pagets to continue to run the centre with rapidly dwindling funds.

With the Fountain Centre now in danger of closing, due to mounting costs, Peter Paget appealed to members for money, the main appeal centering around an offer in the form of an extended subscription to the magazine, for a £100 life subscription. Not surprising, no-one took up the offer.

From issue four onwards, the content of the magazine became more New Age with articles on such subjects as Astrology becoming more prevalent. Possibly as filler material, Peter Paget began writing the *M86 Notebook*, a rather poor attempt at a science fiction story.

Fountain Journal

I myself, was a member of the Fountain Centre and stayed there on a number of occasions, and was involved with the *Fountain Journal.*

The number of members re-subscribing to the *Fountain Journal* was by now dwindling, and it wasn't until the British newspaper, *The News of the World* ran an article on the centre, that for a time at least, the magazine enjoyed a brief resurgence.

UFOs: Key To Inner Perfection

Indeed, issue eight, sent to the original subscribers contained a supplement that Peter Paget produced for anyone who enquired about the centre via the newspaper article.

By now it was early 1977, and the Warminster phenomenon was very old news, and a new area of the UK was hitting the headlines. In south Wales there had been a rash of UFO sightings around the Havorfordwest area, which soon earned the locality the name of **"The Dyfed Enigma"** or **"The Welsh triangle."**

It was during a stay at the Fountain Centre that I, along with a friend, Chris Butler, had, to this day, the most unexplained sighting of my time spent in Warminster. It was late afternoon, and both of us had retired to the 'Green Room' at the top of the house. Chris was lying on his bed, just gazing out of the window. I sat on my bed reading a book. I had mistakenly assumed that Chris had fallen asleep, but he suddenly jumped up off the bed and ran to the window crying out, "What the f**k is that?!" I got off my bed, which was in a corner of the room, and joined Chris at the window.

Over Cop Heap, slowly traversing the sky from right to left, was a silvery cigar-shaped object. Chris fumbled for his binoculars, and through the lenses could see a uniform elliptical object. He passed the binoculars to me and I confirmed what Chris had seen. I handed the binoculars back to Chris and began to rummage through my camera equipment. This was too good an opportunity to miss. As I started to screw on a 400mm telephoto lens I left the room, running down the stairs into the back garden of Star House, where I knew there was a clothesline post. As I was using a long, heavy lens I needed to avoid camera shake. I hadn't brought a tripod to Warminster with me, but I could use the post in the garden to brace the camera.

During the week I had changed the film in the camera from slide film to negative film. This film had a rating of 400ASA (one of the fastest film speeds commercially available at that time), so I was certain that I would be able to catch the object in mid-flight, without any blurring. I reached the clothesline post, lined up the camera and carefully focused it. The object was in the viewfinder, with blue sky and high, light grey clouds in the background. I carefully took three exposures, manually winding the film, refocusing each time, before the UFO went behind the trees on Arn Hill and out of my view. As I finished, Chris yelled from the bedroom window, binoculars still to his eyes "There are people on the hill, and they're pointing at it too... it's got to be a real object!"

When we informed Peter Paget of the sighting and photographic evidence, he offered to get the film developed in the town, that day. For reasons too long to go into here, but which is well documented in my book, **UFO Warminster: Cradle Of Contact**, we were both suspicious of Peter Paget's motives, thinking that he

UFOs: Key To Inner Perfection

would use the images for his own gain. Both of us made the hard but sensible decision to wait until we got back home to get the film developed.

The film was developed when we returned home, but when the film came back; there was blue sky, white clouds but no UFO!

On the left bottom corner of the final print were the tips of the trees on Elm hill. To this day, this is perhaps the most striking evidence of the 'Warminster Mystery' we never had! I assure you I had the object dead centre in the viewfinder, and the exposure was obviously correct. Just what was it we had seen? I had, at the time, my own enlarger and printing equipment at home. Both Chris and I spent a good few hours looking at the negatives through the enlarger, at different settings, and at no time did we ever see any sign of that UFO. But we believe that what we saw was a real tangible object… How else could the golfers on the course above the house have seen it as well?

Due to what I assume were mounting debts, Peter Paget planned to move from the large and costly "Star House" to a more manageable property, "Fountain House," in the summer of 1977. Sadly for the Pagets this was not to be. With mounting pressures on them, and the local UFO researchers becoming more hostile towards the Fountain Centre due in part to Paget's lifestyle being funded by the dwindling members of the organization, and Paget's now isolationist stance due to the fact they had closed the doors on the centre to all but known visitors, and those within their inner circle. The publication of the **"Fountain Journal"** became more sporadic. The magazine became much thinner in both content and volume. Issue 11, dated only 1977, was the last to be published.

Tucked away on page three was an apology for the late publication of that issue, and a further apology informing readers that issue 12 would be late too.

Soon after the publication of issue 11, not surprisingly, the Fountain Centre folded. There were a number of causes for this. The first, and major, was that another research group, UFO-Info, had set up in the town, towards which, I feel, there was a certain amount of hostility. It was as if the Pagets felt they had the exclusive right to be the official voice of the Warminster UFO scene. It also didn't help matters when Arthur Shuttlewood allied himself with the new group, which, unlike the Fountain Centre, was run and staffed by unpaid volunteers. The second cause was that sightings in the area were, as I previously noted, by this time declining, and public awareness of the Warminster phenomena was rapidly dwindling.

Shuttlewood had two further books published in the late 1970s. **UFO Magic In Motion** by Sphere books in 1978, and his final book, **More UFOs Over Warminster** was published by Arthur Baker in 1979. It was after the publication of

UFOs: Key To Inner Perfection

this book that Shuttlewood effectively retired from active UFO research.

Two years later, Peter Paget's first book, *"The Welsh Triangle"* was published in the UK by Granada books. Soon after this, a second book, **UFO-UK**, was published by New English Library. This book contains a lot of material that had originally appeared in his *"Fountain Journal"* a few years before.

UFO-Info folded early in the 1980s. It is interesting to note that one member of the organization, Ian Myzryglod, went on to form the Bristol based Probe, and now lives in the United States where he is a paranormal investigator.

With the closure of UFO-Info, all research effectively ceased in the town. Warminster over the years began to fade from public memory.

Arthur Shuttlewood died in Warminster in 1996. The passing away of the sole champion of the enigma went unreported by the major UFO publications. With his death, the last lingering memories slowly faded away.

Now, in the new millennium, the people who were around during those heady days are either dead, unwilling to talk, or are sadly, even with the use of the internet, untraceable.

Warminster, however, refuses to die. Late in 2006, a woman walking her dogs outside a town some ten miles from the centre of Warminster saw, in the distance, towards Cley Hill, which is another notorious local UFO hotspot, a series of red lights, performing acrobatics. After a few minutes, they formed into what she claimed was a triangle shape and shot off at great speed. Despite the local Somerset press checking with the Armed Forces, the police and the nearby Centre Parcs, no explanation was forthcoming.

Authors Steve Dewey and John Ries published a book in 2005, entitled **In Alien Heat**, (Anomalist Books, 2005) a critical overview of the Warminster phenomena.

Dr. David Clarke's and Andy Roberts' new book, **The Flying Saucerers**, (Heart of Albion Press, 2007), a social study into the history of Ufology here in the UK was due out in April 2007.

One thing is certain however. Despite all the new research into the phenomena in this quiet Wiltshire town all I can say is this: something strange did happen there. I know. For a time, I was part of it.

UFOs: Key To Inner Perfection

CHAPTER 2

"The relationship between Man and the Universe surrounding him will be perfectly understood when the essential truth is grasped that he is an integral part of the all—just as the all is integrally linked with the ultimate destiny of Mankind everywhere..."

Arthur Shuttlewood; UFOs: KEY TO THE NEW AGE, page 35

It was only a short distance from Arthur's home to Cradle Hill. As the taxi drove up a very narrow road only big enough for one car, I noticed many other cars parked alongside the drive in the tall grass. I was amazed at all the people with the same objective, all hoping to sight a UFO. There were people from all walks of life, from a Duke to a street cleaner, scientists from Cambridge and Oxford, as well as BBC-TV cameramen and commentators. There were about a hundred people gathered together on Cradle Hill, waiting to witness a UFO.

Arthur touched my hand and gestured with his arms as if to embrace the multitude. He smiled and said, "Look at all these good people. So many come to see. So many people have seen. Russian physicists have come over; French aerodynamic engineers; Americans such as your good self; New Zealanders and Australians from the other end of the earth; people from all over Europe. It's so lovely to hear how excited they get!

'Yah, yah', you Know, 'Wunderbar'. And another will say, 'C'est Magnifique', you know, 'Mon Dieu'. 'What is it?'

You get all these accents. It's lovely. There's one thing about Ufology, that's perhaps a poor term, but I can't think of a better substitute, there's no class distinction. There are no sides. There are no social barriers. From the refuse collector right up to the millionaire or Lord Bath, the Marquise of Bath and The Duke of Somerset. Or just people who are mildly interested and happen to live around here. It doesn't matter who they are. They all come together for a common purpose, to be a UFO witness. They weld together in observation parties. It's wonderful to be among them, to listen to them talk and to walk around even if a UFO

UFOs: Key To Inner Perfection

isn't seen on a particular night. There's a feeling of friendship, a pattern of good, decent human behavior which perhaps we've lost."

I experienced a true feeling of universal brotherhood and warmth that evening despite the cold English weather. I was not prepared for forty degree temperature in the middle of August, and had come to Warminster with a light jacket. I relied on my years of breathing practice and Yoga training to keep out the chill.

Some of the group had telescopes set on tripods, others had binoculars and cameras ready. Everyone greeted Arthur warmly, as one of the family and he introduced me, "This is Bryce Bond, a psychic investigator and radio announcer from New York City."

I was instantly surrounded by this friendly group all asking questions. Microphones were pushed forward and before I knew it, I was the focal point. I discussed mediumship, healing, and some of the other subjects I teach at my weekend parapsychology classes. Again that feeling of deja vu came over me. I felt I had had this same discussion with these same people at this place but at another time in the past. We talked about developing psychic techniques, UFOs and other strange phenomena.

I asked one lady why she thought all these people were there this evening. She answered, "Some are curious. Some are thrill seekers. We get these young guys down from London on their motorcycles looking for action. Others just enjoy being with this warm, loving group, sharing stories and conversation. Truthfully I'm here because some friends decided to come. I really don't expect to see anything unusual, though some of my friends swear they've seen these strange objects come out of the sky with flashing lights. Sounds pretty mysterious, doesn't it?"

I don't think all my goose bumps were from the cold air. I felt "electric" tingling vibrations enter my body causing me to shiver. Imagination? Or expectation?

I again located Arthur Shuttlewood who was off to my left talking with some people. I asked him, "With this amount of people around, Arthur, do UFOs usually come?"

"Oh, yes," he answered. "Yes, normally they announce their appearance so there's no doubt that they're not a satellite or high flying aircraft. It's as if they know we want to measure, to probe, to gauge, to cut to pieces, to find out what makes the universe tick. We are that sort of people. They give some sort of definite signal, move in some specific way, so we can be sure."

UFOs: Key To Inner Perfection

"Do you think they'll come tonight?' I expect my voice sounded anxious.

"Yes, I think the low cloud cover is going over a bit. I think we may see a UFO tonight; but it won't be close up."

I wondered if Arthur could see my disappointed look in the dark. He continued, "When, perhaps, two or three dozen people are here, in the depth of winter, they come in very close. And, indeed acknowledge our torch signals. They'll stop. They'll hover and the whole body, the whole lighted body of the 'craft' will echo back the signals we flash them with our torches."

"Why," I asked Arthur, "do you think they're manifesting at this particular time in history?"

"That's a good question, Bryce. It might sound hackneyed and trite, I suppose, and, of course, dogmatic science would not like this sort of excuse or reason at all. But, just look around at all the poisoning, the pollution poisoning. Scientists have been researching the Irish Sea for the past ten years. It borders England and Wales. We now know that all life in that sea will be dead within five years from now! You know, the fish are scarred. If you draw a fish out of the sea now, it's scarred. It's below par. In fact, it's not eatable. There will be no more life in that wonderful, dear little sea in five years. This is a very sobering thought. We've only got to look around at other seas, of course, to see this happening. I'm not punning here by saying, 'SEE. SEE.' We can postulate and theorize but all the signs are around us, aren't they? Pollution in the atmosphere? Environmental disease? Unwise use of pesticides? Drug addiction in the young? Why this sudden swing to false stimuli of the self? See what I mean?"

"I certainly do see. The problem is just as serious in America, if not more so," I agreed. "But perhaps a glimpse at something beyond man can make him see that a change is necessary, can make him wake up."

"Bryce, that's precisely what the UFOs are trying to do, wake the people up. I've come to feel over the past eight years of UFO experience that these 'craft' are not tangible, physical structures as such. They are a wonderful, universal power. There's a warmth. There's a tingling warmth from them that you get progressively. They re also awakening us to the possibility of harnessing a new kind of energy, or power, that's all around us. You know about 'ley lines'?"

"Yes," I answered anxious to hear his view of this strange anomaly.

"Our little orb of earth spins at one thousand miles an hour. It's also traveling simultaneously around the sun at one hundred thousand miles an hour.

"Makes the mind boggle. We also know the Earth's motion diffuses and pushes out tremendous belts of electromagnetic energy. If only man could harness more of these energies, we could be self sufficient. We could solve the energy crisis. Here is virginal territory, hardly tapped by science. There are signs here on earth. We feel that the barrows, ancient burial mounds that dot the landscape in this area, are signs of these lines of electromagnetic energy.

"If you look at the barrows from a helicopter as I have, you'll see that they form definite patterns. You can see among the chief or King barrows, as they are called, that you've got round, cigar and bell shaped mound formations—all very similar in shape to UFOs.

"Barrows are forms four and five thousand years old and they appear to be the same shape as flying saucers. Strange? People think they are only primitive burial mounds. We don't feel this is so, because King barrows, in many cases, mark many constellations that we see in the sky at night up north.

"Ursa Major, or the Great Bear, as it is called, is one that is clearly marked on the ground which you can see if you go up in a helicopter. The barrows are perhaps there to make us use our faculties, to begin to think deeply about what sort of power was on earth in those days. And, possibly, much much earlier than that.

"One does not have to be a biblical student to suppose, or imagine, that Ezekiel's wheel in the middle of a wheel was a UFO and the four living creatures he saw were extraterrestrial entities. The star of Bethlehem? We know that no star can come into our system without overturning us, overturning the axis-tilt of the earth. We would have been destroyed if a star came in. Even if a comet came too close it would have effected our little earth. So, we know it couldn't have been a star. It was a UFO. Ezekiel, Elijha, those prophets were taken up in Chariots of fire. UFOs! Even the burning bush of Moses, when he was given the laws that should govern human behavior, many thousands of years ago in the beginning of civilization as we know it, was a UFO.

"When opened, only two percent of these so-called burial mounds around here have shown any human remains or bones. So we can say there's something more. I believe they form a pathway of power that's known to the Ufonauts."

Arthur echoed my earlier supposition. I felt strangely as if Arthur was tuning me in with his words, like a giant antenna, to some still unknown energy. In spite of the cold and late hour, I stood rooted next to Arthur, magnetically drawn to his every word.

His words echoed in my mind like remembered thoughts from some far distant past of my own. I found my mind spinning as I again picked up the thread of Arthur's conversation. I seemed to have lost a sentence or two while reflecting.

UFOs: Key To Inner Perfection

". . . on the other hand, we've got great gravitational anomalies and distortion areas around here. We've got one at Maiden Bradley. The Duke of Somerset will confirm this. He lives there. The water flows up hill a mile and a half. The incline varies along the stretch of this particular stream, or minor river. The Duke will show you. In some sectors, it seems to flow three feet above normal points and then suddenly jerk upwards.

"There's no spring at the bottom. So, here we're faced with a gravity anomaly. Scientists would say, if they're open-minded enough to concede the possibility of UFOs existing, 'Well, at Heaven's Gate, or around that area where this distortion is, there could perhaps be a window or gateway which can warp the space-time continuum.'

"Heaven's Gate is a peculiar name isn't it? Could this be a breakthrough point where other dimensional forms can come through at specific times and converge with ours? Another dimensional form! This is how we, or certainly I, look upon UFOs. Not from other planets as such, but coexisting with us, here, at this moment. They have just moved on, far from the physical mold of things, into a part of the universal structure.

"They are always here, but they manifest themselves before our eyes at particular crisis points or times of emergency in our civilization, at any period in time."

Could it be now, I kept thinking, my mind still racing. Only an hour or so had passed since we arrived on Cradle Hill. Yet, I felt caught up in an endless stream of time; hours, days or just minutes could have passed. I looked out over the sea of people all waiting, the same as us, for some sign; all patient and expectant; all in small or large groups chatting quietly with one another. I again experienced an overwhelming feeling of brotherhood. Yet, I kept wondering why they were there. Was it just curiosity? I voiced my concern to Arthur.

"Unfortunately," he answered, "I think most of the people come for kicks. They think it's a gimmick. They come in a light hearted way and think, 'Well, is it all true?'. But, then when they find out that it is true, they change. Then the whole world can laugh at them as individuals, but they couldn't care less. They have their own truth. This is very sobering, very vitalizing and very important to the person. So, the majority now, after eight years of sighting, are sincere seekers, very genuine people."

UFOs: Key To Inner Perfection

One of the many UFOs observed over Warminster

UFOs: Key To Inner Perfection

CHAPTER 3

"The term 'flying saucer was first used by a Texas farmer who saw one over his ranch in 1878..."

Arthur Shuttlewood; THE WARMINSTER MYSTERY, page 42

The sky was clearing. Arthur suggested that we motor over with some friends to Starr Hill a few miles away where there would be less people and perhaps a better chance of sighting a UFO.

We drove over with two friends, Reginald Bradbury and Diane Mathews, both avid UFO watchers. This was to be Reg's first trip to Starr Hill, but he had been to Cradle Hill twice. It was his third effort at sighting and his expectations were high. Diane had started viewing a year before, last August. To date she informed us that she had seen nineteen UFOs.

"Wow," I said, "That's quite a lot. All here in Warminster?"

"Yes, yes! All in Warminster," she answered. "In fact, my best sightings were here on Starr Hill."

Diane's statement sent a charge of some unexpected force coursing up my spine making me again shiver. Her comment hit me with the force of a premonition.

Starr Hill is another ancient burial ground. It is a sector the Roman's had built upon and a few of the remnants of that civilization are still in evidence. When we arrived there were only a handful of people. We were sort of down in a valley with wheat fields all around. Surrounding us were high hills, each dotted, like an oasis, with a copse or thicket of small trees.

We remained in the car to keep warm and wait. Diane, a lovely, very British lady related to royalty up in Bath England, came well prepared for UFO watching with a large urn of hot tea in the back of her station wagon.

Bless Diane.

UFOs: Key To Inner Perfection

By this time my throat was tightening and I was losing my voice. I really had not come prepared for England's cold, damp weather. The tea was more than welcome.

Facing the wheat fields, we searched the horizon and the skies through the windshield. Reg and Diane had gotten out of the car to greet some friends, and to offer them some hot tea. Arthur was still reassuring. I asked him about his new book, "What is it called?"

"***STAIRWAY TO THE STARS.*** I'm not sure why I chose that title. It's the fourth book I've written and its got hundreds of sightings from all over Britain.

"Many of them in the last two years. Many more people have come forward to claim sightings. Even though they know they may be laughed at. They know that the hatchet men of cynicism are going to come cutting their way as soon as they open their mouths and state firmly, categorically, 'I've seen something that fits nothing conventional or orthodox that we know.' I admire these people. Their moral courage is tremendous. They're often branded as cranks. Even their families are pillorized and often ostracized. No one likes to be laughed at, or made to appear a prevaricator, or a liar.

"That hurts and I've had plenty of hurt in my nine years as a researcher in this. I've been very, very serious about it all because I've always believed that unless you possess your own truth, you dare not try to give truth to anyone else. This is very important to a journalist."

I decided to ask Arthur about something that had been troubling me since becoming involved in UFO investigating. "I've always wondered, Arthur, about so-called 'Men-In-Black'. I've heard said that when a person gets too close to a UFO, he's visited by these 'Men'. Is there any truth in this?"

Arthur sat quietly for a moment or two as if thinking through his answer, "I think you know people who are probably ... well, I'll put it this way, 'Men-In Black' to be quite blunt, I think, are the dark people of the earth. You meet light people, people you take to immediately. They are lovely people. They exude love which is a great universal force. Then there are the dark ones who push out negative charges and give off negative impressions. But don't forget the principles of polarity of the whole universe. Positive normally attracts negative and there is the third part which is the reaction or the off spring. This is true scientifically as well as humanly. Our human existence is one of duality. Often the negative makes us more aware of the positive.

"There is a lot of dark thought pervading the world today. It's an over permissive age. I'm not being prudish. I'm not being biblical. I'm not a student of the bible. But I do think that the spiritual overtones of all this, and all associated phe-

UFOs: Key To Inner Perfection

nomena with UFOs is very, very important and should be weighed carefully."

I, too, have had the growing feeling that UFOs are here as spiritual guides and also as protectors of the earth and its inhabitants. We have been destroying the land on which we live. I don't believe a UFO has ever deliberately injured or killed a person. People usually get hurt when they panic due to lack of proper education about extraterrestrial 'crafts' and their crews. There are thousands of reports where out of fear UFOs have been shot at, even by the military. We have to imagine how we would react if we went to another planet, dimension, universe, or time period. We Probably wouldn't be as careful and gentle as UFOs are to us.

Television and motion pictures show creatures from outer space coming down from the heavens to devour, murder, rape and destroy. Is that a true picture of their intent? I do not believe so. Arthur, thank God, shared my view.

I asked Arthur if it was possible that some UFOs are man made.

He answered, "Well, I know at least four people, or groups of people in England at the moment, who are working very, very hard on electromagnetic devices which they hope will take off one day. They invited national newspaper reporters and photographers to a launching but they never got off the ground. I have never seen anything earth-made that's risen into the air and done anything spectacular. To be frank, I know there are groups that are very close to making it happen. There's ionization. There are all forms of possible propulsion media, nuclear devices, of course.

"I know there are certainly the pioneers who are trying desperately hard to do something of this nature and get to the moon by using energy which is already in this atmosphere. And, I think it could be done. But that's getting technical and mechanical minded which I don't believe the UFO force, the predominant UFO force anyway, today is, at all. A minority may be purely physical and come from another planet, or planets in our galaxy. Of course, this is quite possible."

As if on cue, there suddenly appeared in front of us sharp glowing lights.

Arthur exclaimed matter of factly, "Isn't that , lovely? Look at those glowing lights!"

I couldn't help but see them rising over the horizon. The night had cleared and they stood out starkly against the sky. We quickly got out of the car to get a better look. Arthur commented casually all the while.

"There's an orange. There's a red and a blue coming from ... look at that, a triangle, a triangle in the sky. Above, there. It looks at this moment very suspiciously like a UFO because it's changing its lights all the time and it's staying over one spot. See, Bryce. See, there!"

UFOs: Key To Inner Perfection

I couldn't help but see, but I could hardly speak. Something seemed to have momentarily taken my voice away.

Arthur continued, "I believe it is a UFO. It's up in the air. Well to the right of the farm house. This is how a triangle light appeared two weeks ago, when we saw three enormous figures down here."

"Three what?" I sputtered, my eyes glued to the horizon.

"You may think I'm being way out now. I'm only a little excited by what we're seeing, though I'm happy for your sake, Bryce. But we've become so blasé and conditioned by what we've seen over the years. But there have been instances recently, here, of contacts with huge figures. I can tell you they are very, very lovely. If anyone's worried about it. It's a very beautiful force."

All this time the lights hung in the sky like a Christmas tree, remaining in the same spot and position. I wished it would come closer, do something unusual so I could be sure. All of a sudden it started to lift in a strange zig-zag pattern and then just disappear.

I felt as if I was stretching all my senses, trying to watch and listen to Arthur at the same time. Huge figures? I could just about absorb the appearance of these strange colored lights in the sky. I croaked out a question as my voice began to return, "What are these figures? Outside entities?"

Arthur kept his eyes turned upwards as he answered, "I think I would call them other dimensional forms. I believe, when the right groups of people get together, people who push out thoughts of love and welcome, knowing that this earth doesn't belong to us, they appear."

We still had our eyes trained to the horizon. In front of us stretched a large open wheat field. There was nothing behind it but a range of hills, some treetops, and one little farm house well to the left of where the lights had first appeared. Arthur felt the positioning of the lights made it very probable that it was a true sighting. We stood shoulder to shoulder for a few minutes. Then Arthur pointed excitedly in front of us.

"There. There it is again. See that flickering? That blue? That blue and white? It's in a different location so it's going sideways now. This could be quite important. I hope it is for your sake, Bryce, and for all these good people. Because everyone who sees something is meant to see it. It can register and stop overtones and undertones of unnecessary fear later on. If man fears anything in the universe, he is doomed, isn't he? If he faces his fear and learns to overcome it then a force such as a UFO can come to him in a loving way."

I felt Arthur was conveying a very deep message to me. The UFO was there

UFOs: Key To Inner Perfection

to physically make me aware of something existing beyond our small universe. Arthur was here to remind me that the force was for the good of humanity, was a loving, gentle force here to help us all.

The intensity of the lights increased as the 'craft' raised itself slowly, did a little dance in the sky, then remained again suspended.

We moved over closer to where Reg and Diane were standing with a small group of their friends. Arthur borrowed a flashlight and sent Morse code to the 'craft'. It in turn sent back the same signals. All eyes were focused in the direction of the lights.

Arthur continued, "At this point it's difficult to know if this is a true sighting. I would say that when we've seen lights from that area in the past, we have had other things happen around us and we suddenly become aware of some sort of presence that you can't touch. On the other hand, as in all new spheres of research, and this is essentially that, you get hoaxers and leg pullers. If anyone knew we were here tonight, this is just a thought, it's possible that someone is working some contrivance. However, if it's a genuine force, then it will show itself in another way that will convince the watcher that it's absolutely genuine. Often it will lift to a treetop level just so as to prove ... well ... we're not hoaxers.

"This is the genuine thing. I still have some doubts about what we're seeing. But if it's the real article, it will manifest again in a different position. But, from that area, that particular area which is very sacred because we've seen so much happen there and then things happen all around us, I believe it is a UFO. Here's Reg. Perhaps he has something to add." .

Reg turned his gaze from the sky and came over to us. He grabbed Arthur's arm excitedly while speaking, "I saw lights. I don't know what they were really. But, when you flashed your light, Arthur, it seemed to answer. Whether it was a fluke or not, I'm not sure. You flashed your light and it flashed back."

Arthur again took the flashlight or as he referred to it, the torch. "Watch," he said, "I'll shine something and note carefully, if you can read morse code, what is said. I'll do it from a different angle. If it's a hoaxer, we'll have him then. Does it switch on and off, Reg?"

"Yes," Reg answered.

Arthur walked over to the edge of the wheat field and began to signal with morse code. The wheat was up to waist level. He sent the code by dots and dashes with the flashlight. The 'craft' again sent back the same pattern of lights. Then just as suddenly as it appeared, it disappeared.

UFOs: Key To Inner Perfection

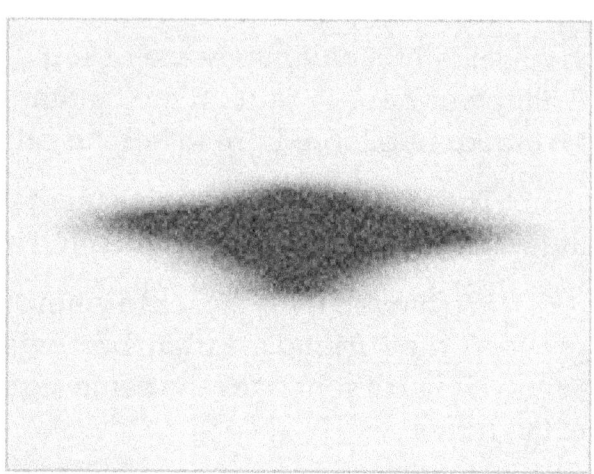

UFOs, lights, crop circles and strange beings appeared in the skies and fields around Warminster, often in broad daylight.

Large triangular shaped area 30 feet by 50 feet found in corn field the day after a landing near Cradle Hill, Warminster.

Depressions could only be seen from an elevated position. Two bar-shaped depressions 12 feet long. In all these cases of a single landing, corn was broken, about halfway up stems, triangular patch swirled round in whirligig style.

UFOs: Key To Inner Perfection

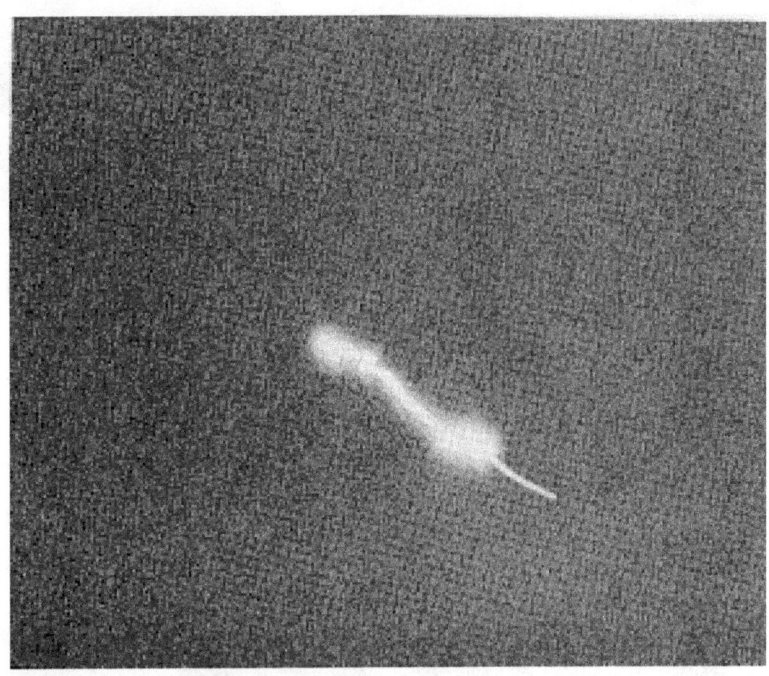

The UFOs over Warminster came in many shapes and sizes - many of them were taken by retired RAF pilot Bob Strong and witnessed by Arthur Shuttlewood as well as many other observers.

UFOs: Key To Inner Perfection

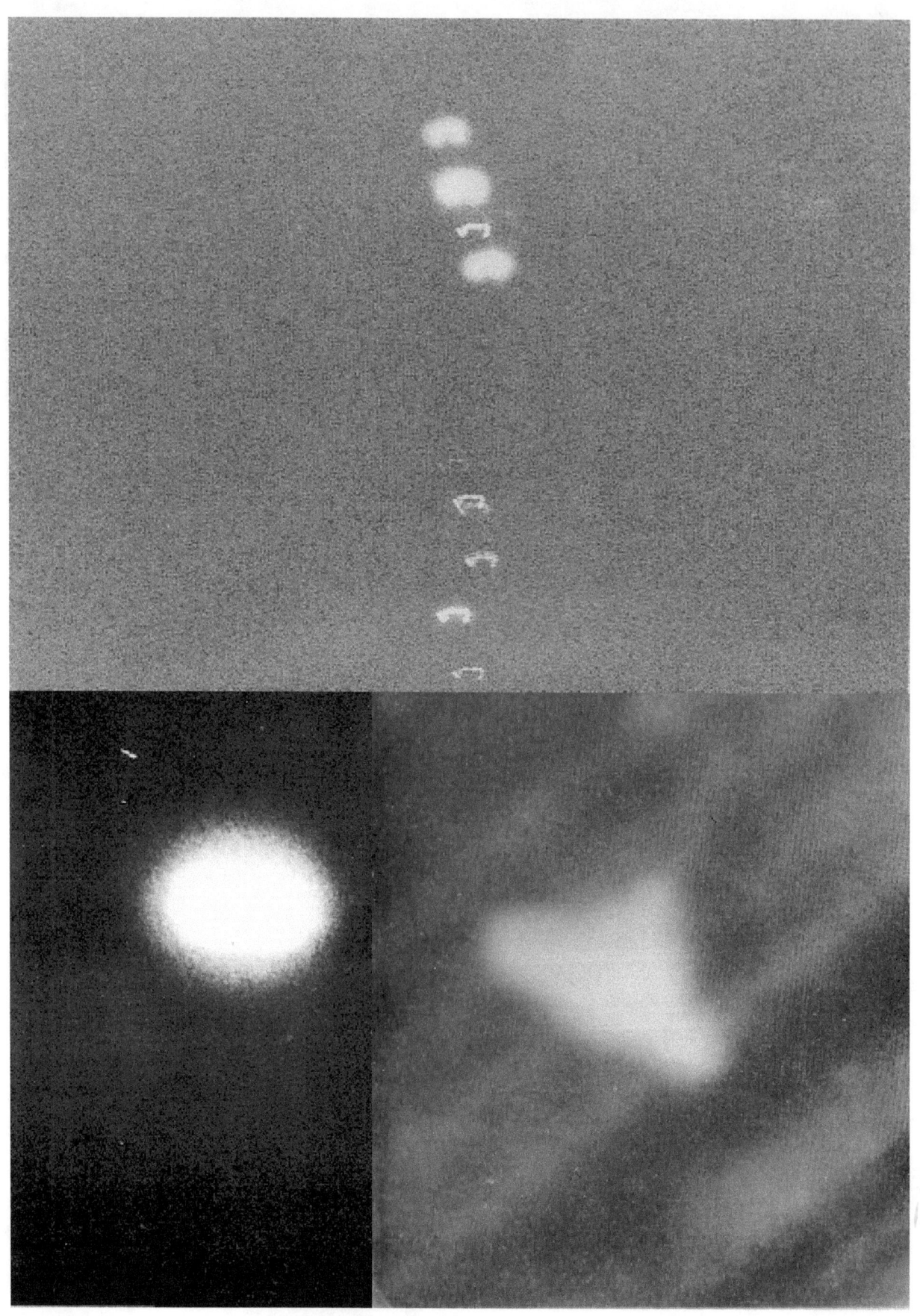

28

UFOs: Key To Inner Perfection

CHAPTER 4

"I can reveal that scorched near-circles and earth indentations are fairly commonplace in our area, nowadays."

Arthur Shuttlewood; THE WARMINSTER MYSTERY, page 125

Arthur excitedly called us over, so we galloped as quickly as we could through the high wheat.

"What's happening, what's happening, Arthur?"

"Stop there. Stop there. Stop where you are. Notice this area."

"It's flat! Reg exclaimed.

"Wow, just like something landed," I remarked almost in unison.

"Yes," Arthur stated, "but there's nothing leading away from it , you see?"

"No," we all seemed to answer at once, "there's not."

There was a sense of awe in all our voices. We stood waist deep in the wheat looking at this large impression of flattened ground.

"It's anti-clockwise brushed around, you see?" Arthur pointed out. "It does look as though something landed here."

"What does that mean, Arthur?", I asked,

Arthur answered, "Well, we found these right at the beginning of the Warminster mystery, back in 1965, before I'd seen any 'crafts'. These sort of impressions were being discovered and always in an anti-clockwise formation. All the wheat had been churned around to the left and there were never any tracks leading to or from it. There are no impressions in the wheat coming off this shape. And the wheat is spun around that way, anti-clockwise. You get that? There's no beginning there at all!"

"It's sort of cigar shaped, isn't it?" I asked.

UFOs: Key To Inner Perfection

"It's the usual shape that we're used to seeing," Arthur answered.

"Could a squall get in this particular spot?" Diane leaned over and brushed the packed wheat with her hand as if checking for an answer through the vibrations.

Her question reflected my own concern for accuracy.

"Well, Diane," Arthur commented, "you do get sudden squalls of energy, of course, that push down wheat, but it's this peculiar way of pushing the wheat down in a swirled mass that makes this different. I've seen banks of wheat go, but usually at the edges or perimeter of the field. And now it's the height of summer and we haven't had any wind lately. We haven't had a storm in ages. It is also rather strange, but I could almost swear it wasn't here a fortnight ago."

I walked around the impression. It was about thirty feet in circumference. On returning, I queried Arthur about the entities he had mentioned earlier. While walking I had had the strange feeling of a presence in the tall grass. "Whereabouts did those entities you spoke about earlier appear?"

"Well, on Cradle Hill they appeared quite near the white gate. Here they appeared around the screen of bushes, which is quite near the farmer's barn." Arthur gestured in the direction of a hollow area about fifty yards away. "At the bottom here are several thousand bees in a bee hive. We'll pop down there because they're quiet after ten o'clock at night, and you might get some atmosphere down at that point there, at the bottom there which fronts onto that hill."

It was now about 2 AM and the night was clear and still. We made our way back to the road side and began walking toward the bee hives.

"Diane," I asked, "did you see anything?"

"I saw some lights over there, different colored lights." Diane pointed towards the horizon where the first lights had appeared to Arthur and me. "I was just trying to work out exactly where it was. It wasn't exactly where the farm was. It seemed to be over and higher up. I'm not sure. It flashed. I believe it was too low for a helicopter or a plane. I don't know. It was a difficult sighting. But there were certainly lights and they seemed to move didn't they? It couldn't be a hoaxer down there, because that's army land and the road is closed tonight."

We passed through a gate and headed over a small bridge. Arthur stopped me and pointed to the left of the bridge on the other side, "Here is where one of the figures stood."

I peered intently into the darkness inwardly trying to will an image to appear at that moment before my eyes. Strangely, I didn't feel any fear. The previ-

UFOs: Key To Inner Perfection

ous sightings had made me feel high and joyous. I felt filled with love for my new friends and fellow adventurers. Passing through the gate and crossing the bridge, I felt as if I was entering a new world.

Symbolically, a gate is an entrance and a bridge means a crossing. One often hears people speak about the bridge between the two worlds. I truly felt as if I was an explorer venturing into new territory.

"Arthur, I wonder, if that impression was a saucer landing, wouldn't there be indentations in the ground from the metal footpads?"

"Not necessarily, Bryce, the 'crafts' seem to float down feather-light. Sometimes we don't even find indentations in the soil, yet, the grass around is all tousled."

We walked directly over to where the giant shape had stood. Arthur elaborated, "The huge figure was between seven and eight feet high. There were six people here and three of these figures were with us for about a half and hour. Some of the people were, naturally, a bit afraid. But when we walked toward the figures a terrific warmth exuded from them.

"You could almost walk right up to them. They were featureless, huge and rather magnificent. Something awe inspiring about them. Giants of the past, we thought. And, then this sweet smell, a mixture of roses and lilies-of-the-valley engulfed us all. It was beautiful, so beautiful!"

"Do you think," I wondered, "if an individual stayed out here over night, a person who was, I would say, more into perfecting himself spiritually, than a thrill seeker, that these entities would appear?"

"Yes, I'm certain," Arthur remarked with surety, "I'm certain of this! Very, very much depends upon the calibre, or quality of the person. I don't mean that in a derogatory sense to anyone. But those who are closely attuned to nature, dowsers, for example, the people who walk with sticks and determine the location of water resources under the earth; and healers, people who believe in love as a universal force, a primary agent, these people I'm sure would see the visitors."

"Could you communicate with these entities?" Again my mind seemed to be racing faster than my words.

"Yes, I'm sure again. This is just judging on personal experience, but it can be backed up by a number of good people around here. I'm sure they do pick up thoughts and that we receive messages through a kind of mental telepathy. There's no doubt at all." Arthur answered me slowly, carefully and affirmatively.

"What happened when you approached the entities?" I kept probing Arthur.

UFOs: Key To Inner Perfection

Perhaps it was just journalistic curiosity, or that deep within myself I was searching for a particular answer that hadn't yet surfaced into my own consciousness. Everything that had been happening that evening had a strange familiarity, as if at some other time, in some other space, all this had been lived before. I felt very close to knowing, deeply knowing, some hidden meaning to my own existence.

Recently I'd had that same feeling during meditation, the feeling of almost touching a significant truth, a truth that I had somehow known before and lost. I had recently begun to delve into the question of reincarnation, of multiple lives, perhaps being lived simultaneously in different dimensions of time. While my thoughts were scattering, a part of my mind focused in on Arthur who was answering my question about the entities.

"...They did disappear whenever the torch beam was focused at them. And, when other people joined us and shown their car headlights. It dispelled the whole atmosphere. Diane and I got here at 9:15 PM and we heard a peculiar commotion in the middle of that bank of bushes near the barn, this side of the barn where I told you they first appeared." Arthur gestured toward the barn and our gaze followed.

"This was just a few weeks ago. We've told very few people because the world laughs at this sort of thing. When you talk about a possible contact they laugh even more. But, I feel I can tell you, Bryce, being a healer and truly interested."

I thanked Arthur for his confidence and asked him to continue.

"Well, Diane and I both heard this terrific noise, so we went into the bushes thinking an animal might be trapped." Both Arthur and Diane gestured towards a small clump of bushes.

"But, there wasn't any animal there. So we left and walked over to the gate where we saw the lights before. Around about 10:15 PM we were joined by two other people, and then, at 10:30 PM two more people joined us. There were three males and three females and we were standing together, the six of us, sending out loving thoughts. Suddenly, the three forms were there, around those bushes, and they were enormous. Weren't they, Diane?"

"Yes, indeed," Diane agreed emphatically.

"And we were quite staggered," Arthur continued. "But, think how truly beautiful it is—the idea that these figures should appear while we were all sending out loving thoughts, each silently in his own way."

"Where do you think they come from, Arthur?" I asked aloud while wondering if the powerful force of love could have attracted these beings from an-

UFOs: Key To Inner Perfection

other space or dimension.

"Earlier that evening we had seen a triangle of lights, much as we saw tonight, over there to the right of the farm house. We also saw two UFOs speed through the air, faster than any plane or satellite, and we were a bit bewildered by this. It was an hour or two after the sighting of the pyramid of lights that everything started to happen with the figures. It was incredible! We realized we could go up to the figures and talk. We actually found ourselves talking to them, welcoming them."

I tried to imagine how I would feel faced with these giant images. Arthur's words, so simply stated, filled me with feelings of love and I could imagine trying to embrace, if only with words, strangers from another time and space. One got the feeling of affinity from listening to Arthur, the same feeling you get when you meet someone for the first time and feel you've somehow known that person and loved them before. There's an immediate happy rapport and familiarity. "Did they physically talk back?"

Arthur shook his head, "No, as I mentioned before, they didn't speak as we know it. All that came immediately was a warm engulfing of beautiful hot air. You felt as if you could sun bathe in their presence. It's crazy, but you felt liberated, somehow. You felt, here was a vast ancient wisdom of beautiful loving power and somehow you wanted to communicate."

Somehow, I felt Arthur knew more that he was telling me and was asking me to listen to what he was saying between the words, to absorb as he had the inner message.

"We were surrounded by waves of warmth and then there was this beautiful scent. I don't know how the others—Diane, Neil, Sally, John or Angela— would describe it. But I would say a mixture of roses and lilies-of-the-valley. What would you say, Diane?"

"Almost beyond description. But, I would say that Arthur is correct, a flower garden in early summer, so beautiful, so very beautiful."

"And there wasn't a puff of wind. Just like tonight when we saw the pushed down wheat, everything still. When we walked away from the figures the warmth and the scent diminished. Anyway we lost sight of them. Someone shown a torch and they disappeared. Then we came down here. Over where Reg is now standing."

Arthur pointed to the left of the bridge. "Over there, is where the tallest, probably the central figure of the three, was standing. Neil, one of the six, stood by the figure. What he said to it I don't know. Perhaps he's here tonight. He might

UFOs: Key To Inner Perfection

tell you, Bryce."

I called over to Reg and asked him if he had seen the chap Arthur called Neil. He answered that he hadn't seen him. So I never did find out what was communicated between Neil and the figure. Perhaps, as I discovered later, we are each to know only what is important to us individually.

"Sorry, Bryce," Arthur continued, "but Neil hasn't wanted to talk about the experience. We could see him outlined against the giant figure for what seemed like ages. We didn't feel we should interrupt. Then he quietly walked back and we all started walking away from here because many headlights from cars were shining over the hill line. I walked ahead of the others thinking that I'd hurry and tell someone. Then something inside said, 'Don't tell too many because people laugh.' As I walked up the hill, Neil came rushing up and he said, 'It was lovely, Arthur, all the way, every step you took up the hill in front of us, one of the figures was by your side.' I know that Neil sees, in the true sense of seeing. It always fills me with joy when others see.

"We are not alone in the universe. Who knows what invisible, normally invisible presences are all around every one of us, in every waking or working step we take in life. And we don't give any credit or credence to that because it's outside the limits, the horizons of our scientific concepts and traditions. It seems so outrageously impossible. We blink our eyes at it, shut our ears to it, and escape into our own little hermitage. But, when it happens, it's incredible, so incredibly lovely!"

UFOs: Key To Inner Perfection

CHAPTER 5

"One must see one of these amazing phenomena to believe it; and there is no such thing as an expert in matters Ufological. Individual experience is the key to all the answers."

Arthur Shuttlewood; UFOs: KEY TO THE NEW AGE, page 21

Arthur, Diane and Reg started back over the bridge toward Starr Hill. I asked if they wouldn't mind if I stayed near where the figures had appeared to meditate for a while. I believe they understood that I needed some time alone to absorb all that had happened that evening. Then, there was always the slim chance that if I sat quietly and sent out loving thoughts that I, too, would see something extraordinary. Some inner feeling compelled me to try and make contact, alone, and quiet.

I watched them disappear into the night. It was around 3:00 AM. I had truly lost all count of time; I sat on the ground in typical Yoga, cross-legged position, did some deep breathing and immediately felt the energy rise along my spine taking my consciousness with it.

I thought only a few minutes had passed as I heard my name being called, "Bryce, Bryce." Arthur was calling me. I looked at my watch, which I had removed earlier and placed in my pocket. It was 4:15 AM. Over an hour had passed since Arthur and the others had left. I called back to Arthur, "Coming."

I truly do not know what transpired while I was sitting in a trance state, totally abstracted from my five sense existence. I stood and brushed myself off, still somewhat dazed. I began to walk back towards Arthur as he began to walk toward the others on the hill.

Then I noticed something strange. The wheat in the field next to me was about waist high. I was walking along the road very close to the wheat when, all of a sudden, I heard a noise, like a thresher cutting the wheat—swish, swish, swish.

I was about three yards from the wheat. I stopped walking. As we remarked

UFOs: Key To Inner Perfection

earlier, there was no breeze that night. The clouds had completely passed and the moon and stars shown brightly in a clear sky.

There, before my eyes, a large depression formed. The wheat was being crushed down in a counterclockwise motion, forming into a triangle. I rubbed my eyes, trying to see what was crushing the wheat.

Little pin pricks of light began to manifest themselves outlining this unusual 'craft'. About twenty feet of wheat from point to point was being crushed down. I stood as if stunned a few minutes to allow what I had just seen to register. I experienced a tremendous tingling sensation all over my body, as if an electric current was being beamed in. There was a sweet smell and I felt engulfed with warm air. Not fully understanding what had just transpired, I found myself running to catch up with Arthur and tell him. I called to him excitedly, "Arthur, Arthur."

Arthur turned and started walking towards me. I sputtered out what I had seen, highly elated and yet, still strangely detached and dazed.

"Well, Bryce," Arthur commented as a matter of fact, "this is your lucky night. I'm glad for your sake. You have just been contacted, and so very close, a very good omen. But you should have stayed. It might have manifested itself. Because you ran away, it must have assumed you didn't want to make contact or you weren't ready yet, so it left. I'm sorry it left because it could have been very, very important for your sake and all these good people around here."

I promised myself that next time—and I knew there would be a next time–I would stand my ground and not get apprehensive. Perhaps, I wasn't ready to face this incredible unknown.

Then Arthur pointed out to me, close to the impression I had experienced, other landing sites. There was a circle about thirty feet in circumference and another long cigar shape. All the depressions were in a counterclockwise position and there were no pathways leading to any of them. I had truly been contacted by more than one "craft". I felt the full impact of the experience as Arthur pointed out the other "landing" areas. Inwardly, I said a prayer of thanks. I felt my mission had been a success. I'd had one of the most amazing, enlightening experiences of my life. Next time I would not just sense but know.

I walked quietly and humbly back with Arthur to the others. He told them of my experience. As he talked, I had time to mentally digest what had happened and to return slowly back to my senses. I felt as if I was coming down from a long, high climb in the mountains, somewhat breathless but elated from the experience.

Diane touched my arm. Her contact seemed to immediately ground me.

UFOs: Key To Inner Perfection

Perhaps, the polarity of male-female was the earth balance I needed to completely return to physical existence.

"Bryce, now that you've made contact, there's something else that happened to me recently that I think you should know about."

There was still more. A labyrinth seemed to be unwinding before me. I could almost see the center, yet, I seemed to know that there were still many paths before the conclusion of the adventure. Perhaps I was just beginning, just entering a new maze of events which would lead me beyond into the far reaches of my imagination. I felt that amazed surprise you get when you find a dream that you've had has become a reality.

Thousands of cases have been recorded of people's dreams literally coming true. We call it precognition, knowing something before it happens. Many people experience this phenomena. But, I didn't need clairvoyance, seeing into the future power, to know that there was still more to be unraveled.

"My experience was in the Warminster newsletter. It's been recorded," Diane began her story. "I was driving Arthur back from a lecture, an excellent lecture he gave at Cerne Abbas that particular evening. It was raining very heavily, absolutely lashing the windscreen. The windshield wipers of the car were just buzzing back and forth and the rain never let up. The lecture lasted a long time and a lot of people stayed behind for a discussion, so we didn't leave Cerne Abbas until around midnight. I dropped Arthur at Warminster at around 2:15 and then I drove on to Bath, where I live. It was a very lonely stretch of road and I was tired and longing for bed. The rain was still pouring down. Then suddenly, to my absolute astonishment, from over a high hedge came a large golden disc and it sailed across the road twelve feet in front of my car and disappeared towards Dilton Marsh.

"No sooner had I recovered from that, when, coming along the road in this lashing rain at 2:30 in the morning, was a very tall man dressed entirely in white overalls. I Know there wasn't a house for miles and I would have given anything for the courage to stop. I went about three hundred yards in the car before I thought, 'Good heavens, I wish I'd stopped and asked the man f he had seen the same large golden disc as I did'.

"Then, I thought, 'How ridiculous. Here I am, a woman at 2:30 in the morning on March the 7th in a dark, lashing rain, would I dare to stop and ask this man this question? And, what on earth, was a man doing walking along the road at this time of night?'

"Absolutely staggering. I shall never forget it. I would have given anything for someone to have been with me, like Arthur, or anyone, to have seen what I

UFOs: Key To Inner Perfection

saw."

"Where do you think this man came from?" I asked.

"I haven't the foggiest idea," Diane answered. "I can see him now: very tall, dressed in those gleaming white overalls, walking through the most tremendous lashing rain. His image will be with me always. I have no idea who he was."

"How about the night when you were with Arthur in the six-man circle and the entities appeared? What did they look like to you, Diane?"

"Very tall, and their heads," Diane pushed her shoulders up until they touched her ear lobes, "They didn't seem to have any necks. Their heads came straight onto their shoulders and it was as though they were encased in a lone cloak. Quite extraordinary."

"How did you feel then?"

"I smelled the same flowery smell as I told you earlier and I felt the warmth. I've felt that warmth on top of Cradle Hill many times. We'd be walking on a blustering, cold, icy winter night in January, along the top of the hill, beyond the white gates. And, suddenly, we'd come into a stream of very warm, quite hot air. We'd often linger there because it was so lovely to suddenly feel warm after being absolutely frozen."

The barn where many gathered to observe the strange lights and objects in the heavens.

UFOs: Key To Inner Perfection

Approaching UFO observation point.
Photo courtesy Steve Wills - Warminster UFO Skywatcher.

Ancient country and ancient stones seem to attract UFOs and strange beings.

UFOs: Key To Inner Perfection

"You mentioned earlier, Diane, that you've had nineteen sightings."

"True, Bryce, and my best as I told you, from here, on Starr Hill."

"How was tonight for a sighting?"

"Well, Bryce," Diane raised her right hand skyward. "I prefer to see the Milky Way overhead. I shall never forget my first sighting here. It was the first day I arrived and I was standing up by the barn at 2:30 in the morning and, suddenly, I heard a shout from Arthur. He rushed down the hill and clutched me by the arm. He raised my hand up to point and where my hand was was this most marvelous great white, pearly disc.

"And it came, well, from Mars, past Venus, and the Moon, right over my head, over the Milky Way, straight to the Plow and then took an absolute upward turn through two stars and disappeared. It wasn't a satellite. Satellites, of course, go along at their own level. But this suddenly took this upward turn, and it must have been going about a thousand miles an hour."

"Fantastic," was all I could answer. Then turning to Arthur, I asked him, "What was your nearest sighting?"

"I remember clearly April 13, 1967. It was over the shoulder of that hill," Arthur pointed again to the right of the farm house. "It was so big. It was so bright. Bob Strong, who is an ex-RAF bomber crewman took thirty-six films of the 'craft' and nothing developed on the plates at all. Yet, it was so powerful. He ran across the fields trying to get at the 'craft. It was just tip-tilting on the top of the hill. It was really huge. It almost blinded us. The nearer we got the more tingling we felt on all the exposed portions of our body, hands and feet particularly.

"Then it just shot away over the tree line, beyond where we saw the light last evening. Then it just hovered there. We are fairly certain it knew—the intelligence knew—the power-force field might harm us if we got too close."

Having come completely back to my physical being and surroundings, I suddenly realized that I was very cold and tired. I still had to get back to London or find a place to rest until morning. It was almost 3 AM. I asked about hotels. Diane Mathews, who lives in Bath, invited me to stay overnight. Then from out of the darkness came Reg. He said he would take me back to London; about ninety miles away, though he hadn't any plans to go. He offered out of friendship and an open, kind heart.

Diane drove us back to Cradle Hill where Reg had his camper van called Elba in which he crusades for his religious organization called Kingdom Voice. My new comrades and I hugged each other and promised to communicate again soon. I knew that I would be returning.

CHAPTER 6

"There is definite evidence of a higher power or intelligence at work in and on our Earth at this vital junction or crossroad of a changing planet; and it behooves us to make up our minds as to which path to pursue from now on."

Arthur Shuttlewood; UFOS: KEY TO A NEW AGE, page 94

On the way back to London, Reg decided we would stop at Stonehenge, on the Salisbury Plain, which was only about fifteen miles from Warminster. This whole area is filled with legend and folklore. We left the car and stood outside the fence. The eerie early morning light cast hazy shadows from these huge stone giants.

They stood outlined against the sky like great skeleton figures, sentinels of the ancient past guarding the future. I wondered who might have constructed these monolithic stone statues. Perhaps their presence was related to the appearance of UFOs and extraterrestrial beings. We may never know who or what constructed these and other magnificent structures, such as the Great Pyramids in Egypt. But they're there to remind man that there may he energies and intelligences at work in the universe far more advanced than we can even imagine.

Reg and I stood in silence, yet, I felt that we were sharing the same questions and thoughts. Our shoulders barely touched, but we seemed to be breathing in unison. We were witnesses, recording through our beings the wonders of life; here to search and experience and, perhaps, one day, to know. This night had made me feel closer than ever to some definitive truth. My years of searching were bearing fruit and I was beginning to know.

Reg broke the silence, "Many fascinating legends are connected with this part of England. A people who were undoubtedly highly sophisticated lived in this Stonehenge area. It is believed that this massive circle of stones, constructed in the Neolithic Age, more than two thousand years before the birth of the Christ, is not merely an ancient temple, but a large and rather extremely accurate computer from which we can work out the equinox, solstices, midsummer days, star shifts and eclipses, as well as the date.

UFOs: Key To Inner Perfection

"Another and larger one exists at Avesbury, north of here, but still in Wiltshire. It is nearly a half-mile in diameter. Do you realize that the construction and use of such a large edifice must indicate mathematical abilities far beyond those of mere Arabic numerology? Who do you think really raised these structures?"

Reg was thinking the same thoughts. "Beats me," I answered, "but perhaps our friends from the sky had a hand in this."

"More than a hand, I would say," Reg answered.

We both laughed.

We stood awhile longer gazing at the huge stones in front of us and then, together, we turned and walked back to the van.

Reg brewed some hot tea over a small gas heater and we toasted our new friendship. The hot, strong tea helped to waken my senses and lessen the early morning chill. Everything was covered with a fine mist which sparkled in the changing light.

We greeted the dawn, uttering a silent prayer to the new day's sun; stretched and returned to our driving.

I felt marvelously uplifted, almost euphoric. Reg capitalized on my happy disposition by taping an interview on the way back to London. He quizzed me about the Bermuda Triangle, psychic phenomena, UFOs and all related topics. He seemed to want to squeeze every drop of information he could from me. Even though I was feeling a little frayed as the morning dawned, I didn't mind Reg's questioning.

He had such a likeable, sincerely enthusiastic personality and he certainly had gone out of his way to drive me all the way back to London. Perhaps he did it for the interview. No matter. I was more than happy to share my thoughts and views and I was sure the information was being gathered to help others to realize themselves and the often stranger than fiction world we live in.

I was happy to be able to return Reg's hospitality by filling his gas tank and making a small contribution to his Kingdom's Voice Crusade. I hadn't heard too much about his mission since he had me answering questions all the way to London. But I felt there would be another time for us to share this information.

We drove into London past Windsor Castle, returning back to the bustle of civilization. The contrast was all the more apparent after the long night with Arthur and friends on Starr Hill. So much had happened. I knew I hadn't as yet absorbed all the consequences of my recent encounter with—as they're aptly called—uni-

UFOs: Key To Inner Perfection

dentified flying objects.

Reg and I hugged each other warmly and said farewell for now in front of Harrod's Department Store. I told him I would probably see him the same time next year. This turned out to be a prophetic statement. I was to return again to Warminster August, 1973, but more on that anon.

Reg headed off towards his Kingdom Crusade office and I walked from Harrod's, a short distance, to my Kensington High Street hotel where I bathed, shaved and, tired but overjoyed, fell peacefully to sleep. But, just before closing my eyes, I uttered a prayer of thanks. "God bless them all, the beautiful people, the sightings, the UFOs, and most of all, one of the most sincere, honest gentlemen I know, Arthur Shuttlewood. Thank you."

Bryce Bond was unique in that he was able to get his courageous experiences with UFOs and his healing abilities before the public through his media connections.

Photo by Phyllis Brinkerhoff

UFOs: Key To Inner Perfection

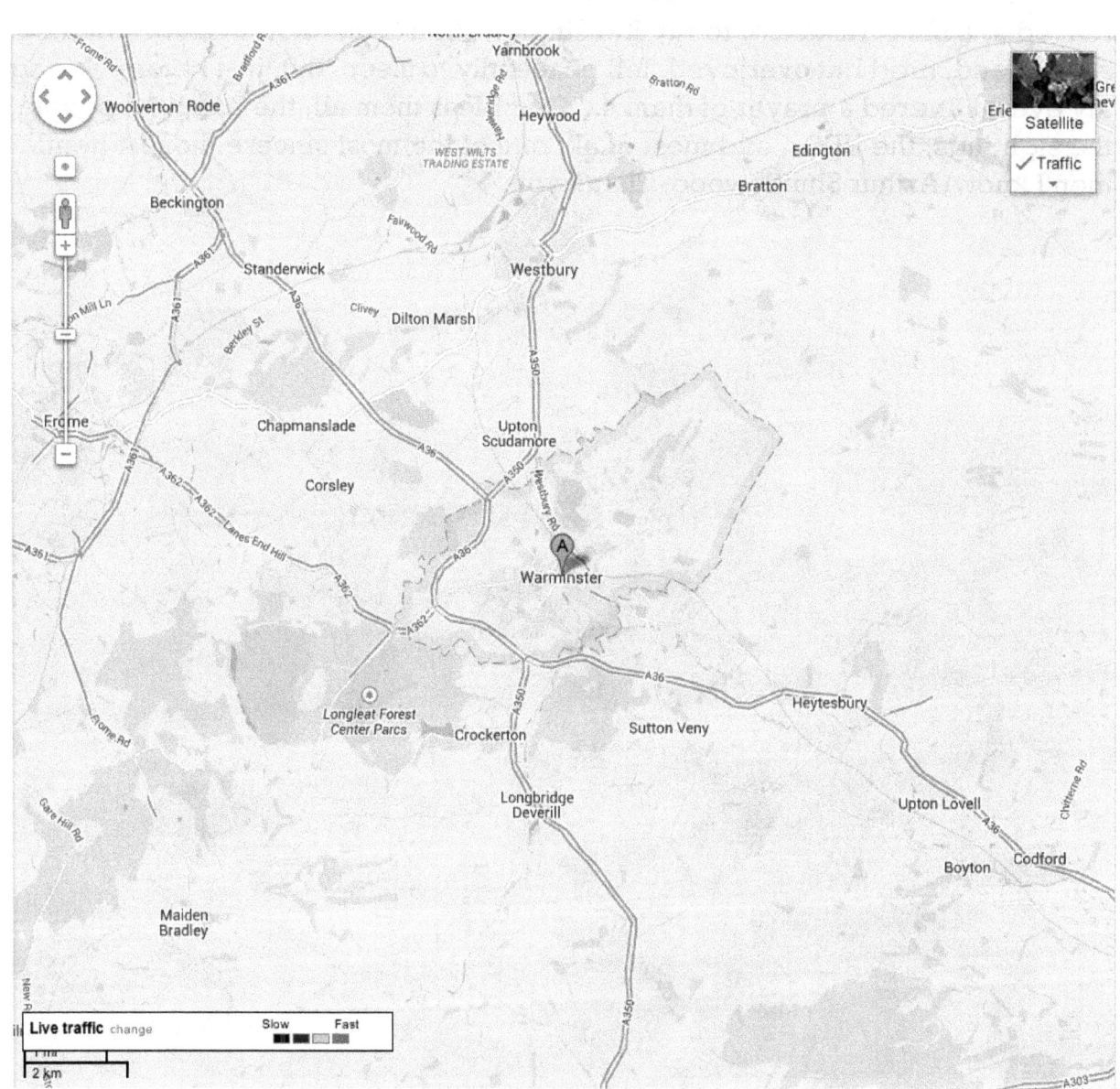

Map of Warminster and surrounding area

UFOs: Key To Inner Perfection

CHAPTER 7

"We of physical form have inevitable opposites in shadowy or reflected form—but it is "they" who could be the Wise Ones of Reality, the Ancients of Days and the Giants of the Past, Present and Future; we are the miniature 'images' or 'likenesses' in embryo of their radiating power and knowledge, until we become as they, without eternal prompting from great teachers. 'The Kingdom Of Heaven Is Within...'"

Arthur Shuttlewood; UFOs: KEY TO THE NEW AGE, page 207

Circumstances brought me back to England, August, 1973. I excitedly anticipated seeing Arthur Shuttlewood again and returning to Cradle and Starr Hills for further sightings. I had kept in touch with Arthur sporadically throughout the year; and had read through most of his material: books, articles, etc. on UFOs.

I was more than ever convinced of the authenticity of UFOs and the actuality of extraterrestrial contact. Further experiences with other UFO investigators, discussed later in this book, brought me definitive acknowledgment of the UFO as a fact, and not the figment of mass hallucination or imagination.

Authentic evidence piled on evidence led ultimately to one conclusion: UFOs were a physical reality. I returned to England with this assurance and with renewed enthusiasm to gain more knowledge and actual sighting experience.

I had written Arthur before leaving for England to inform him of my schedule. I again had a series of interview appointments in England with healers, mediums and other psychically gifted individuals. Arthur and I planned to meet on August 18th, at his home.

Ethel DeLoach, healer and Executive Secretary of the Jersey Society of Parapsychology was also in England at this time. She had been accompanying me on some of my interviews as a very gifted and knowledgeable friend and fellow healer. Being also a fellow seeker, Ethel asked if she could accompany Bill Dysart, my affinity brother and me to Warminster. By all means, I told her, knowing that Arthur would appreciate her gentle sincerity and dedication to helping those in need both physically and spiritually.

Bill also asked along a good friend of his, a lovely English lady by the name

UFOs: Key To Inner Perfection

of Florence Kemp. Florence is a member of The Aetherius Society, which will be fully discussed when we relate our adventures with Dr. George King.

Florence's husband didn't completely share her interest in the spiritual world and so chose not to join us. Florence offered the use of her new Rover 2000, which made the trip to Warminster very comfortable for us.

Ethel DeLoach, Bill Dysart and I left London on Friday, August 18th, by railway, heading twenty five miles to Amersham to rendezvous with Florence.

We admired Florence's charming English country house, her friendly chow companion, and her beautiful well tended gardens with their tall hedges, fruit trees, herbs and flowers. Florence is a gentle spirit. Though petit, she has the enthusiasm and joy of a person of enormous stature with a heart bigger than she is.

After a quick cup of tea, we packed Florence's Rover with food, blankets, tape recorders and cameras; and with Bill at the wheel drove to Warminster, a couple of hours North-West of Amersham. The drive gave us a chance to get acquainted and to share further knowledge of the area surrounding Warminster. (I have included a map so the reader can follow me visually.) 4 Warminster is situated in the center of a triangle formed when Salisbury is connected in a straight line through Amesbury and Stonehenge with Avebury in the North and then West to Glastonbury and back South to Salisbury. (See map page...) These straight interconnecting lines are called "ley lines"—lines which align many points of ancient historical interest.

It is believed that holy places of immense spiritual power with their highly charged sacred edifices, stone circles, barrows, earthworks, and other significant monuments, were erected with an awareness of existing invisible lines of electromagnetic energy. It appears that early civilizations were aware of this energy which they utilized for physical and spiritual benefits by specifically structuring "religious" sites at certain significant points along these power-lines, referred to as "ley lines".

Bordering and within the triangle surrounding Warminster are at least fourteen intersecting ley lines, all aligning over five historical points and some aligning more than thirteen. It is speculated that UFOs are magnetically attracted to "ley lines" and use them as a power source or navigational pathway.

One feasible explanation for UFO's seeming spontaneous appearances and disappearances is that they enter and exit at points along these lines. Perhaps, stretching our minds a little further, entities from other dimensions, time continuums, or universes originally created these earth structures as physical signs and metaphysical guide lines to their existence.

UFOs: Key To Inner Perfection

The structure of the area as seen from the air, reflects on the ground the constellations in the sky. Marked out across the Somerset landscape, when viewed from above, within a circle of ten miles across lies the famous Glastonbury Zodiac, ancient Temple to the Stars. It seems as if these towns were designed in this special way as a reminder that as above so below; man is a reflection of the heavens.

We did a lot of speculating on the ride to Warminster. We stretched our minds and imaginations. You could almost feel the excitement build in the car as we neared our destination.

Bill, Ethel and I strongly voiced the hope that we would experience something special. Florence, quiet soul that she is, wasn't quite sure why she was with us. Then Bill asked her to tell us what had happened earlier in the day when a gypsy lady had come to read her fortune.

Florence related, "Well, she comes once a year. Today she came earlier than usual. I was too excited about this evening and wasn't really in the mood for her, but I listened anyway. Upon looking at my hand, she exclaimed, 'I must do something for you! It's tonight. Tonight. It has to do with a planet.' She was all excited but she really didn't know what she was reading. I do hope she has gone to her healing church and is doing some praying for all of us. For we have quite a long journey."

Yes, my thoughts replied silently, whether we were aware of it or not, we were all being guided on this incredible voyage which may turn out to be just the beginning for all of us.

Bill added to our expectation, by relating the story of the disappearance of a man in Shepton Mallet, (also contained within the triangle, as is Maiden Bradley where water runs up hill for a mile or more). It was during the winter. There was snow on the ground and no footprints. A man walked out onto his front porch and disappeared off the face of the earth. Just a story? We didn't have any proof at the moment, but I made a mental note to check Arthur on this one later.

I vaguely recalled having read something about this phenomena in one of his books, but I couldn't remember exactly where. The plausibility made us all shudder.

Florence was the first to voice our concern, "Don't think I'd like to just disappear, but then there's not much of me to go." We all needed that interjection of levity. Laughing, we entered the Warminster area. We arrived much too late to call Arthur; besides, I was certain I remembered the way to Cradle and Starr Hills, having been there just the year before. To make double sure, we stopped at a truck station and asked if they could direct us. These people didn't even know

UFOs: Key To Inner Perfection

where Cradle or Starr Hills were, yet they were natives of Warminster. What's more, they'd never heard of a UFO or a sighting. I guess we only see what we want to see and acknowledge what we want to know. It's amazing how we can block out knowledge when it's staring us in the face. But then, we all do this as a form of self protection. I've certainly blocked out knowledge when it gets too close to a truth I'm not ready to accept. All in good time, as the expression rightly goes. All in good time.

It was about 1:30 AM when our adventure truly began. We took the wrong road. Facing us were signs saying: Keep Out. Do Not Enter. But it is just this kind of warning that will make my dear friend Bill Dysart, bless him, move forward. He's a very stubborn, adventurous man and quick to answer a challenge.

He drove right through the signs and we found ourselves on military property in what was obviously a marine corps training ground for tank maneuvers. The tank treads were visible all around us. We were going down a bumpy road. I felt the ladies getting apprehensive though they seemed to be too absorbed in what was happening to say anything. I was getting wild impressions and vibrations. An inner voice was loudly telling me not to go any further and I found myself shouting, "Stop Bill, for God's sake, let's not go any further."

"Yes, what if the military found us?" Florence interjected nervously.

Yes, what if they interrogated us. How would we explain why we were there. Perhaps they'd think we were out to sabotage the area. Bill heeded our pleas and turned the car around and began heading back. Then he decided to abruptly turn onto another roadway and then about a hundred yards away he turned again onto a dirt road and we found ourselves facing a huge concrete ramp. Perhaps it was there to park the tanks.

Somehow we all felt more comfortable with the car stopped. We waited quietly inside the car for some kind of signal. It's as if we all knew, without voicing it, that we were there for a reason and that it was all right.

It was now about 2:00 AM, another chilly August night in England, cloudy and about forty degrees. This time I had remembered to bring a sweater to wear under my jacket. We got out of the car separately and wandered around for a while; and then we all walked slowly over to the ramp. Without speaking we formed a metaphysical circle: man, woman, man, woman.

With regard to the electromagnetic polarities of the body, men are positive and woman are negative, much like the north and south poles of a magnet. We joined hands and united in our circle sent out thoughts of love and welcome. Instantly, Ethel, who is a very, very good clairvoyant was getting impressions. It was a dark, cloudy night, yet the air seemed to be filled with sparkling particles of

UFOs: Key To Inner Perfection

light energy, perhaps what is called, "orgone energy," waves of light emanations rising from the ground like a mist. Although it was dark, I could see the texture and pattern of my jacket clearly in the strange, vibrant glowing light.

We were surrounded by hills that seemed to be floating in a pearly, opalescent mist, yet, there did not seem to be any fog on the horizon. All we could see were the tops of the hills, the small groups of trees that cap the hills. From a distance, they seemed to floating like hovering UFOs.

We stood silently in our circle each experiencing the electrical matrix of energy all around us. Holding hands, a tingling sensation seemed to travel around and through our bodies uniting us as we each, in his own way, kept sending out thoughts of acceptance and love.

Suddenly, as if from no where, four or five large translucent egg shaped objects, almost invisible to the naked eye, appeared and hovered about two feet off the ground on the outer periphery of our circle. These "craft" just seemed to manifest out of no where. They projected into our conscious physical dimension for a brief period of time and then they disappeared.

I felt that all of us were experiencing similar sensations. Each seemed to nod at the same time and squeeze the hand of the person next to him. Then Ethel broke the silence softly saying, "They're here."

Entities, tall shimmering tubes of light beams seven to eight feet in height were faintly visible. They manifested into form all around us out of the darkness. I could not be sure if they emerged from the "crafts". They just seemed to float into perspective.

We stood rooted in our circle clutching each others hands. We were together, as one, in the experience. No one moved away. The tall, whitish, translucent entities formed a circle around our circle. I'm not sure how many of them there were. No one bothered to count. We stood still concentrating our energies towards uniting in spirit with each other and our visitors. I know that none of us felt any hostility. We all felt warmth and a tingling sensation on our skin. We were encompassed by streams of warm air. The air made us feel protected, as when a parent or a loved one covers you with an extra blanket in the middle of the night when you're half awake and aware that someone is taking special care of you. One had the feeling that these beings were being especially careful not to harm us.

Tingling vibrations kept passing through us and from hand to hand. There was a faint, delicious scent of roses and lilies-of-the-valley in the air. You could almost taste its sweetness.

UFOs: Key To Inner Perfection

Waves of protective warmth continually surrounded and penetrated our circle. I had the feeling that the warm energy was "speaking" to me. Out loud I voiced a prayer, nothing religious, just a spiritual plea that we be united in love with these higher intelligences. The others echoed my words.

Next, at Bill's suggestion, we broke the circle, dropped hands, and stepping backwards as if to meet the entities, we expanded the circle to contain them. Instantly the entities were in the middle of the circle where we could see them. These seemingly faceless, almost transparent beings are perhaps the angels spoken of in the Bible. Perhaps those shimmering, gossamer-winged beings were really extraterrestrial entities like our visitors. Actually angel in Greek means messenger. Were these strange intangible entities messengers from another time and space?

It seemed that without speaking, we were all experiencing the same sensations at the same time. I wasn't sure if we all physically saw the same things, but I felt a community of feeling. It was as if some telepathic message was being beamed to us and we were each receiving the message separately but simultaneously.

None of us seemed to feel fear. Perhaps we didn't have time for fear, or perhaps it just didn't exist in this dimension of consciousness and contact. In order to feel fear one must be aware of being fearful.

We were so surrounded by pleasant sensations that there wasn't any room in the experience for a contrary feeling. It's difficult to hate and love at the same time. When you're really loving, hate just doesn't exist. This was the same experience. We all agreed later that we had experienced something approximating the ultimate bliss Yogis speak about when they discuss reaching nirvana.

Perhaps these beings created a state of samadhi, the experience of ultimate union with the source of creation, called God, higher consciousness, the Supreme, whatever the name, the feeling of total oneness is the same. One knows in this sublime condition that nothing can hurt you if you're walking in the pathway of the light. Somehow we knew we had been guided to this destination at this specific time to make contact with these extraterrestrial intelligences and to share in this extraordinary experience together.

The entities formed a circle within our expanded circle and then other entities joined and formed a circle outside our circle. Now there were actually three circles. We were surrounded without feeling enclosed. I had a strong feeling that all my faculties were being expanded. I felt great surges of energy reverberate through my body as if I were a giant accordion; and some strange, powerfully beautiful music was being played on me. Those silent sound waves were being transposed by my mind into a message which would unfold its patterned melody

UFOs: Key To Inner Perfection

in the months to come.

We know that the air around us is filled with high frequency sound waves that are beyond our range of hearing but often animals can tune in and react. Earlier, in Warminster, when the residents heard those loud sonic booms, animals reacted violently to the noise.

I have always been interested in sound vibration and I teach and practice a form of breathing called sonic breathing, actually an ancient practice that involves voicing certain sounds from different centers of the body, much like chanting but with special focus on parts of the body.

Voicing Amen or Hallelujah is the same as the Indian Om or Aum. Each sounds a prayer to a higher deity. However, this was a silent experience. No words or audible sounds seemed necessary. This was a magnificent, awe inspiring presence and we all felt the power of the contact. Wherever they came from; another planet, a parallel existence, a vibrational world existing within our own. I don't believe any of us know for sure, but that night, that very special night, they made their presence on this earth known to four human beings and we have all been subtly changed by the experience. I know that my world has never looked the same since.

But this is just the beginning of a weekend filled with adventure.

Dr. Hynek (right foreground) and other UFO devotees.
Dr. Hynek examined more UFO events than any other person in the world.

UFOs: Key To Inner Perfection

CHAPTER 8

"The only Heaven worth striving for is the assurance that all Men shall have in their hearts, minds and consciousness, love for one another; and within their very Soul portion the eternal qualities of Love, Peace and Inner Serenity."

Arthur Shuttlewood; UFOs: KEY TO THE NEW AGE, page 213

Ethel, Florence, Bill and I stood silently awestruck by what had just transpired. The atmosphere changed abruptly when we all turned in the direction of a loud bang coming from just in front of the new Rover two thousand. Ethel was the first to witness a tall entity appear in front of the car at the moment of the noise. I, too, saw the faint outline of this being.

Then Bill and I noticed, along one of the inclining hillsides, what appeared to be thirty-five people coming down towards us. By this time we were apprehensive, thinking perhaps that the military might be patrolling the area and might have spotted us and the car. Perhaps they had come to investigate the loud noise, thinking it might be a gun shot. We told the girls to return to the Rover.

Bill and I decided it would look best if we went to intercept the figures that appeared to be moving towards us over the horizon of the hill, rather than appear guilty by seeming to retreat. Strangely, as we walked toward the figures they became smaller until when we got up close, what appeared to be huge lurking forms from a distance, turned out to be nothing more than six-inch high stunted pines, just little twigs lining a roadside. We laughed with relief and discussed the tricks the senses can play. Can we ever be completely sure of what we see?

Often things aren't what they appear to be. We compared our earlier views of the entities. Bill wasn't sure if he had actually seen entities, though he had felt a strong flowing energy. Here, we had both believed that these tiny trees could be human beings. Bill and I are not people who accept what we see as actual facts. We both have enquiring minds and are aware that the physical senses can be easily fooled by conditions of distance, lighting and perspective. Optical illusions are common occurrences.

UFOs: Key To Inner Perfection

But, in the earlier experience with the entities, we both agreed that we felt a deeper significance to their appearance and disappearance than just what the surface senses might have recorded. Our inner sense; or sixth sense as it's called, had truly witnessed most unusual apparitions. Could the entities have been an illusion?

We speculated, knowing that we could not possibly perceive all the answers at that moment. All that had transpired would have to be correlated later when we had time to connect all the circumstances.

We both stood there shaking our heads and laughing, not just at the joke played by nature, but to release the incredible energy we had accumulated during the evening's intense experience with the entities. With a sense of relief, we joined the ladies back at the car.

We tried to tell them why we were laughing, but our words came out scrambled, and we laughed even harder. You know the feeling you get when you're telling a very funny story and you keep laughing all the way through it because you already know the punch line? Very frustrating to the listener, but a hard thing to control once you're into it. I managed to sputter out, "We'll explain later."

Once we had calmed down, we decided to try again to find Starr Hill. I still felt I could locate it. We found ourselves driving back and forth to no avail.

The road was hilly and bumpy and the darkness of the night obscured our vision. We decided later that we had passed the roadway to Starr Hill many times, but we were apparently not supposed to find it at that time.

It was now approximately 6:00 AM on Saturday. We were about two or three miles outside of Warminster, seemingly going round in circles.

All of a sudden the engine stopped. The brand new generator was burnt out. Was this related to the loud bang we heard earlier when we noticed an entity in front of the car? We couldn't be sure. But there didn't seem to he any evident mechanical reason for generator failure.

Florence and I left Ethel and Bill resting in the car alongside the highway. Still feeling adventuresome and too keyed up to sleep, we decided to walk the few miles into Warminster to see if we could get help.

We walked silently, breathing rhythmically to our footsteps. By concentrating on our pace, walk became a meditation and we soon found ourselves entering Warminster. Though the sky still looked overcast, the town looked peaceful and quiet in the early morning light. We came to a petrol station and the attendant sleepily told us that they wouldn't be open for service until 8:30 AM and that we should return at that time.

UFOs: Key To Inner Perfection

We wandered down the quaint narrow streets in search of another station or someone who might be of help. Some merchants were already languidly opening their stores. They greeted us pleasantly even though we both must have looked rather dishevelled. Florence's clothes were all rumpled and I had more than a day's growth of heard. Perhaps they thought we had been romping in the hay, especially when they discovered I was American. Little did they realize where we had been and what we had seen.

We couldn't find another gas station but we did locate, with the help of a resident, a public restroom. We both felt somewhat better after washing our faces. We then went over to the local police headquarters.

The policemen were just getting ready to start their rounds. We explained our car problem. They tried to be helpful. They, of course, knew Arthur Shuttlewood; but they were not too knowledgeable about UFOs. Their main concern was the heavy traffic in Warminster since the original sonic booms and the subsequent sightings.

Things hadn't been the same since and there were so many strangers in town. Why, there were people from all over the world coming to Warminster. People camping on the hills and sleeping at the side of the road. While we were talking, a patrol car came in and reported a car stuck on the road outside of town with two sleeping people in it. We explained that that was our car and that our friends were resting while we went for help.

Fortunately, they didn't make us feel like intruders. The policemen directed us back to the petrol station. Florence and I went to get some coffee and by that time the garage had opened. The tow truck drove us back to the car. We woke Ethel and Bill who had been sleeping soundly. The truck hitched us up and towed us back to the petrol station in town. We waited for the mechanics. Around 9:00 AM they surveyed the problem and informed us that they would have to go to the next town to get a generator for this particular car. It would take a few hours.

We walked around town and spent the morning consuming quarts of tea and coffee to keep ourselves alert. We seemed to evade talking about the happenings of the night. Perhaps we were too tired to talk, but I rather think that each of us wished to digest the experience without being influenced by the others.

At 11 AM we returned to the station. The car was again ready to roll. Since no one came with cash, I found myself literally pounds lighter after leaving the garage. Luckily I always carry spare bills in case of an emergency. Sometimes exceptional experiences can be costly in every sense of the word. Perhaps, this was a warning to be careful and not push ourselves too far or, like an overloaded fuse, we might have a blow out.

UFOs: Key To Inner Perfection

That's exactly what happened. We had not one but three blow outs on one tire, all in succession. We decided to go to Glastonbury since it was still too early to contact Arthur. But it seems there was a fair somewhere between Warminster and Glastonbury, possibly in Shepton Mallet. The traffic was unbelievable.

Stop-go. Stop-go for miles. In the middle of the traffic we got a flat. No sooner did we get the tire changed and the flat fixed when we had another blow out and then another. The petrol station was getting tired of seeing us. Three strikes! We decided Glastonbury was out for the day.

As it turned out, if we had pushed ahead, we might not have gotten back to Warminster in time that evening to experience what was to follow. We accepted the blow outs as warnings and spent the day in Warminster.

Florence suggested a picnic. She had prepared for the possibility of being stranded in some out of the way place by packing hampers of food. So as soon at the tires were fixed, we headed out of town with Bill at the wheel. It was almost 2:00 PM and all traces of clouds had disappeared. The day turned out to be crystal clear with a brilliant sun shining, a beautiful August day in the country. Our spirits were high and the car was finally running smoothly.

Bill turned off on an unmarked dirt road. We found ourselves in a secluded area with no houses or people visible. Bill pulled off the road onto a thick grassy spot and we all got out of the car to look around.

There were fences on both sides of us. To one side was an open cow pasture and to the other was a wooded area with tall, fat oak trees covered with hanging vines. Directly in front of us was an almost ripe wheat field and we noticed a large landing impression near us in the wheat pushed down in the same counterclockwise manner as the ones I had seen the year before and there wasn't any pathway leading through the wheat to the depression. We had instinctively picked a landing spot for our picnic.

With this realization, we settled ourselves in a cove created by the tall trees and overhanging vines. Here we were out of the direct sun and heat of midday.

Florence spread a feast. From out of the back of the Rover she produced a banquet of sandwiches, tinned meat, cheese, fruit, biscuits, as well as a heater to make hot soup, tea and coffee.

Florence also surprised us with battery-powered portable phonograph and a stack of classical records to choose from: Tchaikovsky, Chopin, Beethoven and Mozart.

We ate to a concert. While eating we all expressed a feeling of deja vu. We began to picture each other dressed as we would have been at another, distant

UFOs: Key To Inner Perfection

time. The ladies appeared to be wearing long heaped skirts and the men pantaloons. We weren't sure of the period of time we were experiencing. The century didn't matter, the experience did. We each realized that we had probably been together at another time, perhaps in another life. We were being transported together and as we listened to the music, the surrounding scenery seemed to change form.

We were in a garden, dancing and playing among the high hedges, behind some elegant Manor House. We were somehow younger and gayer.

All these thoughts were expressed by each of us as we sat on a thick blanket of grass, in the cove, under the vine-covered trees.

Then, one by one-to the strains of "The Midsummer Night's Dream," we all fell soundly asleep. Florence was the first to awake to the sound of the scratching phonograph needle. She changed the record and we all awoke to the lively strains of Chopin's Scherzo, almost a revelry.

We had probably slept for about two hours. The sun was beginning to set. We cleaned up and packed the car. The food and music must have attracted the cows because when we returned to the car they were lining the fence. There was a whole herd of beautiful animals.

Ethel was ecstatic, "The farmer is really going to wonder why he's going to get so many extra gallons of milk at the next milking time. You know cows will produce better when they're given music in the barn? It's a fact. They've done studies. Look at them; aren't they fantastic? Hey, Bossy, over here," Ethel called to the cows lovingly, "Come on Bossy. Hi girls. You're a beautiful audience."

Bill got into the act; jumped over the fence and cavorted among the herd. They watched lazily, uninterested as if mesmerized by the music. I got out my camera and photographed the happy proceedings.

On this note of levity, we headed back towards Warminster. We stopped at a roadside pub and sat in the garden with the clotheslines bedecked with the morning wash. Here, as the day drew to a close, we talked quietly about the experience we had shared together just a half a day before.

Ethel started slowly, hesitantly at first to explain what she saw, "Many clairvoyants, like myself, and I'm sure Bryce would agree, see spirits or entities daily around people and we get used to it. But, I certainly was not prepared for what I saw this morning, that we saw upon the hill there, Cradle Hill, I believe. Wasn't it? It's almost indescribable."

"Yes, Ethel," Bill answered. "But we weren't on the usual part of Cradle Hill, right Bryce?"

UFOs: Key To Inner Perfection

I nodded, not exactly sure of the location but pretty sure I could find this spot again.

"I believe," Ethel continued, "that we were directed to the place by forces we were not aware of. I also feel that what we experienced there has not been completed. I really wish I was an artist so that I could sketch what I saw."

"Ethel, you were the first one to see one of these large beings," Bill stated, "but, I know we all had a strange feeling that something was there; and when we formed the circle and prayed, we felt tremendous energies surging through our bodies and you, and Bryce, saw several beings. I saw the aura of each of you expanding beautifully in that incredible glowing light; and I felt strange things happen to my arms, if you remember."

"Yes, I certainly remember. It was an incredible experience to see those entities join our circle," Ethel seemed to be trying hard to connect together pieces of the experience to form a cohesive whole. "The very tall one seemed to stay behind but two shorter ones , joined us; one got between you, Bill and Florence and one between Florence and Bryce. Of course, I felt them all around me. But then I saw the tallest one, who was a good head taller than you, Bill and you're over six feet?"

"Yes," Bill answered, "about six feet one inch."

"This entity was at least a head taller than you," Ethel continued. "He seemed to be of greater importance since he made his presence felt the strongest. The entities were all unsmiling, but I had a very friendly warm feeling of love and acceptance. They really seemed to want us to know that they were there."

"Did you look into their eyes?" Bill asked.

"I couldn't see the eyes clearly enough especially in the large entity."

"Too much energy, perhaps," Bill was trying hard to grasp the full significance of Ethel's words.

I had not been able to distinguish any features, perhaps the light emanating from these beings was too strong and obliterated the details.

"I think I'll have to describe these entities more in detail later before I forget what they really looked like, because I think this might be helpful in corroborating the evidence we're collecting together, perhaps more than we realize..." Ethel's voice seemed to trail off as a concerned inward look came over her face seeming to close off her outward senses. She was obviously looking within for an answer.

UFOs: Key To Inner Perfection

Bill, who hadn't physically seen the entities, seemed to be trying to make contact with them through Ethel's image. He continued to probe, "One of the best ways human beings can convey power and knowledge to one another is through eye contact. It's a very basic form of telepathic communication. Certainly obvious when you watch two people in love. Their eyes seem to melt into each others. Imagine, if you had in fact seen into the eyes of one of those entities, the beauty would have been such that you would have wanted to become part of it. It would have been like being in samadhic trance, I believe. What ecstasy!"

"The beauty of the entire face was so full of indescribable wisdom that it makes me think that I shouldn't have looked." Ethel's gaze was still directed into herself.

"Perhaps, we shouldn't even be talking," Bill rejoined.

"Perhaps," Ethel almost whispered. "It almost seems too much to feel that you are privileged to see and witness beings like that. Well, I'm going to have to think about it later when I can really sort out my feelings about what I saw and felt and put them into more exact words."

We all sat quietly. Ethel seemed to sum up all our feelings. Florence looked a little bewildered and we didn't question her. I had been happy to sit back, observing and listening. I, too, felt that there were many pieces of this intricate puzzle to fit together and somehow, we were just beginning. We drew closer together as the twilight grew around us. We had a snack and a beverage and all took advantage of the washroom.

It was very quickly time to meet with Arthur Shuttlewood.

UFOs: Key To Inner Perfection

Bryce Bond and others felt that Warminster was a portal or window through which the UFOs and their crews entered Earth dimensions.

UFOs: Key To Inner Perfection

Marc Brinkerhoff & Bryce Bond, visiting the Monroe Institute, Faber, Virginia. Bryce interviewed Bob Monroe for his TV show, 'Dimensions in Parapsychology' 1990.

Photo by Phyllis Brinkerhoff

UFOs: Key To Inner Perfection

Bryce Burleigh Bond

Photo by Phyllis Brinkerhoff

UFOs: Key To Inner Perfection

CHAPTER 9

"Love is undoubtedly the most potent force in the entire strata of existence everywhere.

Arthur Shuttlewood; UFOs: KEY TO THE NEW AGE, page 62

On seeing Arthur Shuttlewood I again experienced that warm, wonderful feeling of brotherhood that I felt with him at my first sighting a year ago on Starr Hill. Reginald Bradbury, the man who had generously driven me to London last year, was there. I asked him how his Kingdom Voice Crusade was progressing, having received his newsletter throughout the year. Arthur introduced everyone all around. There was quite a group of friends and fellow UFO watchers present. Arthur had apparently prepared a welcoming party for us, with tea, cakes, biscuits, cheese and drinks for those who imbibe. I prefer to keep my senses alert without the stimulation of alcohol or tobacco, but do not socially condemn either.

Arthur, Bill and I sat off a ways from the others and discussed the events and thoughts that had transpired over the past year. Arthur seemed anxious to share his discoveries with us.

He discussed the state of the world now as he sees it, "I think we're at a turning point. I think it's going to hit man straight in the eyes that he's going the wrong way in life. He's going to get a blinding flash of inspiration, in a practical form, like seeing and not being able to deny the existence of UFOs."

"Do you feel they're here to wake man up?" Bill asked.

"I think this force has come at crucial points in time," Arthur replied. "When man has taken a wrong turn, perhaps through over self dependence; when he starts taking things into his own hands, instead of leaving them to the will of the great designer, the great architect of the whole universe. I believe they come at those times, and at times of what, perhaps, we would term natural disaster. We don't know much about Noah's ark and the flood, which is perhaps an allegorical tale, and yet, obviously has a substratum of truth in it.

UFOs: Key To Inner Perfection

"We've had a number of catastrophes, world wide, in the past, and these are signs. It says in the New Testament, quite clearly: 'I will lift up mine eyes unto the hills, from whence cometh my help'. I believe that appears in the 121st Psalm. So the old truths, to me, are crystal clear as absolute truths today. The more one ponders them, the more true they are."

"We do have a lot to learn by observing and paying close attention," Bill had been listening carefully, as I had, to Arthur's words and they had obviously penetrated deeply. "There's so much we don't know."

"Yes," I interjected, "and it seems the more I think I know the less I seem to really know. I have begun to feel so insignificant with regard to dimensions and universes of existence far beyond me. Perhaps there really is a God, or what we call God."

"Yes, Bryce," Arthur answered, "I think the UFO intelligence is essentially of God. But man must sink his ego Before he can get the truth. He must be ready to learn from every man, negative or positive. You know, there's the old story: 'He that is without Sin among you let him cast the first stone.' No one can. No man can set himself up as God, obviously, because no man can ever cast the first stone. We must first learn our lessons.

"Look how many marriages and partnerships have split up, how much discord there is in the world. Even here on the hill. You get negative stories about malevolence, about poltergeist activity, ghosts and all. It really depends upon the mental and spiritual frame of the person who goes to the hill; their motive and what they're seeing. UFOs test the weaknesses and frailties of man.

"I know I've changed since going into the hills and sighting. During the war I would have killed. Today I couldn't kill a fly. Now when I'm on the hill, I have my coat tugged by invisible presences, I've had all sorts of peculiar things happen that at the time caused me fright. But when I've braved that fear and pushed out loving thoughts only, knowing that love and fear can't live together anyway, beautiful things have happened."

Hearing Arthur, I recalled the thought I had had when the entities had appeared to the four of us. "When you're filled with love there's no room for fear."

I felt slightly out of sync, to use a broadcast term, or disoriented with regard to the twelve hours or so that had passed since our shared experience with the entities.

In certain states of consciousness, time can be somehow expanding while compressing: moments can seem like forever and yet, forever seems to be contained in a second. Time becomes very subjective; one has an incredible sense of

UFOs: Key To Inner Perfection

timelessness and of being suspended in space. I tried to focus in on the exact feeling but it evaded me. Arthur was answering a question about fear. I tuned back in.

"If you give way to fear you shrivel up and die physically—you're doomed. But why worry. There's always the next time around. My experiences have convinced me of this. Fear and love are such unhappy bedfellows. I think it was John who said that perfect love casteth out fear!

"If man has any fear within him, he still has a lot of weakness he's got to get rid of. This is probably the whole meaning of 'look within for the answers'. The UFO intelligence will exploit all our weaknesses until man realizes what's meant by being one with God. Do you see what I mean?"

"Yes," Bill and I answered together. We hadn't as yet related our experience to Arthur so he didn't know how clearly we saw what he meant.

"UFOs are simply telling you," Arthur continued, "that all things are not physical as you would like to think they are. We have not even begun to touch the boundaries of our scientific horizons. If you ponder a little deeper, you begin to realize that there may be presences around us all the time that we know nothing about as yet. They're here to guide and help and if you can overcome fear, perhaps you can make contact."

Bill started to tell Arthur about our shared experience. Arthur wanted to hear, but first he wished to tell us about a friend of his who had had a most unusual occurrence with some extraordinary people. It was as if Arthur knew that something special had happened to us, but he wanted to add strength to our experience by supplying this knowledge before we came to any conclusions. Before beginning, he called Ethel and Florence over. Some other visitors, Reg included, joined us as well.

"This story was told to me by a friend of mine named Marion. She's a pilot's wife and every day she commutes from Andover to Bristol which means coming through Warminster. On this particular day, she was attending a panel discussion at a TV studio. I believe George King of the Aetherius Society and some other chaps were speaking. Well, the program was going quite well until one of the men, spoke about this UFO he was watching change into a robed figure of Christ in the sky.

"Then, the back room boys who were listening to this, belonging to HTV, that's Herlech Television Bristol Studios, burst into laughter behind the scenes and said, 'stupid'. They do this when you mention anything religious. They feel uncomfortable so they snicker.

UFOs: Key To Inner Perfection

"Well, on her way back from Bristol that night, the train stooped as usual at Warminster and two young students get on. Both tall—about six feet. One with long flaxen hair, parted in the middle, down to his shoulders, slim, wearing tight fitting jeans. The other chap was burly with wide shoulders. He had horn-rimmed spectacles and thick bushy black hair brushed back and cut shorter than the other fellow's. They both had blue eyes. They looked like typical students. They even had duffel bags which they pushed up onto the rack.

"They sat down opposite my friend in a fairly crowded compartment. She was reading a book when they got on so she didn't notice them. But, just after the train pulled out of Warminster and going in the Salisbury direction towards Andover, one of the young men politely leaned forward and said, 'Do excuse me, but would you mind looking out of the window and telling me what you see?'

"Marion looked out of the window and said, 'Yes, a very steep hill.'

"'Yes,' he said, 'but what's at the bottom of it?'

"'Well,' she answered, 'a peculiar oval shape. It's absolutely white.'"

"'Yes,' he said. 'Would you believe that that is the impression left by a UFO?'

"Ah," she answered, 'it could be I suppose.'

"They both looked at each other and smiled much as to say, 'Well, that's nice at least she knows what a UFO is.'

"Later, in their very fragmentary conversation, they told her, 'Well, look for it in the future.'

"Marion has been looking for it every evening and every morning as she commutes back and forth. Neither the UFO impression or the hill seems to exist. And she had marked the features of the hill very clearly in her mind. She can't find either.

"Also during their strange conversation, out of the blue, you might say, the darker one asked Marion, 'Well, you know what UFO means. What did you think of the program?"

"Marion answered spontaneously, 'Well, one man was quite good, you know, until he mentioned that Christ appeared from a UFO.' Later Marion realized that she hadn't mentioned the program. But at the time she didn't think too much about what was happening.

"Then the young men got out at the changing point, she thought, 'Well, they're going to Southampton. I suppose they're students at the University there.'

"The last thing, however, that the fair-haired one remarked to her was, 'Why

UFOs: Key To Inner Perfection

is it that people laugh when the word God or the word Jesus Christ is mentioned?'

"Now it dawned on Marion that she hadn't mentioned the program and certainly hadn't mentioned the laughter. How did they know? Who were they?

"Marion is a very sensible woman. The day after this happened she called me. She was quite plainly worried and had to tell someone. The few friends she told in Bristol had laughed at her. Her husband, a senior pilot in the air force didn't laugh; in fact he agreed that she should call me. She felt a bit foolish about it all and wondered what was happening.

"I asked her if the boys gave any names. She said, 'No!' But when she gave me the descriptions, they matched perfectly Micah and Joab, two young men who had called on me in 1969 and accompanied me in their car to Cradle Hill."

Yes, this was an incredible story. But, reflecting on our own remarkable experience, I wondered if the two young men were real, physical people.

"Oh, yes, physical people as they were on the train. But the important thing is what they can induce into one's mind and what they can do physically."

"What can they do?" Bill asked anxious to hear more.

"Well, we were in the car broadside the main gate which fronts you as you're up on the hill. Micah was in the back with me and Joab was at the controls in the driver's seat. It was a big American car with a left-hand wheel. I gazed up into the turbulent sky and forecast, 'I'm awfully sorry, but I'm afraid we won't see anything tonight. There's no guarantee of a sighting in this weather.'

The fair-haired lad, Micah, who was in the back with me and nearest the gate, said quietly as he wound the window of the car down on his side, 'Arthur, why do you worry so muck about what people see? Why won't they use their other senses? Listen!'

"As soon as he said, 'Listen!' the whole car shook. Instantly, it was as if this large vehicle was ` transformed into a ship in a tumultuous sea with huge waves buffeting the sides. And it sounded as if a hundred people were around the car hitting it with buckets of gravel all over the chassis and metal work.

"But there wasn't anyone there. Ultra realist that I am, I looked at Joab at the wheel to see if he was fiddling with any controls or playing with the ignition and he wasn't. Joab was looking back at me with a slow smile on his frank face. It was matched by Micah.

"'You see," said Joab, "one does not have to rely on seeing to the exclusion of hearing and the other senses, to know what all this means at the present time.

"Somehow with all this happening I felt completely at ease with these two

UFOs: Key To Inner Perfection

lads. It was lovely to be with both of them. There were no inhibitions. I felt that I could say or do anything and they would understand perfectly."

"How do you think they rocked the car?" Florence asked shaking her head as if bewildered.

"Well, they didn't seem to have what I would call a mastery or control over natural forces, but rather an absolute affinity. It was as if a catalyst was set up immediately between natural forces and what they wanted to convey to me at that particular time; as if they simultaneously adjusted their thought vibrations to exactly synchronize with that of the car. A perfect tuning of thought with action.

"Another thing. They had with them a large full plate photograph that perfectly matched the person I call my Special Visitor. He came to me Sunday morning, August 27th, 1967. I called him that in my second book, 'THE WARNINGS FROM FLYING FRIENDS'. Most people derided me, but the feeling was so strong, I know I would follow him anywhere, not just the ends of the earth, but any earth, anywhere. I wouldn't say that about anyone else I've ever met. But you know what I mean? I would follow those eyes. If only the eyes could speak and say, 'Follow me', I would go."

"What did he look like?" Ethel asked.

"Hard to describe. It was the same face as the photograph, but my visitor had violet-blue eyes and russet-colored hair. This photograph showed a dark-skinned, brown-eyed face. But it was the same, the same expression in the eyes.

"They both asked if I knew him. I said that I did and I didn't. They asked me to explain. I told them what happened and I'll tell you now. I had taken the last train back from Caxton Hall where I had given a lecture. It was 11:30 on a Saturday night. I wasn't sure how the talk had gone. I had brought religion into it and I wasn't sure how the hard nuts and bolts hypothesis boys had liked it. I felt a little depressed when I got home. I arrived late and the wife was a bit annoyed. I sat alone here in this room to gather my thoughts and emotions. The light was dim, but suddenly the room was filled with brilliance. Then a figure just appeared. I've never seen anything like it in my whole life—this life anyway. When I tell people, they say, 'Well, that was Christ.' It doesn't really matter. He just appeared. A moment before, I had been thinking, 'I'll pack up the whole thing. I'm not going to do any more'. I was adamant about it. We'd taken so many photographs; very few had developed. I wasn't getting anywhere, so much sarcasm from people, so many nasty remarks. My child at school had been bullied by other children who said, 'My father and mother say your father is mad so you must be, too.'

"That hurt. So I was going to pack the whole thing up and let other, braver people tackle whatever it was on the hill. This happened in the early days. He just stood there in front of me with a mute appeal in those eyes. It overwhelmed me. I couldn't face it. That was the beginning. I could not betray those eyes. I had to continue to watch and write.

"I told Micah and Joab what happened with my visitor and they smiled a knowing smile at each other. For a moment I thought they didn't believe me.

'You don't believe, do you?'

"'Just the opposite. We know you speak the truth," they answered, because while you were telling us about him, you were no longer in this car with us. Only your flame was in the seat.' That was the proof they wanted.

"I asked them about their names. They are very old Biblical names. Reg, would know far more about Micah and Joab than I would."

"Micah was a minor prophet and Joab was a captain of David's guard. Both are mentioned in the First Book of Chronicles in The Old Testament," Reg related.

"They seemed to be such old souls, if you know what I mean," Arthur continued. "I had the feeling that I knew them very well. They stayed over night in a little hotel around the corner. The next morning I thought, 'Well, at least I'll buy them a meal.' I took them along to the George Restaurant near here. All they had was a glass of milk, one home made scone each and no meat. They were vegetarians. When I asked them what they were doing in this part of the country, they answered that they were retracing the footsteps of two thousand years ago. They had already been to Cornwall, Devon, Somerset, Glastonbury and Stonehenge. '

"This all happened in the early days. Well, I got out of the car and walked a few feet over to the gate and I could hear them talking together from the open window. I just heard, 'It will be water here.' That's all I heard. We can make what we like of it, a cataclysm in the future, perhaps...?" Arthur's voice ended with a question that sounded more like a statement of fact than a chance possibility.

"So you see why I got so excited when Marion described the two young men on the train. They exactly fit the description of Micah and Joab. So they are still here among us, still watching over us. Micah, the fair-haired one also said to Marion as they left the train, "I suppose you would laugh your head off if I told you that my friend and I do not come from this planet at all.' Then he bowed politely, shut the door, and off they went. Strange? I know Marion will never forget them and neither will I."

"What a story," I replied, realizing that this was a true story and not just the figment of someone's imagination. This was all happening in our physical five-senses world.

UFOs: Key To Inner Perfection

"Here's another strange tale and this has been carefully recorded with officials. There was a landing in a place called Gwent in Monmouthshire. It happened on April 5th of this year, 1973. Two little girls and a GPC engineer, their names and addresses are recorded with the police in that area, witnessed a daytime landing of a luminous 'craft' that came down into a field in Wales.

"One of my officers in the last war was Lord Carrington, who is now our secretary of defense. He knows this story. The special UFO investigating air branch, I think it's S4-A of the Air Ministry knows this. I have a friend who works for them. I'm not mentioning his name, obviously, but he keeps me well informed. There's no doubt about the authenticity of this, because I've checked with the Air Ministry and they won't deny it at all. I've even offered my help in an advisory capacity, in a humble way, to go around and talk to units of the Air Force and Army, whatever they like. Some of the lads do worry about the things they see when their exercises are rendered chaotic and interfered with.

"Well, to get back to the story. Now, on this particular occasion in Gwent, the two little girls saw this object land. They went up to the field. They looked over the hedge and they were scared because the object didn't look like a plane. And it was giving off this fitful halo of, you know, electromagnetism, as most people would call it. So they ran home and on their way they met a neighbor, a GPC engineer. He asked them to show him. They went back across the field. When they were within seventy yards of that flying object which had landed, it didn't suddenly tilt up and away very fast as we've seen them do here in Warminster when they're very close to the ground. It literally, and this is in the report, disappeared. On the ground. Dematerialized. They combed the field for quite a while looking for it. Of course the little children were quite relieved that it had gone. But it was probably still there.

"They went straight to the police and reported the whole thing. Now the police are very conscientious about this. They got in touch with my friend's department and I got the full story from my friend. I, of course, wrote to Carrington. I figured I'd go right to the top. I started off with some nostalgia about the good old times we had in the guards, the 2nd Battalion. I reminded him that I used to drive his tank. Then I told him about this particular case and that I've been interested in UFOs for several years and knowing, I hope, my character I wouldn't lie about these things. I offered him my services to talk to the troops. I do a lot of lecturing in the evenings. "I told him I had some very good photographs and that many were from his department, thank you. I feel that the government has a moral duty now to tell the people the truth about UFOs."

I recalled hearing that our American Astronauts have taken pictures of UFOs from their space crafts. They can be obtained by writing to NASA Headquarters,

UFOs: Key To Inner Perfection

but of course this isn't publicized. I voiced this knowledge to the group.

"They're certainly not going to admit that UFOs come from God. They're in a real dilemma. And what would they say about the giant figures that have certainly been seen on the hill by psychic people."

Arthur had given us the cue. But first I asked him about the disappearance, Bill had mentioned earlier, of the man in Shepton Mallet.

"True," Arthur revealed, "material things, as well, have often disappeared and then strangely reappeared in a completely different place. Many strange phenomena have been happening, more and more every day. But please tell us about your experience. Teleportation was not a subject he seemed to want to discuss at this time.

"Our experience took place in what seemed to be a tank training ground. We apparently missed the Cradle Hill entrance. I thought I knew the way but was obviously mistaken."

Bill continued, "The seeming loss of direction is, I think, a very important factor in terms of the balance of karma and in the relative obstructions, shall we say, in trying to reach the light. Often our path is changed radically. We may choose one direction but 'they', the powers that be, will often select another. We tried to go one way and ended up in the wrong place. We turned off onto this dirt road and came to a ramp of concrete. We parked the car, got out and wandered around a bit."

"Sounds as if you were near post five. There are three copses in a straight line there. You must have been on the center one. We say the two end ones are positive; and the middle one is negative. Horses won't go near it." Arthur interjected, "Yes, yes, carry on."

He seemed very excited about the location. We had unwittingly stumbled into a very important sighting area.

"Yes," Bill continued, "that must be the place because when you look around it appears you are seeing three or four spacecraft, in terms of those burial mounds that are on top of the hills.

"Well, after wandering around, we instinctively came together and formed a circle alternating male and female: negative and positive. Bryce and I are Sagittarians and the two ladies here are Pisceans. We stood silently in the circle and, each in his own way, sent out loving thoughts and feelings. Then suddenly Ethel saw these entities, one taller than me; seven feet at least. We all felt energy, as if an electric current was passing between us and we all, apparently, saw each other's auras which had become, within the etheric body, a beautiful blue and, as

UFOs: Key To Inner Perfection

it went out became white. Absolutely marvelous! There was no shaking it off. One didn't want to shake it off."

"Yes," Arthur smiled, "that blue is a lovely color. It is sometimes flecked with gold. Do you know that the entities often manifest in that color?" His voice had a note of wonder.

"That's what it was," Florence, who had remained quiet now responded eagerly. "I thought I was seeing things I've been trying to figure it out all day At first I thought the blue light was just an emanation from one of the auras, but then, I saw this blue mist form into a separate humanoid shape. That must have been an entity. One moment there and then the next moment it was gone. Was that it?"

"Sounds like it," Ethel responded.

"I really wouldn't know," Bill continued, "I don't think I saw any of the entities. But at one point when we separated the circle to include the being, my whole hand went pins and needles. The large finger of the left hand became almost numb and it throbbed. But it wasn't painful, in fact, it was a beautiful sensation. I felt the energy flowing through me. Now Ethel and Bryce observed that these entities came and stood between each of us to form a larger circle. I believe they joined us to feel at one in the never-ending circle which is the symbol of God, or the absolute. They also might have entered the circle because it is a shape in which powers can be gathered into one nucleus and then directed according to it's need."

We shook our heads in positive agreement. Ethel volunteered to do a healing on Arthur, especially upon his eyes. One eye had been giving him a lot of trouble. He believes it might be a warning to discontinue sighting and look deeper within himself for the truth. He no longer goes to the hills, but remains at home working on his writing. Ethel made her magnetic passes over Arthur's eyes and down his body. We all prayed that he would be completely healed, knowing deeply and truly that "Thy will be done". There are often reasons for physical manifestations that are beyond our intelligence.

It was time to head for the hills. Arthur entrusted me to be his emissary. We steered our car again in the direction of Cradle Hill.

UFOs: Key To Inner Perfection

CHAPTER 10

"No one Man holds every particle of Truth in an ever-changing Universe and every Man is our teacher. As a Man thinketh today, so he becomes tomorrow..."

Arthur Shuttlewood; UFOS: KEY TO THE NEW AGE, page 208

Cradle Hill was packed with sky watchers. The expectations were great. There had already been a few sightings but very high in the sky. Many people were ready again with telescopes, binoculars, cameras and flashlights, watching and waiting for something to happen.

Bill and I decided to venture beyond "Heaven's Gate", as it's called, and go up on top of one of the barrow mounds located in a blocked off portion of a military reserve. A lot of UFO sightings have been made from this particular spot and many entities have been seen walking in this area. On the hill the vibrations were totally uncanny. Aside from a generator of sorts on top, the barrow was empty of people of houses. Our whole bodies were tingling with electromagnetic energy so strong that the hair started standing up all over the skin. I had the strange feeling that we had been followed up the hill by invisible entities.

We came down elated. Ethel and Florence joined us and we all ventured over to Starr Hill where I had had the strongest impressions a year ago. There were fewer people on Starr Hill, but there was a pack of thrill seekers on motorcycles looking for action. Fortunately one came racing down the road shouting, "Hey, there's one in the field about three miles away. It looks like a haybinder but it isn't." On hearing this, the whole group revved up their motorcycles and took off in a flurry of dust, sparks, and gas fumes. Thank God.

Other sky watching devotees remained but eventually, when nothing was sighted, they also left.

Remembering the gate and the bridge from a year ago, where Arthur had first sighted the higher beings, I decided as his trusted liaison to return to the spot. Bill and Florence decided to join me, while Ethel remained in the car to rest.

This time as soon as we passed the gate I felt a terrific chill. Shuddering inside, my teeth started to chatter, and I instinctively rubbed my arms, hugging

UFOs: Key To Inner Perfection

them close to my solar plexus as if for protection. I don't know what caused the chill and Bill and Florence didn't make any comment about feeling cold so I guessed that I was the only one experiencing this sensation. However, as soon as we squeezed through the gate and walked over the bridge the chill left me and as we walked together up the hill I got warmer and warmer. We walked past the area where I had been a year ago and climbed to the top of a very round, tall, steep hill. It was shaped like a pyramid with tiers or steps winding up along the sides.

We joined together and again sent out thoughts of love and welcome. We tried various metaphysical formations being a triangle this time of three: two male, one female. The energy got very strong. Again, the electrical matrix to the side, above and below became very pronounced and the area seemed to be filled with pin pricks of light. We all exclaimed at the luminous mist that started to surround us. We walked together another twenty-five yards to the very pinnacle of this round-topped hill or burial mound, as it's called; and we came upon the grassy knoll, or copse, that tops the barrow. As soon as we stepped onto the grassy area each of us gasped, realizing that we had perhaps stepped into another dimension, another space-time continuum.

We all began to feel strangely detached from the physical. We all started to space out as if we were all on a trip together. According to what I've heard and read the sensation seems to be similar when one is high on drugs. However, the highest trips I've had have all been without artificial stimulation, pure mind blowing adventures. When consciousness naturally separates from the physical, I assure you, it is an ecstatic, magnificent experience of total freedom; still with the feeling of being in control and clearly knowing what is happening.

Drugs may simulate these feelings but there is a definite lack of control. When one walks the fine line between the two worlds one should truly have his wits about him; be totally centered and consciously open. Then the experience raises one's level of evolutionary awareness. Timing is essential.

I felt that we had each been prepared for what was happening and therefore, we could fully benefit from the total experience, in fact, our mental awareness was heightened. We were all filled with joy. Everything around us became alive with light; the air began to sparkle like fine silver dust. I began to feel weightless. My imagination began to expand so that when a "craft" suddenly appeared rising over the horizon, it seemed to wink at us, tip on its side like a giant smile and then disappear. Oh, I thought, I'm really seeing things! But I immediately realized from Bill's and Florence's expressions of glee that a "craft" with a blinking light had actually appeared and had the appearance of a tilted saucer.

Drunk with the heightened energy of the experience, we began to make our way down the hill. Florence commented that she felt as if she was floating and

UFOs: Key To Inner Perfection

with that, tumbled and fell, rolling down the hill. We deliberately tumbled after her; three delightfully high children. We reached the bottom so happy and relaxed that none of us felt the fall. We caught each other in a circle and spun around laughingly, bound together by a deep feeling of unity and love. I remember thinking that the higher intelligence must have a marvelous sense of humor. Though I'm sure we were all aware of the seriousness of the sighting, especially in the light of the present day state of the world.

I believe that UFOs and extraterrestrial beings want us to know that they are there to protect and watch over us; and help us, as fellow children of the universe, to avert any impending catastrophe.

When we stopped spinning, we all noticed that the field in front of us, at the base of the hill, had over thirty large depressions crushed down in the wheat in a counterclockwise motion without any pathway leading to them. They were circular, triangular and cylindrical in shape.

Perhaps the "crafts" and higher beings were there and were not manifesting into discernible form. Suddenly Bill stopped in his tracks. He stood perfectly still as if listening to some indistinguishable sound. He seemed to be in meditation, or tuning in to some inaudible vibration. All of a sudden I saw Bill separate into three distinct parts. I felt that the three images I was witnessing were Bill in the middle; his astral body on one side; and his etheric body on the other. I don't believe I was hallucinating; some incredible manifestation was taking place in front of my physical eyes. I felt there was a definite reason for this to happen.

The reason became clear when from directly behind Bill I saw appear, silhouetted against a pearly grey opalescent mist, an entity seven to eight feet in height. I could vaguely make out his features. He was humanoid in shape.

Not being sure of what I was seeing, I decided to try to get closer. Walking out of the line of sight of Bill, who stood rooted to the one spot, I began advancing toward the entity. I motioned to Florence to remain where she was standing. The entity, witnessing my movement toward him, slowly turned around and walked back into the mist. I believe he was acting protectively, because as I came close to him the vibrations increased to such a degree that my body began to shake uncontrollably. It was not an unpleasant sensation since I have experienced the same vibrations course through my being just before separating in astral projection.

I have always felt extremely elated at these times of conscious projection outside the body. I didn't experience any fear, having probably been prepared for the intensity. In fact, I felt ready to make close contact. But this was obviously not my decision.

UFOs: Key To Inner Perfection

That unearthly globe appeared overhead, accompanied by several shepherd globes, popping on and off. I was mesmerized by the globes, unaware of my surroundings.

There was only me. There was only the lights. How long I stood there in awe I cannot say. I vaguely remember a fragrance of flowers...

UFOs: Key To Inner Perfection

I retraced my steps back to Bill. He seemed to have merged into his body upon the disappearance of the entity. He walked with me out of the field somewhat dazed. We joined Florence and returned to the car. Bill, who is usually jovial and outspoken, remained quiet. I believe something he was perhaps not yet aware of had profoundly happened to him while he stood near the entity.

We woke Ethel. Florence made us some strong, hot English tea. What a love, always unselfishly there to tend to our needs. After tea, Bill and I decided to venture forth again.

I led him to the hollow near the farmer's barn. We again passed through the gate and walked over the bridge but this time we headed towards the fields near the barn where the farmer keeps his beehives. We climbed over a fence and found ourselves in a field of dry grass.

Suddenly, by some unknown signal, Bill and I parted and began walking away from each other at a ninety degree angle, as if heading for the outer points of an imaginary triangle. When we were approximately ten yards away from each other, Bill disappeared from sight. The night was again filled with a strange vibrant glow, yet, when I turned to see Bill, he seemed to be surrounded by a mist of darkness. As I tried to understand his disappearance, my attention was drawn to an unusual phenomena occurring over my head, just in front of my line of vision.

A large, self-contained globe of light, about ten feet in circumference, began popping on and off. When I turned to see if I could locate Bill, I noticed a globe of light flashing over his head although I couldn't make out his form. These lights seemed to be guiding each of us in opposite directions. Feeling they were a sign of protection, I returned my gaze forward.

When the lights went off they created loud popping sounds. Now these lights did not bleed off into infinity as a light will when the air is damp and misty as it is in this area of the country. They just popped in and out like spots of brilliant yellow luminescence. They flashed momentarily in the sky just over my head as I walked, and then pooped out. They did this about five times.

All sound, except the loud popping seemed to be stilled. Perhaps I was so tuned to the current over my head that I was not aware of the noises around me. Later, I realized that we were walking through heavy stubbles of grass with dried branches and rocks underfoot, yet I heard only the melee caused by the lights.

I speculated about their origin. Were they a manifestation of electrical plasma, St. Elmo's Fire, ball lightning, swamp gas or some other physical phenomena?

Having witnessed them, I knew this was a different form of manifestation.

UFOs: Key To Inner Perfection

My conclusion, as a research investigator, was that they were a sign of a higher intelligence, products of an advanced sophisticated technology. Where did they originate? It leaves a lot to the imagination and to postulation.

Were they being projected from my own mind, from a different parallel existence, a past or future time continuum, or another planetary system?

I believe I am a person with a cool, sane head. I am skeptical end don't readily accept even what I see as fact.

Both Bill and I were being subjected to multiple experiences perhaps to sharpen our mutual passion for truth. But with each experience, I know when we correlated our separate experiences, that we both felt overwhelmingly that contact with some higher intelligence had truly been made.

When I reached the zenith of my walk, I stopped and immediately the lights started popping all around me at once. They appeared to make a half crescent arch and went off with a very loud pop.

When they did this I felt a tremendous surge of energy course through my whole body. My knees began shaking and I found myself kneeling and meditating in a prayer-like position. I then rose and again, as if by signal, turned and started back towards the spot where Hill and I had parted. Bill must have gotten the same signal because we seemed to come together at the same point at which we parted. I noticed Bill moving towards me when we were again about ten yards away from each other. We just came together at the apex, and without saying a word, we joined ranks and began walking side by side back to the car.

We stopped suddenly near the bridge and three large entities appeared in a very faint translucent state. Bill gasped, so this time I realized that he, too, was seeing them. Perhaps his inner vision had been awakened while in the fields. We both physically, mentally and spiritually saw these beings. The physical sees with the outer eyes, the mental sees with the inner image and the spiritual knows and receives telepathic communication. We both felt we were standing there only a minute and a half but later realized that we must have been there over an hour.

I am not sure what transpired during this time of intense meditation. I feel that information was beamed to both of us telepathically and the knowledge is being released much like a Contact cold capsule, a little is released each hour, but for us it seems a little is released each month.

Upon coming to, I experienced a slight apprehension, as if I had perhaps ventured too far into the unknown. There is a point of no return that one feels sometimes when exploring the inner/outer spaces of consciousness; there is a feeling that once having passed this point, there is no return.

UFOs: Key To Inner Perfection

Perhaps it is the point beyond the speed of light for there is an intense feeling of being hot and cold at the same time, similar to touching a piece of dry ice. The body begins to shake as if the atomic structure is being ripped apart, followed by a feeling of being drawn out of one's body into a whirlpool of darkened space. Perhaps this is the doorway or window out of the galaxy—what astronomers refer to now as a "black hole." Total human annihilation!

It seems to be beyond the light referred to when one speaks about the light of God. The other side of the moon is dark and no one has ventured there in human form. There seems to be worlds even beyond our wildest imagination; I know I have only begun, in my limited physical condition, to tap these realms beyond the mind.

Apprehension, however, disappears when I realize that I am being carefully protected and guided on this journey. I am only experiencing what I am prepared and ready to experience. It is better to follow the natural God-given route for sometimes we can push the doors of perception open too quickly, and then spend ages, perhaps eternity, working off the consequences.

Many people flip out by using drugs and playing with the powers that be. If Bill and I were playing a game it was deadly serious. As these thoughts went out, as if to assure us that all was well and as it should he, we were engulfed by warm flower-scented air. The trancelike state broke suddenly for both of us. We headed back to the car and the sleeping ladies.

Bill and I could now talk freely and we exchanged perspectives. Bill had gone up to the hillside, right up to the fence that surrounds the top of the hill. He felt drawn to a presence and contact was definitely made. He had seen the popping lights. Then he saw, as clearly as one sees a physical person, a man with long, flowing hair and eyes filled with love. Perhaps the same man Arthur had seen in his living room.

Bill did not say what knowledge the image imparted. I did not press him, feeling that if he wished to tell me, he would. It was his own private message. My experience was different. But then each of us experience differently. We have each been patterned by time and circumstance into unique physical, mental and spiritual beings. We are all multiple facets of the same reality, so perhaps there are as many reflected facets in the universe beyond our knowing at this time. As we expand, our knowledge expands infinitely. Perhaps if we could face the so-called black hole of negative space, without fear, it would turn out to be positive. One step at a time. One step at a time.

We arrived at the car and woke the ladies. We briefly touched on what had happened to us while they slept. I walked over to Reg's van, Alba, to say goodbye

UFOs: Key To Inner Perfection

to him and to ask him if he or any of his companions had seen the lights popping. One young man said he had seen some lights in the direction of the wheat field but Reg and the others apologized, explaining that their gaze had been in the opposite direction.

I left Reg and, walking away by myself, lay the wheat field to try to gather together all of the last two days. I immediately felt the pleasant separating sensation one experiences when falling gently to sleep.

I awoke suddenly with the feeling of having been yanked back into my body. My head pounded. The girls were calling. I noticed that it was almost dawn. I scrambled back to the car. They were all packed and ready to return to London. I was filled with renewed energy from my short "nap" in the field.

We all seemed to be a little slap happy and joked our way back. By eight in the morning we arrived back at Florence's house in Amersham. We were all feeling a bit weary and grubby from our two days in the fields.

Florence graced us with a large English breakfast and clean, fresh country-smelling towels with which to wash. We sat eating and reflecting on the wonders of the world, both physically, mentally and spiritually. What an incredible adventure and what a wonder to be alive. The world is opening, expanding and we are just beginning to venture into the depths of the inner and outer space.

One thing is for sure, sharing an experience of this magnitude really puts you in touch with a supreme sense of love. If we could only take this universal love and put it into service for all of man, what a glorious world we would be living in.

Perhaps all my years—over twenty three—of training as a radio and TV broadcaster and photographer, all these communication skills, were only to sharpen my ability to translate the message from above to my fellow travelers here on earth. I feel that I am only an instrument, a vehicle, to help spread the message. Often I have a sense of rebirth, as if this being, developing rapidly into spiritual realms of parapsychology and metaphysics, has only been here on this earth for perhaps two or three years.

After washing and eating breakfast, Ethel, Bill and I caught the British rail back to London. As soon as we got into Paddington Station, we sent Ethel by cab back to her hotel to get some much needed rest. Bill and I took another cab and headed towards his apartment in Chelsea. We showered, shaved and spent most of the day talking and reconstructing the events of the last sixty or so hours.

We only hope that every one of you will someday experience something wonderful, something that will open your awareness of the worlds beyond. And we pray that when this experience comes you will let it happen, without fear, with

UFOs: Key To Inner Perfection

only love and welcome in your hearts. For we are only here for experience and we grow and become aware the more we open to experience. From birth to birth, point A to point B, we journey through life gathering new knowledge, exploring new adventures.

We hope reading this book has been an experience that, at least, will make you wonder and perhaps question the beliefs you've held on to, perhaps because you have felt that you must have these beliefs for some kind of protective security. We all blanket ourselves, at times, in a cocoon of unawareness. I remember, as a child, covering my head at night, completely believing that no one could see me in that state. I, too, have hidden, but now that I've seen and experienced, I wish only to go further, and so I shall.

I only ask you, the reader, not to close this book too quickly, not to be too hasty to jump to conclusions. Believe me, the material presented here is real and tangible. Perhaps, my friends and I can only touch the experiences recorded here in our minds, but that does not mean that they are not valid. Know that there are things beyond our five senses that truly exist and are out there for all of us to search and explore. Open the Kingdom within and all will he revealed. So before making up your minds and hearts, consider carefully the possibilities set before you.

UFOs: Key To Inner Perfection

UFOs: Key To Inner Perfection

HIGHER TECHNIQUES TO INNER PERFECTION

ACKNOWLEDGMENTS

To GOD for manifesting my creation on this planet, to gain the experiences, to learn the lessons, to create and to eventually manifest his perfection within and without, so I might be able humbly to reflect his divine awareness.

To my friends on both realms, I give THANKS for your support, and those very special beings who worked so closely believing that these thoughts had to materialize, that others might gain a new access route to their own personal enlightenment.

To a very special brother, FRANK DON, who had the courage of his convictions to collaborate with his wisdom and sharing, on this project.

To you all, my LOVE, and heartfelt THANKS.

PREFACE

There is no place where mind cannot travel, penetrating a curved universe into a spheroid of shaped mind desire. Mind desire gives birth to physical manifestation in matter. Matter forms in the shape of evolutionary mind of spirit desire constantly gestating in cyclic time. Time and space are frozen in form by non-energized mind desire of the one mind expression of exploding compression.

Mind desire manifests mind power which creates energy compression to manifest shaped matter. It holds itself into a freeze frame of mind to awaken mind desire into pulsations of electrical rings of mind, creating patterns between the freeze frames of mind desire! We form our thoughts by the ever changing thought patterns of electrical energies created by Mind Desire.

UFOs: Key To Inner Perfection

We are the reflection and expressions of our thoughts; created thought forms made manifest in physical bodies. Whatever we think, we become. Our physical bodies begin to be programmed by our thinking process, and we will portray that reflection until a new thought structure begins. And when a new thought pattern begins, it expands consciousness. It builds a superstructure to awareness.

For all ideas, thoughts, and the expression of emotion are building blocks toward self-revelation, awakening, and lifting the shutters of the mind, the storehouse of all thought and past life experiences. We merely repeat the cycles unconsciously as a mirror looking back at itself. We are in all reality mirrors to each other. Most individuals do not like what they see in themselves by the mirror reflected by others.

If we mirror the highest of all life forms (GOD), we would see only perfection in ourselves and in others. We would be free of judgments, for how can we see darkness when we stand in the light?

The darkness dwells in our inability to forgive ourselves for our judgments, our hates, our angers. The CHOSEN ones are CHOSEN in their own judgement!

Turn on your light by allowing it to be seen by others. Today is your last day on earth. Tomorrow is the rebirth. Let rebirth be FREE, PURE and TRUTHFUL. If others live through spiritual lack and limitations, allow them their choice. REMEMBER, you cannot share your pearls before time!

One day in the future they will make a great decision to change. Change is constant, and must not be stopped or harnessed. It is a cyclic pulsation of the continuum and expression of consciousness of all creation, a creation that has never stopped, a creation that has always been. Man represents the small specks of imperfection that resists change, to the point of static inertia.

Allow your mind to permeate the atmosphere of your soul; allow it to open to receive the gift of creation that is in continual flow. Keep the mind moving forward, seeking change, manifesting and expressing true perfection within the continuity of life.

Any impression that takes form in the mind and becomes deeply seated will take physical form and manifest itself accordingly. Again, whatever we think we become. We can hold back diluted ideas with procrastination, because they were not desires or honest beliefs; they were only random thoughts swirling about going nowhere, caught in the kaleidoscope of energies within the life-streams which envelop our planet.

We must be able to become focused with our thoughts, and not allow random thoughts to intrude upon our centering and focused consciousness. If they are true desire fixations where intent is clean and clear, then you do give life to the thought forms that we all create.

In turn, these will put us in harmony with the collective vibrations which manifest themselves in the others. These electrical energies (THOUGHT FORMS) create patterns. From these patterns come desire, will, and the substance that brings all these collected energies into the accomplished desire form.

More and more individuals can see the light, and hear the approach of those spiritual beings; they can read the sign of the times, and there is a sincere desire to help their fellow men, their brothers and sisters. They have reached turning points in their lives and now are reaching in the direction of GOD.

You see the manifestation of the final act in the drama of life expressed on this beautiful EARTH MOTHER now made sick and diseased and tilting on its axis, like yesterdays hangover. She is in her final hour. Can she, in one last fleeting effort, stave off the inevitable transformation of this planet?

If all men and women collectively could stand side by side, balanced in harmony and love, equally, we could correct our world over night. WE COULD! Women are the polarity that will make it all work, the blending of the two. Man must rid himself of his own distorted view of women, for he keeps peace from happening. When will man grow up? When will he realize that women are equal, in every way the opposites of men? Yet two equally polarized electrical energies manifested in the image of the FATHER—MOTHER merged as the one GOD of all that is. GOD remains the same; only man changes in a constant cycle through the evolutionary spiral of eternity. If you stay in the past, you lose the future!

When we completely surrender to the highest concepts within ourselves, with unquestionable FAITH, miracles begin to happen. But what is a miracle? A miracle is a mode of understanding that when you break through fear, you find love. When you break through darkness, you find light. Each negative provides a positive. Within torment there is peace! As night gives way for the day you can see again. Everything is attracted to the light.

The light of GOD is so bright that many squint their eyes and DIM the reality of their vision, and their souls. You lock a man in TOTAL darkness for a year and he will die. Lock man's consciousness in darkness and that, too, fades into oblivion. We must now more than ever before open our consciousness, and risk the fear of the unknown to the beauty to the LOVE, joy and peace that is our birthright. The gifts are always waiting for you. Pick your time (LIFETIME-PAST-FUTURE-PRESENT)

UFOs: Key To Inner Perfection

and give yourself a preview You will never look back. You will first discover your own beauty your own wisdom, your own true peace.

You will come to realize there is only one path, and one road, and it leads back home to the loving FATHER. At that glorious moment in time, you will be ALL light. Never again will you ever walk in darkness.

Bryce Bond interviews chief Druid, Dr. Thomas Maugham, D. Sc., who has been a great inspiration in the author's knowledge of metaphysics.

UFOs: Key To Inner Perfection

SELF-DISCOVERY

Why are we here? What is the purpose of life? Some people say we are here only to eat, drink and be merry for tomorrow... Ah, tomorrow. Waiting like a phantom in the wings, tomorrow for this type of person seems fraught with radical, devastating change on their inexorable march to the final step: death.

Do you believe that?

Other people say that life is to be lived to the fullest. And I agree. But to get while the getting is good? That's what many people believe. For we have been taught, as one television commercial paraphrases it, that we only go round once in life, so we better grab for all the gusto we can get. This type of person believes living life to the fullest is like some kind of monopoly game where we try to acquire all things material, then store and hoard our "goodies".

What do you think?

I happen to believe that you, the reader, with this book in hand, has a clue to something beyond these perspectives in life. I believe there is something awakening in you, a quickening taking place that demands an answer to the nagging question: Why am I here?

Maybe you have been successful in the material world. Maybe you have realized your wildest dreams, but in your success have found the experience not a sweet taste but rather a taste like bitter ashes. Consequently you may have turned from your habitual ways, and in the quiet of the small voice within, asked your self: Is that all there is?

Or maybe you have toiled the fields, always trying to be the good Samaritan, helping others along the way. But for all your efforts, for all your good intentions, you feel a certain sadness that your efforts have gone unrewarded, whether the reward be that of commendation, praise and approval from others, or the reward of increased self-esteem. Stymied by the lack of apparent reward, perhaps you have asked yourself the question: why?

UFOs: Key To Inner Perfection

And like Job beseeching the heavens for the answer to life's apparent inequities, you have demanded some logic or rationale to your own life's work and efforts.

Do you know people who feel overwhelmed by life's complications? People who feel their life has been a series of tragedies? And, when compared to the lot of others, their share of pain and hurt seems so unfair to them. These type of people are likely to say that they feel old and tired, and they have been through enough.

Whatever the reason for asking the question, the questioning of life's purpose begins the first step on the journey along the path.

What path? you might ask. The path of evolution—the beginning of your journey toward growth and development through living. All the experiences we go through, that continually changing montage of life's incidents and events—they all have one purpose. And that purpose is to hone us and refine us in our evolving as a human being.

By coping with personal trials and tribulations, your experiences bring you closer to GOD and closer to the consciousness of realizing yourself as the child of GOD.

So when you become stymied by life and you stop to ask yourself the purpose of your life, do not despair. For you have begun your journey: a quest in search of the answer.

When you have become aware of the personal conflicts in your own life, as you begin to wonder about the choices you have made, you awaken to surging thoughts that reflect upon the purpose of life. You start to question life—your life. And the questions flood your mind. Questions such as: Why am I here? What is my purpose on this planet? Why do certain things happen to me, and not to other people? .... What am I supposed to learn? .... Is this all there is? .... Why is life so painful? .... Why must so many suffer? .... Why can't I make a go of it? These are just a few of the countless questions raised in the minds of those who are unaware.

Although the rampage of unanswered questions may throw you into despondency or total confusion, it is an important time. Remember, confusion is the starting point of wisdom. For what is a question? It is not a quest, a search for understanding?

With all thy getting .... This quest, with its nagging questions, is often triggered by some negative event. The incident may be traumatic, even life-threatening. Or it may come quietly to you, like a subtle feeling within you that something is wrong.

Whether traumatic or subtle, these challenges are to be appreciated. They

UFOs: Key To Inner Perfection

are truly blessings in the disguise of pain. Some people may ignore these blessings by saying they have learned to live with their pain. They are making excuses. They are looking the other way. They do not want to change. But why?

Because these of people find change too difficult to express. Change to them is an unsure journey of forsaking the known for the unknown. And what if the unknown is worse than the known? Instead, they put off until tomorrow what they could be doing today. And when tomorrow comes, they will find other reasons not to change. Perhaps they will justify their actions with "I only live one day at a time."

Such rationale depicts the person who is totally unconscious, who has no conception what time of day it is, unaware of who he is or where he or she is. This person thinks life is just one long procession through painful hardships, unpleasant experiences and often he or she believes he or she is the only one suffering.

Even this person will change. Eventually the pain and torment of their condition will force a change. A change either instigated by themselves or forced upon them by the outside world. Painful experiences provide catalysts in your evolution. They dictate a change. And then the quest begins. Do not worry if you feel at times as though you do not know what to change. Do not be worried if the road toward change seems overwhelming and poorly marked.

The catalyst is the seed of dissatisfaction. Some little thought may be tiny in the beginning, has entered your mind, and your consciousness has started to respond. You are no longer satisfied with your life as you have lived it, and you want something more.

But what? Is it a new car? A new house? A new job? A lover? If you believe it is any of these, then, as you follow your urging, you will find you have started a circuitous course that leads you back to the same general sense of dissatisfaction. The real quest is not a transition from one material goal to another. It is a search for peace of mind, for enlightenment, and wisdom.

But how do we get there? We get there by walking the road, by living our life.

Through all the joys, all the sorrows, we look beyond the ephemeral to the real. There are many guideposts along the way; any number of markers leading us in the right direction. Each person's path is different. Each person has his or her own unique set of experiences to go through. These experiences are the lessons of life by which we learn about ourselves, about our true purpose in life, about the errors of our ways in the past so we may correct them in the present.

If you look for the answer in the ways of other people or functions, then you

UFOs: Key To Inner Perfection

are likely to get on the wrong track. Why? Because every person's lesson in life is different. Life is experienced differently even under similar situations. For each of us is a unique entity with the divine spark indwelling within each of us, waiting to ignite through our own efforts.

There is much illusion to cut through. Hindu philosophy talks about this illusion as the veil of maya. In Western terms, we know it to be the deceit of appearance. What appears to be real or true may only be a mirage, a distortion of true reality.

Why do we buy into such illusion and distortion? Because from our earliest days, through our parental conditioning, later on by the schooling process, we are taught inaccuracies, distortions and falsehoods, all under the guise of truth and reality.

If you feel yourself to be different, enjoy the sense. For you have begun to pull away from the mass consciousness, away from the accepted opinions and standards of society, it may seem a lonely space for you. You may rebel against it. You may wonder what's wrong with you, being different when everyone else is so much the same.

They are really not the same. We are all different. But in our society, in our learning processes, we discover that to be different is to become the target of some perverse pecking order. Our society demands conformity for conformity breeds acceptance of the ways and mores of social conditioning.

Is conformity effective? Yes, indeed it is, for it has purged the spirit of individuality within the person seeking to change. We have all experienced it in our own lives. Perhaps it started with our parents; they wondered why we couldn't be more like our brother, our sister, our uncle Eddie or our aunt Bernice.

May be we have had the idea drummed into us that what is good for the goose is good for the gander. "Do not make waves, do not be different." And with the brute force of the collective consciousness as our adversary we battled for our right to be different, to be individual, to be true to ourselves.

But it is a battle, and some of us may decide we are not strong enough, that it is not worth it, that it is like banging our head against the wall until we finally stop and give up, and give in. If we do that, we may condemn ourselves to a life that may be socially acceptable but not fulfilling. We have to remember that misery loves company.

UFOs: Key To Inner Perfection

SELF

Today the way you live, what you do, the manner of interacting with others, creates the patterns of your tomorrow. For it is a law of the universe that whatever is set into motion must work itself out. In biblical terms we know it in the parable "as ye sow so, too, shall ye reap." It is in karma that our tomorrows are built upon what we do today.

If you lie, cheat and steal today perhaps you will get away with it. Momentarily. But over the longer haul, tomorrow or the day after, your choices in action will come back to haunt you. Take advantage of someone else today and you will get your turn at being taken advantage of tomorrow.

In the manner of JESUS the CHRIST, we are told to "forgive them for they know not what they do." Unconsciousness, the lack of awareness, may be an excuse for wrong action. But it is truly only that: an excuse. People who seek such excuses feed upon the phrase that ignorance is bliss. But ignorance is not bliss. It is only ignorant.

As individuals, living in the collective stream of consciousness, we are growing toward awareness. We are expanding our consciousness and eventually will gain understanding. When?

When we use the pain and hardship of our life experiences as the catalysts to our growth; for correcting our inappropriate behavior, for remedying our past ways of action. Will we take advantage of such golden opportunities? Or will we, instead, decry the slings and arrows of outrageous fortune?

Will we, in that supposedly blissful state of ignorance, accept the belief that we are the only one suffering as if we were personally picked by GOD to bear the brunt of life's misfortunes, while others were out having a good time, enjoying themselves and acquiring and hoarding material goods?

If we fail to take advantage of the labor pains in the process of our own rebirthing, then realize that those guides along the way may look at us in a detached manner and utter the word of the one who proved to mankind the victory of spirit over matter.

"Forgive them, LORD, for they know not what they do." To believe that GOD has personally picked us out to experience the scourges of the world is highly egotistical, and is in truth an inaccurate attitude. It is a martyr role, and one that deserves all the misfortunes it programs for the person. If you buy into this attitude, then you are likely to feel completely thwarted.

And indeed, you will be. For such an attitude forces you to build up some very heavy limitations, self- imposed, that instigate a sense of blaming the world for all of your hardships.

If ever there was a cop out, that's the one. And it is an excuse used by those who are too lazy, who do not want to grow or work through this lifetime. Instead, they make excuses for why they can't take hold of their own lives. With a lack of self worth, and low self esteem, these people cannot love themselves. Nor can they truly love life. Instead, they blame everyone. They blame their parents for being bad parents, for not raising them right, for pigeonholing them into some specific role for which they feel unsuited.

And the one who is likely to get the greatest share of the blame is the one who can give us the most: GOD. But these people lash out, blaming anyone and everyone, except the true culprit: themselves.

It is only when we own up to our responsibility for our evolution, for our progress through life, that we address our readiness to evolve in this life experience. It takes time. It takes time to grow into awareness. As it takes time for a mighty oak to grow from an acorn, so too, do we need the time to progress in our consciousness, expand our awareness.

Perhaps we do not see the time factor as necessary. With societal conditioning and present attitudes, where we have instant breakfast, instant coffee, instant gratification and instant enlightenment, we lose sight of the true process of reality. At this stage in human evolution, one outlet for this instant phenomena craze is the fundamentalist Christian attitude of the "born again." This attitude allows a belief that we can expiate all our past sins, all our wrong actions, with one quick conversion process—being "born again!" While we should not deny the possibility of such a conversion, one profound example is the experience of Saul of Tarsus on the road to Damascus, when he experienced the CHRIST and by this revelation, had a conversion to be the true apostle—Paul. In our day while such conversion remains a definite possibility the experience has been misapplied by those "false prophets" who proclaim against the universal law: The real truth of harvesting what you have sown from your past actions.

UFOs: Key To Inner Perfection

Time is an essential component in our growth process. You would not expect a child in kindergarten to master university studies. Within the child is the seed which may well grow into the young man or woman ready to engage a university education. The same is true for ourselves and our level of consciousness. We cannot expect someone who has not evolved to the moral action to be moral and upright in their dealings. It is beyond them. So too is our development of consciousness.

Our growth, our development, takes time. For time provides us with the opportunity of experience. True growth comes from experience. It cannot be learned merely by the abstraction contained in some book of knowledge. It must be used; applied. It must come through our errors, our backsliding habits, our realizations of the consequences of past actions we have previously employed.

In our life experience it is important to appreciate where we are right now. Why? Mainly it gives us the awareness of our self as we truly are. We look at ourselves in the clarity of our present life conditions, without the distortions of ego games, the manipulations of our very being through our wants, needs, and desires, many of which are expected to shore up our sense of insecurity, our lack. Then too, by truly looking at where we are in life, we appreciate the process, the various levels we go through as we advance in life, both through time and in the expansion of our consciousness.

Let me give you an example. Have you ever planted a seed in a paper cup and watched the process as the seed takes to the soil, gestates, germinates, then pops its tiny sprout through the soil to grow in the sunlight, branching out, reaching higher toward that light? At each step of the way, if we are like children sensitive to the wonder, there is pure delight.

In our lives, we continually rid ourselves of the many dragons which live within us. These dragons are the wrong attitudes and wrong actions that we have adapted. The slaying of these dragons is facing and owning up to the results of our human emotional ego, the collected clutter of our personality state.

Today is your first step into your tomorrow. Today is the day you can make a firm commitment to free yourself. Free yourself from what? From all the limitations, all those dragons that clutter your path and block your way. If you will make that commitment, you have already begun the process of cleaning out. It is almost like reprogramming yourself, cutting the cord of a habitual response pattern. So when the negative force comes back knocking on your door, no matter what form it may take, you do not have to react the way you have done in the past. Instead, like a warrior ready to slay your own hangups and blockages, you can forcefully shout out: SORRY, THE DRAGON DOES NOT LIVE HERE ANYMORE!

UFOs: Key To Inner Perfection

What a glorious experience! What a cause for celebration! Untangling some of the lines of the constrictive webs we have woven for ourselves. Like Gulliver, freeing ourselves from the Lilliputians that would keep us restricted, keep us in an attitude of lack, the behavior of fear.

Like the phoenix, that mythical bird of resurrection, burning upon the pyre all our outdated and dying forms and beliefs, freeing ourselves from our own past limitations, opening up to a rebirth within ourselves, to soar even higher. If you are anchored to the ground by weighty burdens, how can you imagine to fly?

The journey within is the pathway to self-discovery It is lived in the context of time-space, in this lifetime, in the lifetimes of eternity—the lives we have lived, the lives we have to live. Along the way are many pitfalls, traps, temptations, seductions and manipulations of ego, personality, the unawakened consciousness, or more literally, the unconscious. To avoid the detours along the path, it is wise to stay in the middle of the road. In so doing, you choose moderation.

And have we not learned the truth in the adage: moderation in all things. For if we have not yet realized that truth, we shall have to learn it in the future. Our immoderation and excesses demand their toll.

Imagine if you will, those of you who drink alcohol and have occasionally tied one on, the hangover of the day after a partying binge. You pay the price. As with everything in life, there is no free lunch. Consequences follow actions, and there is no avoiding it. How about the times, the feasts of national holidays, when the focus of our bountiful blessings is symbolized in the gargantuan displays of food? Who hasn't gorged himself with incredible amounts of food? Eating well past a sense of fullness, to a point of exhaustion and bloating. And the consequence? Indigestion.

We accept a belief that having a good time means running at our limits because we have been conditioned to do so. But sometimes we forget to link up the price we have paid for our actions.

The two examples above are obvious and I am sure you can imagine your own consequences from the above actions. But what about subtle immoderation, those excesses that we may not see as excesses, those seductions that may seem so right, but in their actions are so wrong— the dragons in sheep's clothing? Can you think of any? How about the ones where we justify our actions because everyone else in doing it? May be we understand, somewhere, deep within our conscience, that what we are doing is not truly right. But we do it anyway because everybody else is doing it and if we don't, then we are just being stupid, and we are creating our own blockages and limitations, and ....

WAIT A MINUTE. The justifications are only excuses. Remember: it takes time to grow into awareness. And the seductions do not go away at any point along the trip. Another seduction, one that ebbs and flows, is one of self-righteousness. You probably know the adage: a little knowledge is a dangerous thing. Indeed it is.

Self-righteousness is running rampant today. Everybody who has turned, no matter to what degree, from total material focus seems to go through a period of running for some perverse kind of sainthood. It is like everybody who is finding GOD has the way. And like missionaries in the cause of divine right they spread the word to the uninformed, unenlightened. While sharing their insights and marvelling in life's creations is a wonderful delight, these people want you to know and accept their truth as your own. And they may go to the extreme in trying to impress their beliefs upon you, molding your mind, your self expression, your own individual growth according to their specifications.

And it is a case of immoderation. Dogma and doctrine speak of a rigidity. Rigidity is a blockage of energy and thus is completely out of step with universal reality. Watch for it. It is coming to your local area, down the street, within your own home. It is a danger.

When people begin to get religious, the message, the meaning, whether it be the teachings of organized religion or an occult group, people seem to go on a mission. In a sense, they are spurred on by those who have sponsored them, the practitioners of their truth. And various teachers and groups are mushrooming, spreading the way of finding GOD, of touching base with the divinity within themselves.

Immoderation in the cause of some glorious goal is one of the greatest seductions, for indeed it is the most subtle. Today it is growing stronger, in the increasing influence of what we might term in the broadest sense "religion." Religion is extending its influence into our lives, but not in the sense of moral teachings of life understandings. Rather, religion, the institutions devoid of their kernel of truth, are spreading their tentacles, demanding that we accept their own specific sense of the true way imposing certain beliefs upon society's accepted standards and how we live our lives. All in the name of morality.

It is a seduction we must learn from, in our own personal lives, and in our communities. Mankind has gone through the excesses of dogma in the past with dire consequences: millions of people consumed, at different times, in different ages, all in the name of righteousness. And at present we see the rising of religious groups, carrying on their holy wars. The fundamentalist Islamic rise in the Khomeini regime in Iran, the invasion of the holy Sikh shrine, the Golden Temple in Amritsars, and the consequent assassination of Prime Minister Indira Gandhi by a Sikh fanatic, the Born-Again Christian movement in the United States with its

UFOs: Key To Inner Perfection

threatening damnation of those who have not found JESUS CHRIST in the same place they believe they have found him.

Religion and morality are both examples of self-righteousness, of the ego's manipulation in allowing you to believe you have the power, or right, to judge another. You may think I have emphasized this seduction out of all proportion. Not really. Because it is essential that we become clear in our perceptions, in order to see Reality as it truly is and not the way we wish to imagine it. We are working toward a phase when we clearly see (clairvoyantly) what is really going on; when we can clearly perceive the seductions, manipulations and the right action.

The seduction in life will push us to the very brink of self-destruction. It constantly pulls us from the path. In elementary school we were taught that the shortest distance between two points is a straight line. It is. But always from abstractions, in life's reality, where we have cycles in action, the inflowing and outflowing, crests and troughs, life's process is more like a lightning bolt, streaking through the sky indicating the shift from one polarity to another, as if seeking the middle point.

When you are pulled from the path by some seduction or another, do not worry about reaping your consequences. You will. You have to. But do not waste a lot of time in damning yourself. Flogging yourself for the errors of your ways is only acting upon your judgement of your ways. It is another seduction.

Life is a constant change. As individuals, we tend to take on the conditions of our environment. We work through those conditions, learning the lessons contained in those experiences, and eventually we move on to another environment, taking on the conditions of that environment, gaining new experiences or different experiences from that environment, eventually learning the lessons of that environment.

Experience is GROWTH. The moment you stop growing, you begin to die. You do not have to, though.

Life provides us with a multitude of varied experiences. Happy times, good times, difficult times, times of sorrow. They are all part of the ebb and flow in life's development. Although we probably all wish for only the good times, the difficult times often provide the greatest catalysts for change, for growth. During the good times, when we feel like we are riding the crest of a wave, it is easy for us to become contended or complacent with our lives.

Then we begin to atrophy, our growth stops, all circuits of life begin to slowly close down. Like a muscle that has not been used, complacency leads to narrowness of vision, a restriction of bodily functions, and a contraction of life itself, so that life becomes like Beckett's characters in "Waiting for Godot"—a tedious wait

UFOs: Key To Inner Perfection

for some Messiah of Savior, a wait that never ends, until the end at death. Not much of a life; not a life worth living.

Friction provides a dynamic energy. It breaks the inertia of set patterns, challenges accepted ways, demands new methods and innovative approaches. It is during the phases of friction in our lives that we are forced to make resolutions.

Our life, our very existence on planet Earth is a series of conflicts needing to be resolved. The duration of these conflicts depends upon our awareness, upon our desire to learn and grow.

We stand on the threshold of great wisdom. However, we must open our eyes if we are to see. We open our eyes when we begin to look inward. Not on an egotistical, personality level, but rather when we start to look at who we truly are. SELF REVELATION IS THE TRUE RELIGION.

The religious teachings, as they are expressed today have forgotten this very key point. Instead, today's religious institutions purport the coming of a Messiah, a wonder person to take away all our sins, a magic elixir, by which we become perfected by someone else doing it for us.

Do you believe that's the way? It is not. The way to heaven is a journey of self-discovery; a self-revelation that comes through learning more about ourselves, a learning that takes place in the various experiences of life.

The two BIG questions you will be asked when this life's work is done are: WHAT HAVE YOU LEARNED AND WHOM HAVE YOU HELPED? Ask yourself those questions right now and answer them honestly Then see where you are, what you have been doing, and in what direction you are going.

When you become consciously aware of the lessons you have learned and, as importantly, the lessons you have yet to learn, you come to a realization that life is a progression of steps through expanding awareness, opening the consciousness to self-revelation, and self-discovery. Whom have you helped? Think about it.

We will discuss this in greater length in the forthcoming pages, but for now seed your conscience with these questions. No matter what you are doing in your life, you have reached a point where self-discovery is becoming more and more important for you. Look for it in your life. Right now. See where you could be manifesting the wonders of self-discovery. It may be subtle. It may be something you consider insignificant. Maybe it is as simple as your reacting differently to a situation that, two months ago, you might have reacted to more negatively (self-destructive).

It may seem insignificant, but it is not.

UFOs: Key To Inner Perfection

On your journey to true understanding, you will find that the spiritual urge is the most powerful driving force in the world. Why? Because it is a force that is in complete harmony with the procession of life. Life is evolving in spiritual understanding. The urge is in sync with the unfolding of life, not in friction with life which can be wearying.

As Luke Skywalker was told in the Star War Trilogy "MAY THE FORCE BE WITH YOU!"

And guess what? It is. To be aware of this force, this energy of the spiritual urge, all you have to do is tap into it. How? First, let go of all your preconceptions, your assumptions, judgments and opinions of reality. Instead of maintaining a running commentary on life's actions and reactions, let go and live life. Live it with an openness, with no expectations, but with the awe of a child discovering a new world for the first time.

It is a unique experience, one we have forgotten. By ridding ourselves of expectations, we allow ourselves to experience life. Truly experience it. Expectations place conditions on our experiences.

Think about it. Think about the times when you last planned some event or activity. Did you have certain expectations about it? Were those expectations fulfilled? Were you disappointed? Now think about the times when you did something spontaneously. Wasn't there more of a sense of excitement, of adventure?

When we free ourselves from our limited expectations and conditions, we open ourselves up to life and to living.

UFOs: Key To Inner Perfection

UNCONDITIONAL LOVE IS
THE HIGHEST FORM OF SERVICE

By giving unconditional love, you free yourself from the slavery of expectations, of rigid limitations. When I say unconditional love, I do not mean solely in your interactions with other people. I also mean giving unconditional love to you, yourself.

Do you love yourself? Oh, I do not mean in a narcissistic manner of loving how you appear. I mean do you truly love your "self?" So few people today really do. Why? Because of the conditions they place upon themselves. The expectations that tell us, "Yes, indeed, I could love myself, IF..."

"IF"—the response of the conditional world. Eliminate the "IF"s in your life when it comes to love. You will find it is easier to love. It is easier to live. Unconditional love is giving back to the world. It is also a magical tonic. If you will love your conditions in life, you change the conditions. Love your environment, and you change the environment. Love yourself, and you change the world.

UFOs: Key To Inner Perfection

NEEDS AND WANTS

What do you need? What do you want? Although some people may think the difference between these two questions is merely a matter of semantic quibbling, there is a profound difference between needs and wants.

We attract experiences, the lessons in events, to ourselves by our needs. What are our needs? Do we really need anything in this life? Do we need that racy sports car? Do we need that person in our life? Needing is a rather negative energy because it indicates a sense of dependency

Wants, wanting, are a more positive force, for there isn't the urgency (or the condition) of dependency. Ask yourself, do you want that person in your life? Or do you need him? Do you need to see that movie someone recommended, or do you want to see it? Do you want to eat that piece of cheesecake, or do you need to eat it?

There are no needs.

If you can become firm in your convictions, you will understand what I mean. The difference between the needs and the wants in your life is essential in your growing awareness.

"I don't need someone in my life as a relationship. I want to have a successful relationship. I want love in my life. I want to eat to live. I want a good education. I want a good job. I want good health. I want a lot of things. But do I need them? Do I truly need them?" NO.

Perhaps we were taught that to want too much is to be greedy. Do you believe that?

If you do, please see that you are looking at life as a fixed commodity—only so much to go around. Yet, life is filled with abundance, not with a lack of it. The only limits are those we place upon ourselves. Self-imposed limitations manifest from a sense of need. Whatever we worship, we attract. If you worship "I can't", then "can't" is what you will receive. If you worship lack, then lack is your reward. If you worship limitations, then limitations are your experience. If you give your love conditionally then you will receive love on condition.

Please realize that when you give hate, you get hate in return. When you give anger, you will get anger. When you give negativity you get negativity.

UFOs: Key To Inner Perfection

WHAT GOES AROUND, COMES AROUND

Give love, and you will get love. Give love unconditionally and you get unconditional love .... from the Universe. In the Universe, there is no condemnation of us for our actions. It is only man who becomes the judge, jury and executioner to his own thinking.

As a man thinks, so shall he become. Thoughts are energy like everything else. Your thoughts constantly are being broadcast. Whatever you are thinking about right now is being broadcast out. And there will always be someone out there picking up those transmissions of yours. Whatever thoughts you are sending out, you are going to receive the same sort of thoughts back.

Like always attracts like. If you send out hostile energy to a negative situation, you feed that situation. By feeding it, all that negative energy comes back to you. And it comes back manyfold. You are likely to become depressed, angry, frustrated. If this continues over time, your thinking is likely to affect your physical condition. Illness will follow for dis-ease and dis-harmony lead to disease and illness. Do you want to be sick? Do you want to have nothing or no one in your life? Do you worship lack?

These are some of the questions each of us must really ask ourselves. What do you want? If you feel caught in a trap, give yourself permission to spring the trap. If you feel there is no way out, reach inward and upward toward the higher forces, the divine spark in each of us waiting to ignite. You are the torchbearer. You are the one who will light that flame to burn brilliantly; just give yourself permission to do so.

Allow yourself to change. Give yourself permission for the things you want out of life. Can you? Will you? '

Sometimes we step back from ourselves, look at ourselves and with all the objectivity of a need masquerading as a want, we say we could, if we were not such a "bad" person. What?! Our lives would be turned around, if what? If the conditions were met. What conditions? Whatever conditions we devise to limit ourselves.

One of the most effectively designed conditions for keeping us from change is self-recrimination—the expectation we have not met, the success we have not achieved, the condition by which we can love ourselves. LOVE YOURSELF UNCONDITIONALLY.

Today, right now, at this very moment, forgive yourself for any guilt, fear or sin you may harbor about yourself. For they are the conditions that hold you back. By forgiving yourself, you slay the dragon within. You cut the anchor cords of negativity getting rid of dis-ease. By forgiving ourselves for what we consider to be transgressions, we are cleaning the temple, the sanctity of GOD in the image and form of mankind. By so doing, we put ourselves in touch with our higher self, where the spirit of truth dwells.

Wisdom in action is forgiveness and unconditional love. Just for a moment, reflect on your relationship with your parents. Do you love your parents? Do you hate them? Do you blame them for the way your life is now? Do you judge them? However you might answer these questions, one question is paramount: CAN YOU FORGIVE THEM?

If you love your parents, there is no need for forgiveness. However, that type of relationship with parents is not universal. Some of us feel anger or frustration over our relationship with our parents. But do we see clearly? Often, we get so caught up in a situation that we tend to see it solely from our own perspective, a perspective of limited self-interest. We see how other people's actions or behavior have had an effect upon us. So it is with our parents.

From the childish perspective that parents are omnipotent and can do no wrong, we forget that parents are people like ourselves, trying to learn their lessons in everyday life, struggling to meet their challenges with their own sets of trials and tribulations.

But we lose sight of that. Instead, some of us are ensnared in the trap that our lives are wrong due to our parents poor job of parenting. Whether such criticism is valid or not, it is still a trap. If your relationship with your parents has been bad, ask yourself whether you have made resolution with it, with them. If you have not made resolution, recognize that you are holding on to a feeling, a negative feeling, that is only blocking your own growth, your own fulfillment.

Therefore, eliminate those feelings. How? First, by forgiving yourself.

"Forgive myself?" you may ask incredulously. Why should I forgive myself when it is them, my parents, who have done wrong? I am the one wronged, the victim. The role of victim, the idea of being victimized, is a trap, a severely limit-

UFOs: Key To Inner Perfection

ing trap. If you want to move on from these limitations, from the bindings that hold you back, indeed forgive yourself for holding such thoughts. Once you have done this, then forgive them. Can you? Will you?

Perhaps it might help if you remember a master's words: "Forgive them, for they know not what they do". If you can forgive them, then move to a point where you can send them unconditional love. Love, unconditional love, is a power that unleashes the abundance in your life.

UFOs: Key To Inner Perfection

The author in earlier days, shown at the microphone at a New York radio station.

UFOs: Key To Inner Perfection

THE BIRD THAT FLIES HIGHEST SEES THE FURTHEST

By ridding your mind and emotions of all negative clutter, you raise your consciousness upward, toward the light, in the warming comfort of unconditional love. But first you must risk everything like the little bird leaving its nest to fly. You must be willing to launch yourself from your morass of preconceived opinions and habitual response patterns. That is the true alchemy of turning base metal into gold. It is the flight of the Phoenix. If you will do that, dear friend, then you will soar on high.

It is a marvelous feeling. For you will find that your perceptions, both inner and outer, are clearer and made more manifest. What we term psychic abilities will become more evident within you. And these abilities will enhance the awareness of your spiritual progression in life.

It is like being in a helicopter. If you are caught in the grid- lock of a traffic jam, you can't see what is causing the bottleneck. But if you are in a helicopter, above the traffic jam, you see what is causing it, where the flow is blocked. The same is true in your development. Perhaps you may feel, or think, that I have laid certain traps for you. You may consider my suggestions as possible only for applicants to sainthood. They are not.

One of the beauties of growth, of self-development, is the unfolding process whereby certain talents or qualities are revealed and made manifest as your progress. It is like the unfolding of a flower bud into full bloom.

People on the path are very evident to each other. Not so much by their actions or what they might say but more importantly by their manner. As you develop, as you progress in your own unfolding, you will find it easier and easier to love. A childlike awe of life resurfaces, a clear perception that regenerates your very being, manifesting itself externally as a certain calm to your presence.

Self-growth will come to all of us. It is a question of time and nourishment. It will come to you. The turning point, as I have mentioned before, will come at the appropriate time. No sooner, no later. It may come in those "healing crises" that

UFOs: Key To Inner Perfection

occur periodically in our lives to catalyze us into transformations along the way. It may come quietly in the night while you sleep. But it will come to you. In time.

Through awareness, commitment and understanding you can nourish your own growth. The moment we acknowledge life as a process of evolution, we take on added responsibilities. The power of transformation. We work with it every day, sometimes unconsciously with possibly dire consequences.

George Orwell is quoted as saying that a person gets the face they deserve by age 52. What he meant was that as we are, so we become. Indelibly etched by that age on our faces, as though chiseled in stone, is the mark of our character, our qualities, our being.

You have seen it. You may have seen it in a person who looks incredibly angry or seen bitterness scrawled in the lines of a face. Distorted thoughts create a distorted body. Wrong thinking can and does take its toll. Wrong thinking and negative emotions lead to distress, dis-ease, and dis-harmony. In turn, they create a diseased body

It does not have to be that way. Do you know that the greatest diet, the greatest body health technique is not some specific exercise program, or a calculated food intake program? It is the mind. The power of the mind is the germinating ground for our later creations. We must protect it at all costs.

If you truly want to be one of the "beautiful people" (in the true sense of the word), then work on your mind. Reeducate yourself. Program yourself to snip all those negative thoughts to which you give form. And instead, tune your mind to the higher self, to the understanding of your life. In so doing, you will be able to forgive, to love unconditionally, to share and help others, no matter who they might be. Even strangers.

UFOs: Key To Inner Perfection

HEAVEN AND HELL

Heaven and hell are not places, no matter what you have been taught. You can't drive to heaven. You can't catch a plane to hell, no matter what people might say. Why not try it? But you can still get to heaven, or you can go to hell. But they are not places, not physical locales. They are states of mind; consciousness or unconsciousness.

Hell is darkness. It is those areas of life we do not understand that are negative. We are all plunged into darkness in this material world. It is done with clear intent and many guideposts along the way. It is done so that we, as individuals, can find the light, attain our own enlightened-ness, enlightenment.

This analogy is repeated throughout man's history and legends. We see the fall from grace in the Bible with the expulsion of Adam and Eve from the Garden of Eden. It is repeated in the tarot system with the Fall of the Fool, and in the cabalistic system, at the crossing of the abyss.

It is the alchemy of spiritual essence into material form. But in the darkness of matter, that spiritual essence yearns to rediscover its true heritage. And the process ensues. The individual begins to seek answers. He does so in time, for there is much of it. He goes on many journeys, through countless experiences, in myriads of relationships and entanglements.

As he goes through life cycles, the individual learns about living. He begins to realize why he is here. And then he develops what he has been given to work with. Eventually, he reaches understanding, and attunement.

One of the beauties of life is that it is all about cycles. We know some of these cycles: cycles of existence-birth-life- death; cycles of earth parameters-day and night, the four seasons; cycles of physical life-youth-adult-age.

Perhaps we are not aware enough of the latter cycle, the cycle of physical life. It is hard for a young person to see the reality of an older person's perspective. And in reflection, older people look at the young and say that youth is wasted

UFOs: Key To Inner Perfection

on the young.

Yet in the past few years, various popular culture books have come out, focusing on certain "crisis" periods in an individual's life. But depicting them in terms of "crises" is to forget the valuable opportunity and potential for sharp transitioning during these times.

Chronologically through life, we go through various cycles. These cycles are broken down into different phases—times when we are learning about specific areas or a certain function. FOR EVERYTHING THERE IS A SEASON, AND A TIME TO EVERY PURPOSE UNDER THE HEAVENS.

Our human life is broken into three cycles that have a 27 to 30 year duration each. Back in the 1960's, student radicals on college campuses proclaimed that you could not trust anyone over the age of thirty. It is ironic that the students were unaware of a profound truth.

Those of you who have passed that time in your life, reflect and remember how that period was a time of tying up loose ends, of going back over certain things that had occurred during your life.

Maybe you remember reconnecting with people from whom you had not heard for a long stretch of time. Maybe you experienced a breakup, or more responsibility or a feeling of weightiness. Whatever you may have experienced, this period was a time of strong transitioning for you, a maturation that changed you significantly

That time frame is the time when we move from adolescence and become an adult, true adulthood. As we enter our thirties, we are moving through the period where we take on our life's purpose in work. This is our productive cycle, where we work in the world, sow our fields, no matter what type of function we may have.

At the age of 57 to 60, we go through another significant transition. It is a time of resolving, and coming to terms with any loose ends of the past 27 to 30 years.

Those of you who have passed this mark may remember it as a sense of diminishing physical capabilities, a sense of age creeping up on you. Death, the prospect of mortality seems to loom during this time, for there is an awareness that the person's productive years are drawing to a close. However, with this transitioning period, there is another significant change, a time of moving from the productive cycle of one's life into the harvest period, the third and last cycle in an individuals life.

The harvest period in a person's life is a phase where the spirit in man re-

UFOs: Key To Inner Perfection

ally comes consciously forward. We see respect for this cycle in the oriental tradition, where older people are venerated and respected for their wisdom and understanding. In societies that are youth-oriented or concerned solely with productivity this third cycle is often relegated to merely waiting for death.

If we could be aware of these three cycles in our lives, we could then live our lives in accord with the purpose and function of those different phases. While our lives can be broken up into three major cycles, there are also seven year cycles in our lives.

We have heard the phrase the "seven-year itch." By that phrase alone, there is a connotation of change nagging to be fulfilled.

UFOs: Key To Inner Perfection

THE SEVEN YEAR CYCLES IN A HUMAN'S LIFE

AGE 0 TO 7: The incarnating soul is still very much connected with the essence of life. This can show itself in many ways. It can manifest as the wonder in experiencing life, the reverential awe of childhood innocence, similar to the biblical parable: Until we become like little children.

The individual in this stage is "en rapport" with mother nature. This rapport may manifest as an ability to perceive nature sprites, elves, or other ethereal forms, and may include imaginary friends.

This first cycle of seven years in human life is the process of the soul incarnating into human form. It is the time in which the child grows physically, his skeletal structure becoming less malleable, more solid in form. It is also the time during which the incarnating soul, its essential quality, is buried by the fall into human personality—the ego quality. The child is conditioned to life by his parents, peers and pedagogues. The child takes on a personality

AGE 7 TO 14: The emerging ego personality starts to express itself. This is a time when the individual develops his creative self-assertion. No longer content to adopt the ways of parents and society the child speaks now in terms of "I." It is the time in which the child begins to challenge the limitations others would try to place on him.

It is also a time of challenge in physical terms, as the child grows into his physical body. In the child's play there is an element of risk-taking, whatever form it might take. Increasingly a sense of personal power develops as the child takes on the growth of his physical body along with the strengthening of his ego personality. This is the period of clarion call to creative self-assertion: I AM SOMEONE.

AGE 14 TO 21: As the child becomes aware of a power of procreation with the new-found sexual energy through the crisis of puberty a differentiation occurs: It is during this period in time when the individual consciously begins to separate himself from the father and mother figures. There is a recognition that the father and mother are not Gods, infallible in their decisions, looked up to for sustenance. Rather, the parents are seen as human, liable to make mistakes, prone to errors of judgement.

The individual now begins to readjust himself for relationships. While this period incorporates a differentiation between the young adolescent and his parents, there is a seeking-out of peer relationships, relationships that now also encompass sexual relationships.

In relating to others, there is now a honing of the creative self-assertion developed during the preceding seven year cycle. Now we look to how our actions impact upon others. No longer just the "I AM" expression, but self-expression in relating with others. It is during this time that the individual begins to question society's terms of relating to one another. It is during this age when the individual works on a social conscience.

AGE 21 TO 28: During this time, the individual moves further away from parental and educational conditioning. The individual is ready to take a personal stand in the world. This is the time when the individual moves from learning to applying.

The individual is likely to finish formalized educational studies, and may move out of the parental nest. During this time, the individual is likely to take on a job, live on his own, perhaps marry and begin his own family. This is the last quarter in the first cycle of adolescence. It is during this phase that the person consciously starts to move into his own life function and system.

AGE 28 TO 35: With the beginning of the individual's cycle of productivity at this age, the purpose now is to express his true individuality. Up to this point, life had been lived in assimilating and living one's life for the past conditioning to cultural parameters. The testing of the waters in self-expression may have been tried prior to this phase, but such attempts were likely to have been strongly influenced by past culture and family considerations. It is at this phase that the maturation of the individual takes place and he accepts responsibility for his actions as an individual.

This is a time of rebirth, with associated labor pains. This rebirth is the maturation of the adolescent into an adult. As an adult, family matters - not the parental family but the family created by choice - become of paramount concern.

AGE 35 TO 42: At this stage in his development, the person seeks to express his true individuality in the various areas of family business, religion and community involvement. This is a time of self-awareness, when the person can realize that he does have choices in his actions. Of course, with choice comes responsibility and during this stage, the responsibility is to be true to one's self.

UFOs: Key To Inner Perfection

While the self-determining individuality is struggling for prominence, the reaction by external forces, past conditioning and patterns, can be one of opposition.

Not only does the individual struggle against the tentacles of past actions and entanglements, but there comes a growing awareness of the polarities between his own internal and external forces. Through the synthesis of these two forces, the person has the opportunity to bring about an integration of self-individuality. Should the opportunity for awareness and self-integration be lost during this phase, then the individual will face the succeeding "mid-life" period as one fraught with crisis and chaos.

AGE 42 TO 49: The mid-life period is a dramatic shifting of gears. At this time in life the individual becomes aware that his external being—his physical body—is in a state of decline. The process of aging becomes apparent, as the parents' generation dies away and this age group takes their parents place as the "older" generation.

People often rebel against change. They do so from anxiety spurred on by a sense that life is fast ticking away and that this is their last chance. As a result, this can be a time when people try to recapture their youth. Some may change their clothing styles to a younger fashion, others become involved with a new romantic partner.

While the physical prowess begins to decline at this stage, this is also the time when the inner forces—the internal being—become more developed. This is the changing of gears. Instead of being solely concerned with grabbing the gusto from life's experiences, the person becomes more reflective regarding the meaning behind events. It is the time when we can become more aware of the spiritual side to ourselves. It is a time when we are better able to see the spirit in matter. But, of course, we must look in order to see.

AGE 49 TO 56: From learning through experience, we gain wisdom. This wisdom is to be shared. This period is a phase of positive expression, of giving back what one has learned. This may incorporate increased social responsibility or the education of others.

From the preceding seven-year cycle, we have touched base with a sense of lack, of failure, of mortality. Yet, if that period has been used constructively, there has also been a regeneration whereby the individual is now concerned with a new quality in his life—spirit.

This seven year cycle is the final quadrant of the productive cycle. As we pass through this cycle, we are moving toward the harvest period, which can include retirement from the productive function. As if in preparation for that major change, the individual now seeks something beyond mere productivity. He seeks

UFOs: Key To Inner Perfection

the quality of wisdom.

AGE 56 TO 63: During this period, the individual transitions from the second life cycle of productivity into the third, the harvest cycle. During this phase, we begin to reap what we have sown during the past 30 odd years.

Another chance at rebirth is possible at this time. Now the rebirth is from an adult human personality into a spiritual repolarization. For this is a time of review and reassessment of what is important, what is essential to life. Not so much life in terms of the individual personality but life in terms of the collective. This is the age for philosophy.

The montage of experiences are seen more clearly for their undercurrents of lessons and purpose behind the events. It is this understanding that can impinge upon the collective consciousness at this time.

AGE 63 TO 70: This seven-year cycle sees a preparation for the afterlife. Either this is done consciously by the individual who opens himself up to new realms of consciousness, and radiates wisdom of the developing spirit, or it is done unconsciously by the individual who becomes bored, listless, and merely waiting for death.

These are the various functions and purposes of each seven- year cycle up to the age of seventy. During these age periods, certain opportunities and specific challenges are provided for us. If we are aware of the meaning of these various cycles, then we can live in sync with the chronological evolution in man. If we are unaware of these different cycles, we are apt to go through life banging our heads again walls, feeling frustrated and daunted at every turn. But it does not have to be that way.

As we noted in the seven-year cycles in man's life, human life evolves from the physical to the spiritual. In this process, that which is not essential drops away. It is all part of the soul's progression. The journey we embark on in life is filled with pain, sadness, emotional chaos, frustrations, rejections .... EVERYTHING YOU HAVE TO MASTER WITHIN YOURSELF

While we are subjected to challenges, we are also provided opportunities. The opportunity to live our life filled with joy, health, understanding, success, happiness, LOVE. The choice is ours. Individually, yours and mine. When we begin to place more VALUE on the spirit than on matter, we turn our lives around. A resurrection takes place, as glorious as the mystery of Golgotha where the spirit in CHRIST gains victory over the crush of matters.

It will happen to all of us eventually. By increasing our awareness, however, we can quicken the process. By making right choices, we accelerate our evolu-

UFOs: Key To Inner Perfection

tion. One such choice is in the right action of mind. Our mind is a powerful tool. It creates our future. What we visualize in our mind we project into our conditions. The power of mind over matter, the power of positive thinking, reflect the laser quality of our mind stuff. .

Too often, however, we let our mind wreak havoc in our lives. One way we do so is by worrying about possible future situations, mulling them over to the point where every calamity and catastrophe imaginable has been built into that future condition.

Or we set ourselves up. We begin a project with enthusiasm and zest. But when we face any form of resistance, any obstacle or obstruction to the completion of our project, we begin to question whether we can actually pull it off.

From where do these worries and concerns come? They come from insecurity... an insecurity about our *self*. Some of these insecurities have been programmed into our minds from past conditioning, past incidents. These programs are like tape loops that repeatedly condition our attitudes and affect our behavior.

Because these tape loops have played for such a long time, we have come to rely upon them to prevent ourselves from getting what we want, rely upon them to ingrain a sense of lack and limitation in our lives, rely upon them to provide us with yet another example of our failure. Some reliance! What a dependency!

Although these tape loops may have become dominant as an instinctual response pattern, you can loosen their grip. Even cut their hold upon your behavior and actions. How? First, through awareness. How aware are you of your actions? When you do something, even routine tasks, do you just go through the motions? That is, is it mechanical? Is your life mechanical, the same drudgery and routine, day in, day out?

Remember the parable: Until you become like a little child, with awe and wonder about life, you will be locked into the same tape loops, the same programs of frustrations and self-defeat. It does not have to be that way. By awareness of your actions, you can begin to see some of the tape loops in operation. Once you see what is going on, you can then initiate right action. What kind of action? Modifying your behavior. Perhaps only in reflection at first. THE MORE YOU BECOME AWARE OF WHAT YOU DO AND HOW YOU DO IT, THE MORE CONSCIOUS YOU BECOME OF WHY YOU DO IT

If the effects are self-defeating, you can change them. Maybe slowly at first. That's OK. Rome was not built in a day, nor is our evolution and development through life done in one day or even in one lifetime. It takes time. Just by starting

UFOs: Key To Inner Perfection

you put into process your conscious evolution, a concentration on your own growth.

Similar to your experiences, my life has been a series of unusual events. Yet, as I began to look, I could see how each event gave me a deeper insight about myself and my direction in this period. OUR LIVES ARE OUR GREATEST TEACHERS.

We sometimes forget this. Occasionally when we have had some remarkable insight into our own lives, we assume it to be a universal truth, readily accepted by others. And so we spread the word. With our new insight, we go out and try to save the world.

We bang on people's doors, trying to wake them from their stupor. There is an obnoxious enthusiasm that often overcomes people when they "get religion." It is a righteousness that is blind to where other people are in their lives, in their consciousness, in their understanding. Before you go out and save the world, SAVE THE WORLD WITHIN YOURSELF.

By your example, you can affect multitudes. Like a pebble dropped into a pond, your growing spurts through life will have an effect upon others. Let your light shine brightly and others will see you as a beacon.

THE DRUID PRAYER

GRANT OH GOD THY PROTECTION

AND IN PROTECTION-STRENGTH!

AND IN STRENGTH-UNDERSTANDING!

AND IN UNDERSTANDING-KNOWLEDGE!

AND IN KNOWLEDGE-THE KNOWLEDGE OF JUSTICE!

AND IN THE KNOWLEDGE OF JUSTICE-THE LOVE OF IT:

AND IN THE LOVE OF IT-THE LOVE OF ALL EXISTENCES:

AND IN THE LOVE OF ALL EXISTENCES-THE LOVE OF GOD AND ALL GOODNESS

UFOs: Key To Inner Perfection

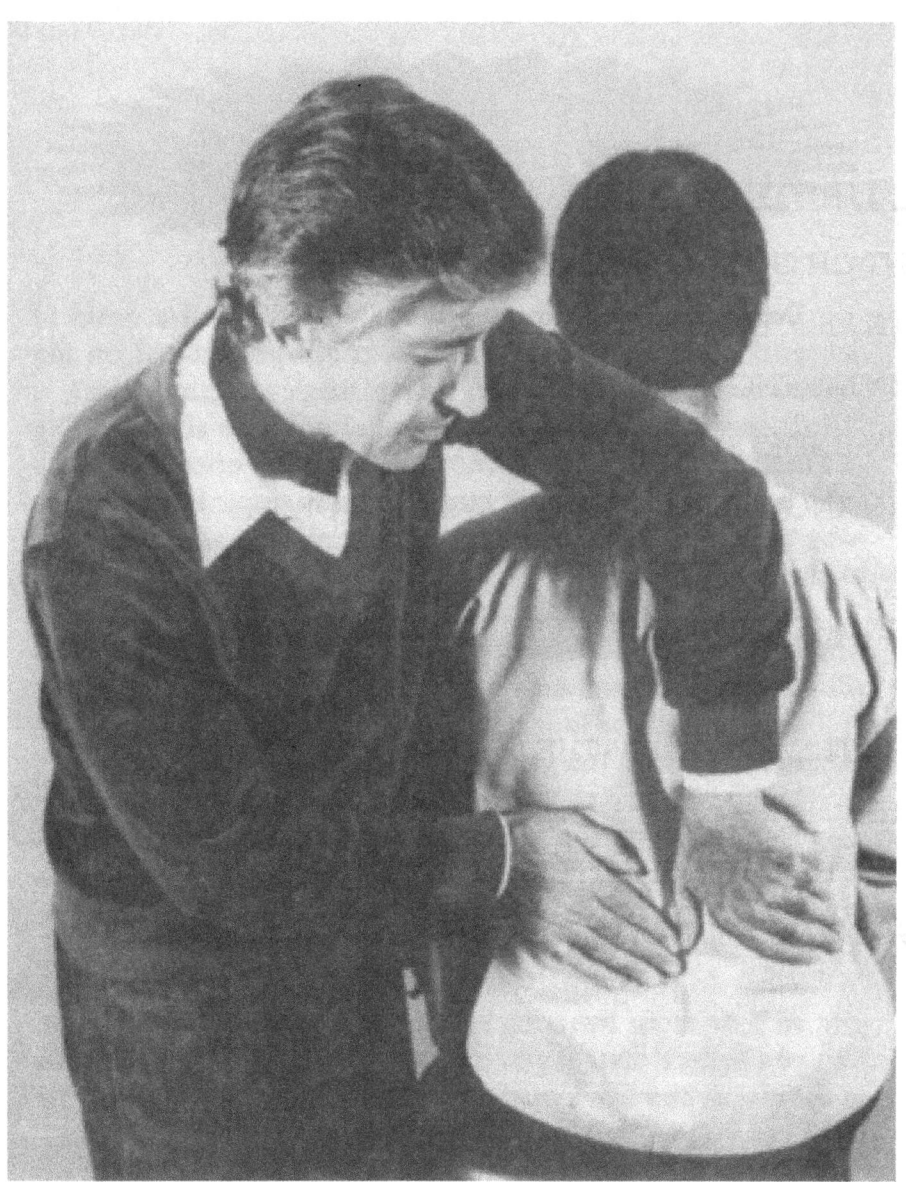

The author demonstrating his special techniques of healing as described in the pages of this book.

UFOs: Key To Inner Perfection

THE MAGUS

Do you believe in magic? What is magic? Is it a series of deceptions or sleight-of-hand? Is it tricks perpetrated on the limitations of our sense faculties? Or is magic something else? To me, there is magic in seeing a butterfly soar after crawling as a caterpillar. I feel magic when I have a client open himself up to be healed, and has healed himself. I sense magic in watching a baby grow into childhood, then adolescent into adulthood and maturity into old age.

For me, magic is a state of change, a transformation, whether it be physical, mental, or emotional. Our world is filled with magic if you will only believe it. Can you believe in magic? Do you believe that you could be a master magician? You can. Magic is in knowing you can change, if you want to change.

Give yourself permission to change. That's a beginning. For then you begin to look beyond the routine drudgery and begin to see what is beyond. You go beyond the limitations and look to the possibilities.

Chance begins with desire.

What do you want? Whatever it might be, focus your energies on it, without wavering in your pursuit, and you will get it. Can you believe that? If you can, you are ready to take your role as the magus and like a master magician transform your life from lacks and limitations into growth and abundance. That is the greatest act of magic we can perform; transmuting the base metal of our character into the radiant gold of divinity. It is perfection; paradise. It is divine.

UFOs: Key To Inner Perfection

THE GOD WITHIN

If GOD really wanted a place to hide, where would GOD hide? Within man. For that would be the last place man would look for GOD. Despite all the teachings to the contrary man still refuses to accept his heritage as the son of GOD. With man's fall from grace, when the essence goes within the ego of the growing child as he takes on personality around the age of seven, man loses the clear perceptions of reality to society's accepted illusions in mere appearances.

As the natural communion with life ends so, too, does man's connection to the continual progression, and evolution, in the life cycle. Look around you and see how man treats himself. Man's physical body is in disrepair, the temple of GOD ill treated by rampant negative thought forms, emotional chaos and self-destructive indulgence. As we think, so shall we become.

As we look around at the state of mankind today it is obvious what we have become. As though caught in some carnival fun house with distorted mirrors, we see etched upon every human being his emotions, his qualities and his character. There is sadness, bitterness, anger and defeat displayed during these times.

The lack of connection to the divine force that lies waiting to be ignited within each of us has sewn seeds of personal discontent, hostility and aggression. Yet having torn down this physical temple, we seek to build it up. True to Western civilization, we do so by looking at the symptoms and not at the essential cause. And, thus, we do not repair our emotions and the negative tape loops running constantly in our minds. Rather, we repair ourselves by cosmetic approaches, facial applications, plastic surgery, jewels and costumes. And we become the beautiful people.

The irony of it. For beauty is not the momentary bloom, or a transitory blossom. Beauty is the entire process of being, in which that momentary bloom is but a phase. And beauty comes not from application. It radiates out with life, love and character. If you seek to be beautiful, to allow the fullness of life into your own life, cosmetic means may get you a brief hit or two, but it will be momentary. To truly

UFOs: Key To Inner Perfection

find, one must search. Not the far corners of the earth. It is not even necessary to get out of your chair. For the search is a journey within.

The moment you truly reach inward and upward for the highest within yourself, your physiological appearance will change. Our external appearance is a reflection of our inner being. If we are confused, chaotic and angry within ourselves, no amount of beauty creams or cosmetics will effectively mask our expression of discontent.

Do you want to be beautiful? Then clean up your act. See yourself as you are. Not your opinion about yourself, or other people's opinions. See yourself as part of it all. As part of divinity. For you are.

REALITY FOLLOWS BELIEF

Which came first, the chicken or the egg? The law of cause and effect is everywhere. It is part of the life process, the transformation of the driving force into forms that continually change. CHANGE. Can you?

REALITY FOLLOWS BELIEF

It bears repeating, for we continually do so. Unfortunately we do so unconsciously thereby caroming back and forth between emotional crises and negative conditions.

UFOs: Key To Inner Perfection

YOUR THOUGHTS CREATE YOUR CONDITIONS

Think negatively, think in a mindset of lacks and unfulfilled wishes, and you will create such conditions. Negative thoughts breed negative conditions. However, if you see yourself as part of it all —part of the process, of this divine plan— then you are less likely to tap into your own personal ego conditioning tape loops that might set you up and cause you to fail.

It takes time. It takes awareness. Similar to any birthing process, it needs constant nourishment and focused awareness. Nourishment in the process of the creative self-expression of the individuality, YOUR GROWTH, takes many forms. It comes through books or discussions like this. It comes through a diet that is concerned with nutrition. It comes through our lessons learned in the natural procession of life. It comes from a respect for ourselves as part of the GOD force. It comes through a life cycle that is more inherently in tune with the cosmic rhythms.

The tidal action of the oceans, night into day; rest into action, breathing in and breathing out. How well do you breathe? Peculiar question? Not really. But possibly one you have not thought of for some time, if at all. Why? Because we take breathing for granted. It is automatic. It comes naturally. We do it all the time.

We had better. Otherwise, we would be dead. Man can go three weeks without food before he dies. He can go three days without water before he dies. But man can go only three minutes without breathing before he dies. Breath is life. Later, we will discuss several techniques to increase the awareness and proper rhythm for our breathing.

Right now recognize breathing as essential, even though it is automatic. And try to focus on your breathing more and more. For inhaling nourishes our body and vitalizes our blood stream. Exhaling allows us to release the toxins, the waste matter within our bodies. You know how people sometimes refer to those who are going through senility as not getting enough oxygen to the brain. Breath is indeed life. The Hindus talk of "prana", the life force contained within the air, invisible to our normal sight perceptions. By inhaling, we take this life force into ourselves. That is why awareness and proper breathing are so essential. It affects our brain. It affects our thoughts. It affects our life conditions.

You will see. The more you put into practice some of our insights and techniques given here, the more you will discover. You do not have to find some authoritative regimen to implement these understandings and applications. Really it is not necessary; just do it naturally. Like the awe of a little child at some new insight or flash that comes to you.

If you will look at your life, at the lives of people around you, and look objectively not with judgement or opinion, you are likely to see how much each of us has to put up with every day. In our day and age, with its fast pace and high technology we are being asked to master more and more situations in different areas of our lives in a much faster time frame. Think about it.

Those of you who have experienced some of this life may be able to see how life has accelerated in the last five to ten years. We are being asked to master financial survival, relationships, parenting, at a quicker pace and with a large degree of uncertainty and anxiety in the air.

There is a Chinese proverb, some would say a curse, that goes: "May you live in interesting times."

Indeed, we do. These times are times that try man's soul and press mankind to the very limits of its resilience. But these are also times that allow us to make quantum leaps in our understanding, in our consciousness, in our evolution. A quickening is taking place. Not only in the life of collective mankind, but in our individual lives as well. For the life of the collective is a reflection of the multitude of individual lives being lived.

If mankind is at war, and at present over one quarter of the world's countries are currently involved in war, then it is only a reflection of the war within the self of the individual lives. We are at war within ourselves. Our personal conflicts, the petty and trivial becoming paramount, are manifestations of our confusion, our ignorance. Did someone really say that ignorance is bliss?

While war rages, both on the external level and the internal, we can go forth as crusaders. First, begin to reevaluate who you are and what you are. Is there a war raging within you? Are there the vestiges of a brushfire deep within your soul that threaten to flare up? Do you have personal conflicts to resolve? Can you see the direction in which you are heading? The direction you want to go? Do you know who you are? And what you are here to do?

You know the answer to all of these questions, and any others that may be nagging within your mind. They are within you. They are not the conditioning

UFOs: Key To Inner Perfection

from your parents or society. They are that true you, your true individuality to be expressed in a creative manner. How? No one can give you the answer, EXCEPT yourself. You know that answer. And you will learn it, if you have forgotten, by listening to that small voice within. It knows. You know .

Like the biblical allegory of the prodigal son, we, too, lose our way. We forget what we are looking for. We ignore the process of evolution in its metronome-like swings between ever lessening extremes. That's why books like these are written as guides along the way.

In your journey through life, hold strong to the process of mankind made in the image of GOD, preserving and mastering through the experiences of earth life, to realize the GOD force within yourself. WE ARE ALL GODS IN THE MAKING. Every one of us. Each of us is part of a great master plan. We may often swear that the chaos of "random" incidents defies any sort of plan, much less a master plan. But that occurs through a narrowing of our perspective, when we look only at a small piece in the larger puzzle and lose sight of the total picture.

Man's knowledge is an extension of his consciousness. We mentioned it before: reality follows belief. There are no limits to mankind's expansion in understanding, only the capacity to which man is open to new insights, new understanding, even when they may be radical departures from previous beliefs and standards.

If we keep in sight the total picture, the total process of development and evolvement, we shall see the grand design in all its intricate workings. To me, one of the most beautiful sights in the cycles of life is that of a tree. For it encompasses and displays the multifaceted aspects of life. From an acorn a mighty oak is grown. Indeed. A seed dropped, perhaps borne by the wind to a distant spot, out from the shadow of the mother oak. The seed held gently by the earth, nourished in the darkness by the moist soil to sprout and grow toward the light.

This tiny shoot grows through seasonal experiences, each year getting bigger and stronger. The tree grows up, becomes taller and begins to take on branches. The tree grows out, the once spindly little trunk standing majestically strong. The winds of change constantly blow through the tree limbs. Rains come, provide water to nourish the tree. The tree continues to develop. As it grows, it goes through basic seasonal changes. In the Spring, the tree's limbs sprout tiny tight-closed buds that later break forth as the foliage of late Spring, Summer and early Fall. Come Fall and the tree loses its leaves in a radiant display of color, to stand apparently lifeless through the winter.

Continuously it grows upward and develops outward. If we look at the cycle of a tree, it provides incredible symbolism to the process of life and living. And it

UFOs: Key To Inner Perfection

records that process. Every year the tree in its widening breadth takes on another ring in its trunk, a wisdom ring which records the conditions of growth during that year.

While we might assume the tree stands alone, there is a larger picture to the puzzle. Not only does the tree provide us with the analogy of growth, a tree may serve many functions. Tree limbs provide nestings for birds. The oak provides acorns for squirrels. In summer, a leafy tree offers shade from the sun's heat.

The wood of a tree gives us building materials for houses, provides us with wood for fires. Fallen leaves decay and become a mulch to revitalize the soil from which it sprang. The interweaving and interdependency in life is a majestic spectacle. Perhaps part of its majesty stems from the fact that too often we tend to neglect the process and look only at one piece.

Do that and you are likely to lose sight of the total picture, and some of the opportunities contained therein. Mother nature provides us with many lessons about living and progression. It is a question of looking, of listening, of being en rapport with nature.

At the turn of the century there lived a black man, born into slavery who grew into a true individual whose depth and sensitivity would highlight his contributions to international renown. This man was George Washington Carver, truly a gentle man. His spiritual communion with nature is legendary He would communicate- with nature, speaking to it, holding it, sensing something in it that others could not sense. And in turn nature made him aware of its limitless abundance and mysteries. Carver called Mother Nature his teacher. It is one of the best. And part of that is relationship.

Bryce Bond and co-host Linda Pelerin from the TV program, Dimensions in Parapsychology.

UFOs: Key To Inner Perfection

RELATEDNESS

Relationships, the act of relating, have become an art in our day and age. For our society reflects an inability to relate. We see it reflected in the divorce statistics, in the singe-parent family structures, in the number of singles who are committed to a singles lifestyle.

Fundamental changes are taking place in the ways we relate to one another. These changes are the result of the present dichotomy in our individual selves. On the one hand, we are evolving as individuals more and more toward self-development and the expression of the true individuality. On the other hand, the techniques and attitudes of our self-development have subtly contributed to an ego reinforcement of the personal "me," a subtle trap and seduction indeed.

Relationships always have and always will provide us with the important lessons of developing ourselves through the process of interaction with others. It is part of man's life cycle. We see it as the child goes off to school; to learn about himself, to absorb rote knowledge, through the interaction with his peers. Relationships begin at a very early age. Before birth, the developing human body is completely dependent upon the mother carrying it for life support systems. Dependency continues after birth and throughout childhood. As we grow older, we take on other types of relationships. Not just parent-child relationships, but relationships with friends, relationships with teachers, relationships with the opposite sex. As we move toward maturity our relationships change.

We have talked repeatedly about change. The same is true in relationships. In your own life, you have probably seen people pass in, through and out of connection with you at various times in your life experience. Even now, perhaps you find yourself gravitating toward specific new types of people. Maybe some relationships are fading, with certain people moving out of your life.

If there are people from whom you are parting, recognize that it is not because you hate them. It is not because you no longer love them. It is because these people are no longer necessary to your personal growth. Does that sound callous

UFOs: Key To Inner Perfection

and too full of the "me" attitude? It does not.

We learn through relationships. We come together in dynamic interactions or relationships in order to discover more about ourselves. When we have learned whatever we can learn from interaction with the other person, we often find the relationship dissolves. Oh, it may do so for various reasons: Death, distant move, lack of continued mutual interests, arguments. Whatever they might be, the real reason that relationships end is because all the lessons to be learned through that other person, at that particular time period and level of development, have been learned. And so, it is time to move on. Whether we so choose, or life conditions insist on it, we move on.

One of the greatest lessons in our interactions with others is to be true to ourselves. Think about it. Relationships are dynamic interactions of various individuals. In those interactions, however, we too often assume that we must follow the habits and ways of our neighbors and friends. There is almost a silent acquiescence to the standards and conventions of the majority. Otherwise, we are afraid we will be branded as different, that we will become social outcasts.

Think back for a moment. Has there ever been a time when you went along with someone else's idea, even though you thought it was a bad one? Why did you do it? Was it because it was the line of least resistance? Was the social pressure too great to say no? PEER PRESSURE IS ONE OF THE GREATEST TESTS WE CAN MASTER.

Under peer pressure we are likely to do all sorts of things we would not even consider doing if we were alone. There is a blindness to our actions we accept when we acquiesce to peer pressure. It is the blindness of running with the pack; the accepted belief that might makes right. The weight of conventionality has lead us down many a winding road. Conventionality is accepted belief. It is largely based upon the premise that what worked once in the past, will work again now in the present, or even into the future. It is locked into a time frame that may be largely irrelevant to present realities.

Yet, hypnotically we accept the idea that what worked in the past will work now as well. It does not always, you know. IN ALL OF LIFE, ESPECIALLY IN RELATIONSHIPS, IT IS ESSENTIAL TO BE TRUE TO YOURSELF. Some of our relationships take the form of adversity. Relationships, nonetheless, but relationships that provide more an element of frustration, pain, hurt, as opposed to our love relationships.

All relationships provide challenges and opportunities.

If we are discussing a love relationship, the challenge may be one of possessiveness—love that is conditional, based upon each other's own expectations,

UFOs: Key To Inner Perfection

and as such limiting to both the people involved. If the relationship is antagonistic, then the opportunity arises to face the conflict not with anger, violence or hate but with awareness and the desire to seek a just resolution.

In relating to others, we get a chance to work out the emotions of our ego. Ego emotions are like heavy anchors. They hold us down. They keep us from truly experiencing or sharing with others because of our emotions. Have you seen love between two people turn sour, even to the point where they manifest hate for each other? It is unfortunate, but it is not a rarity. It is unfortunate because the two people involved are unable to come to terms with the negative emotions that have sprung from a soil once nourished in love.

And what are some of these emotions we have to master in our relationships with other people? Hate, anger, jealousy fear, animosity rejection, envy, pride, vanity, unworthiness, ridicule, judgments, and frustrations are some of these emotions. And each of these emotions is but another anchor to weigh you down and hold you back from self-mastery through relatedness.

The most powerful force in the universe is love. LOVE IN ACTION manifests GOD on earth. If you want to clean up your act in your personal relationships, unconditional love is the way. For unconditional love, the ability to love expecting nothing in return, is the highest form of love. It is the love that JESUS taught, when he said to love your brother as yourself.

Loving people unconditionally is to accept them the way they are, without your conditions, or your expectations, or what you want them to do for you in return. One of the great clues in relationships is to recognize that we tend to see the other person according to our perspective. In looking at someone, we often see only a mirrored image of ourselves. If we happen to see in someone something that we do not like about him, recognize that quite possibly what we are disapproving of is the same quality we do not like about ourselves.

Before we judge a person by their actions, question whether those actions seem so dreadful to us because of our own unconscious sense of guilt over similar behavior. Quite a morass in which we move in our relationships. Quite a mess, one that parallels our present day and age, where we are just incapable of sustaining "good" relationships. Swell, you might think, disheartened by such a suggestion. So much for a successful relationship only found in the pages of romance novels, or on the flickering images of the television screens. Not so.

The fact of the matter is that all we have to do is turn the gears of our behavior patterns. The moment we forgive a person for the faults we imagine they have, and send that person our unconditional love, at that moment, no sooner, no later, we sever the cord of negative emotions toward that person.

UFOs: Key To Inner Perfection

Unconditional love is free of judgments. It holds no opinions. It truly wants the very best for an individual, no matter what the personal conflicts are between the two of you. Unconditional love is being able to rejoice in another's success before your own. It is the ability to love a stranger as you do yourself.

LOVE. Love your conditions, and you will change those conditions. Love your environment, and you change that environment. Love yourself, and you change the world. We change those around us by changing ourselves first. Look not for the change in your brother or sister, look for the change in you. By your changes, you will affect changes in your relationships, in your life, in your loves. You might argue with this point, and say, perhaps, that the other person should change his attitude or behavior. And perhaps with your sense of rightness (a. k. a. self-righteousness) you will go forward to change him, correct his ways, in the name of love.

Have you ever thought about the calamities and deaths caused in the name of "love", in the name of "GOD"?

To try and change another, no matter what you use as a rationale, is an ego manipulation. What you are doing is placing conditions on your love. It is the carrot-and-stick routine of relatedness. I will love you more, if you will .... I can't love you, if you won't .... Conditions to our love are restrictions upon our selves. They place limits to our sharing, to our experiencing. Accept people as they are. It is quite a test, no doubt about it. But is essential to be able to do so, before you can truly love the other.

Another master test for all of us is the ability to forgive. It was intoned by the mater JESUS as he hung nailed to the cross when he called out: "Forgive them, for they know not what they do." It is a powerful affirmation, reinforced by wise understanding. Forgiveness is a phenomenal healing tool. When we are wounded or hurt in our experiences through life, there is the possibility that we might allow that pain to embitter us from similar situations in the future, or even to life itself. You have seen it. Ride a city bus some time, and see the bitterness etched on some faces.

The face is an incredible map. On it becomes etched the life pattern, the individuals reaction to life itself. All kinds of emotions are etched on people's faces. What will you enscrawl upon your own? It is your choice. In being able to forgive someone, it is not a question of forgive and forget. It is forgiveness and awareness. A dramatic difference.

Forgiveness is letting go of a situation, not holding on to it. It is the recognition that people have to act out their emotional imbalances, coupled with the strength not to get sucked into it. If someone is outlandish in their actions, are we

UFOs: Key To Inner Perfection

going to match their bizarre behavior?

Are we going to come down to their level and retaliate? If we do, we give that person incredible power over us. For we are reacting in a manner similar to their own. TO THEIR OWN. Important words, for they remind us that everyone of us is a unique individual entity on various levels of development. You cannot ask a child of three to have the knowledge of a Nobel physicist in his sixties. You cannot ask of people who know not what they do reason and understanding in their actions, much less so in their interactions.

But can you forgive them? If you can, send them unconditional love. This does not mean you forget, for lessons are to be learned. But if you truly can forgive them, you will feel as if a weight has been lifted from your chest for, indeed, a weightiness has. You will have severed the connection to the ego emotion and the negative situation.

Sending unconditional love, like a prayer, will provide the one who hurt us with a healing, and may help him move to a higher understanding. There are many wounded souls out there in the world today. You do not have to be one of them. There is an old saying that goes: When the student is ready the teacher appears. It is a very simple but very wise saying. Unfortunately people tend to believe their teacher is likely to come in raiment of gold cloth, hailed as the Messiah himself. This attitude is akin to the expectant coming in the Jewish religion, and the second coming of the present fundamentalists. If we accept that belief, what happens is that we become like characters out of Beckett's "Waiting For Godot"—waiting expectantly, ever waiting.

Meanwhile, the teacher may have come and gone. WE ARE ALL TEACHERS, WE ARE ALL STUDENTS. As you begin to realize the truth to this statement, you will begin to see the varied lessons to be learned in our different relationships. For that is the importance of relationships: SELF-MASTERY THROUGH RELATEDNESS.

Not everything is black and white. In fact, few things are. Consequently clear-cut decisions often necessitate weighing of many factors before the actual decision is made. This is also true in our lessons through experience. Often, you won't find your situation or incident clearly marked with the label: "the lesson of this experience is .... "

That is true of all of life. And relationships are no exception. During moments of floundering, wondering what is the right action, we can go back to the masters, the world teachers who have passed through this life and impacted human culture. No matter what our personal bias or cultural background, the truth is expressed in many forms, in many different manifestations. The teachers are in

UFOs: Key To Inner Perfection

the multitude. They are the teachers such as JESUS, MOHAMMED, MOSES, CONFUCIUS, ZOROASTER, LAO TSE, BUDDHA.

Their words, their wisdom, can be like guides for our decisions, for our actions. If we question what to do or how to act in a situation, reflect back on the understanding expressed through these various teachers. For myself, I find the teacher I turn to is JESUS. When I find myself perplexed, caught up in frustration or anger, I stop for a moment and ask myself " What would JESUS do in a situation like this?"

The answer comes instantly He would forgive the intrusion, he would give love, and then he would continue on his way. Try it. What have you got to lose? Only your anger, frustration, and disappointments. And you have got so much to gain. There is a technique I use, and one that works every time when I am confronted by a negative situation. Let us say someone comes up to you in a state of anger, wanting to put you down, reject you, or insult you. First thing to do is to look directly into their eyes. The eyes are the windows to the soul. Then, evoke the eleventh commandment, the one that affirms: "Keep Thy Mouth Shut!". Third, in your consciousness say to that person silently without moving your lips: "I love you."

Within five minutes of working this technique, and applying it sincerely you are likely to find the other person dumfounded. It is as if he does not know what hit him. Either he may apologize for his action, or he may just walk away.

Let me share an incident I experienced in this regard. It was many years ago, during the early days of my career as a radio broadcaster. I was heading to work one hot Friday afternoon in August. It was about 3:30, and I was leaving Manhattan for Long Island by the 59th Street Bridge. I was feeling on top of the world at the time. I really enjoyed my work, and I liked my job. I had just gotten a new car at the time. I was feeling really good about myself.

Of course, bliss without awareness gets back to the old ignorance bit. And so I was at the time. For while I was feeling great about myself and my own personal world, I had lost awareness of what was going on around me that Friday afternoon on the bridge. Leaving New York on a Friday afternoon in August for Long Island is like joining an exodus of lemmings racing for the shore. The traffic was heavy, the situation complicated by ongoing construction on the bridge. Due to the construction and merging lanes, traffic narrowed down to a feeder lane to the upper level of the bridge.

Because of my happy state without awareness, I did not notice all the pent up anger and frustration around me that the other drivers were feeling. So I was driving along, moving toward the narrowing of the roadway. Usually cars will al-

UFOs: Key To Inner Perfection

ternate in a merging situation.

However, several taxi cabs in their race to nowhere pushed ahead of me. In all, I let three cabs go ahead of me. A fourth one came up, trying to push ahead of me. We were side by side, heading up the narrowing roadway. I decided not to let him in ahead of me, and he was just determined to do so. We were inching along side by side as the roadway continued to narrow. I could see the cabdriver was very agitated. There was a fare in his back seat.

I smiled at the cab driver. He responded by showing me his index finger. I smiled back at him. In turn, he screamed at me very loudly some profanity about my mother. I looked back over at him. I could see his face was livid with rage. He was clutching the steering wheel as though he was strangling someone. The fare in the back seat was freaking out by what was going on. My eyes and the cabdriver's met once again as I was about to take my turn at the merge. I looked at the cabdriver, smiled, and mouthed the words: "I love you."

His reaction was completely insane. Whether he thought I was homosexual or what, he went totally out of control. He drove his cab forward, refusing to yield the right of way. Instead, he was driving his cab for about fifty yards along the metal divider, and as his cab scraped the metal barrier, sparks were flying. It would have been simple for him to have turned the wheel to the right and disengaged his cab from the barrier. But he was in such a rage that not only did it blind his thinking, but his entire equilibrium.

This would not be much of a story if there was not a follow-up. After we had gotten off the bridge, several miles down the highway the cabdriver and I happened to pass again. But this time, when we passed each other, the most extraordinary thing happened. Instead of swearing and cursing at me, he was waving and laughing. For at least a moment, the power of love had transformed him.

Try something like this. It works. Say nothing, just let the power of love be felt. Can you? Can you forgive and give love? Our relationships show a paradox. It is a paradox similar to the old chicken-egg controversy: what came first, the chicken or the egg? The same thing can be said of relationships. And that is: HOW CAN YOU LOVE ANOTHER IF YOU CANNOT LOVE YOURSELF? You can't. Not really. Not in the sense of love. That's why it is so important to become aware of ourselves. That is why it is essential to appreciate our qualities and respect our character.

However, this does not mean we should give license to the self-aggrandizement of the ego personality where people try to convince themselves and others, often through conspicuous consumption, that not only are they "good" people, but that they are "better people."

UFOs: Key To Inner Perfection

Such an attitude is not grounded in love for one's self. Rather, it is an attitude fostered and festered by the sense of insecurity by a discord and disharmony within the self. And it is an attitude born of ignorance, a lack of understanding and awareness. So much for the ignorance is bliss bit.

However, by growing in awareness, you provide fertile ground for the true development of the self to be realized. As you start to see divinity in material manifestations (recognize the spirit in matter), you will begin to understand the truth to the affirmation that man is made in the image of GOD. With that increased understanding, you will be better able to love yourself.

Love yourself not in the sense of the mortal ego personality but rather as a child of GOD, the striving spirit of the eternal soul. When you can truly love yourself, then you can truly love another.

How often have you heard people say to one another: "love you?"-Despite what we might presume, this phrase is incredibly hollow There is no substance to it, because it is impersonal by the lack of the "I". Without the "I" there is no commitment in the statement. Only a shallow expression.

I LOVE YOU. These are powerful words, for with the "I" we honestly express ourselves, our feelings and our commitment. Many people fear these words, however. And why? Because they are afraid to commit themselves, in case commitment becomes attachment and obligation. It does not have to. For our primary commitment is in the evolution of ourselves. And relationships provide us the ground for self-mastery through relatedness.

LOVE is the most powerful force in the Universe. And when we see how effective the expression of love (unconditional love) is, we surely realize its phenomenal powers of transformation. There is one story I would like to share with you that illustrates this power. As a healer, I find many people come through my door. There are many wounded souls in the world today, some seeking help, sometimes in desperation, come to me for healing. One such person was Janet.

Janet was desperate when she came to me, for her physical body had become cancerous. The medical doctors she had seen had given her six months to live. This six months death sentence might be commuted, the doctors told her, if she would undergo an extensive operation to remove the rapidly spreading malignant growth on her left side. After the operation, the follow-up would be a regimen of chemotherapy and radiation treatments.

Janet was in total panic. She was touching base with that very fundamental issue of personal survival, and she was terrified of death. If she went into the hospital for the operation, she believed she would never come out alive. The medical doctors she saw were not supportive. The outlook was bleak. She went to various medical doctors, hoping their diagnosis would be different. But each of them predicted the same result.

Although at her wits end, Janet was determined to find an alternate way of treating her problem. She investigated the various options open to her, and decided upon healing. She had heard about my method of healing, SPIRITUAL HEALING. Believing she had nothing to lose, she gave herself permission to try it. After all, she rationalized, if healing did not work, then she would accept her medical doctor's advice and submit to the operation and chemotherapy treatments.

Guided by her own personal instincts, Janet called me and set up an appointment. Whenever I meet a client, I first make it crystal clear that I can promise nothing, that I guarantee nothing. As a healer, I am only a channel for energy that flows from GOD. I am not the one who heals. It is he, the patient, who is the healer and the physician. Secondly I never suggest that he should stop his medical treatment, no matter what it is. For that is not my decision to make, it is the patient's. After all, it is his life.

And in his life, he is the outward reflection of his inner condition. Therefore, when Janet came to me, I understood that Janet herself was the mental architect for the basic foundation, structure and creation of her disease (dis-ease). Janet was the cause of the cancer manifesting in her physical body This is not to imply that all cancer is created or manifested by psychological rules. All of us have cancer cells within our bodies, and all of us have the ability to manifest a latent condition into reality. However, my point here is to share with you a certain type of the cancer personality.

By casting light on our attraction of the possibility of cancer, we can lift ourselves above the causation, and become aware of the psychological traps from our conditioning environment. When I met with Janet, she expressed the sense that her whole life was deteriorating. She had been dealt a cruel hand. She believed GOD was punishing her. Instead of looking within herself, she blamed everyone and everything around her for her problems.

She explained how her problem had started. It all began when her husband of 27 years ran off with another woman. Not that she presumed their life together was paradise. On the contrary she told me that their relationship was an uneasy one. Their life together had not been all that loving. Both made demands on the other.

The day her husband ran off, he told her that he wanted out, that he did not love her, that he was tired of his existence with her, and that he was in love with another woman. Janet exploded. Emotionally her security was shattered. Her whole life was about to end. Despite the conflicts and the lack of love between the two of

UFOs: Key To Inner Perfection

them, she had learned to live with the nagging emotional pain. Perhaps she was dissatisfied, but she was content to live with the situation.

So when her husband confronted her with his feelings, when he told her of his intent, and when he packed his bags and left, Janet locked herself into a mental closet. Day after day her thoughts were angry, hateful and filled with tremendous jealousy. All of these damaging, negative thoughts collectively triggered a massive biochemical change within Janet's emotional-physical system. The shock to her bio-computer in the brain reached a dangerous level. And her adrenaline released into her body a psychological awareness of discomfort, sensations of heavy depression and the fright of being alone. The awful moments of disorientation, the bodily rushes of anxiety which she experienced increased her body tension and created a violent collision with the immune system. Janet became a living wreck.

Every day when she returned to her apartment, the breeding ground of her discontent, she would review her life over and over again. She replayed all the old tapes. For in the apartment was her husband's picture, his favorite chair, his books, the walls he had painted. The reflection of his presence was everywhere in the apartment. And in that environment, Janet would sit down and feed hostile, negative thoughts to a negative situation.

As they do, all the negative thoughts she sent out came back to her tenfold. But she was not aware of this. Instead, she would send out hateful, jealous thoughts. She blamed the other woman for taking away her husband. No matter that their life together was less than conjugal bliss. Every waking moment, Janet projected hate and anger. She was in a state of emotional turmoil. She was feeding a negative situation, negative energy. Things began to happen. Janet lost her job. Friends stopped calling her. The walls of the apartment seemed to be closing in on her. She developed a pain in her left side. As the weeks went by the pain became steadily worse. She sensed something was growing inside of her. The pain continued to worsen. Finally in fear, she consulted her doctors. And they gave her the news. She had cancer, and six months to live.

When she came to me, I remember how heavy with depression she was. It looked like she was trying to crawl back inside herself. We talked. We talked about her life, about her marriage, about her likes and dislikes. All the while, she sat very rigid, listening, hoping that her prayers would be answered.

From her personal experiences in life, we moved to a discussion of life itself. I began telling her why we are here on this planet, and why things happen to us. We talked about how every life was different, and how each of us experiences different events for the varied lessons to be learned. I mentioned that when something has outlived its usefulness in our lives, it is taken from us.

UFOs: Key To Inner Perfection

In our personal interactions, relationships are taken from us by death, divorce, rejection. Any of these creates a very painful experience. In personal relationships, you cannot have an experience solely by yourself. Both partners share, extracting differing experiences. At this time in her life, Janet was going through a very profound experience. She was filled with two very destructive emotions, HATE AND ANGER, which were eating her alive, and the causation of her cancer.

Janet and I talked about life as being like a classroom. We go into a new grade, take on the conditions of that grade, the conditions of our environment, the conditions of the collective, and our classmates. If we pass the test, we graduate. We go on summer vacation. As we talked about what we have learned, what we have yet to learn, it became apparent that Janet was a fast learner. She understood the philosophical concepts about reincarnation, about cause and effect, about karma, and lessons to be learned.

We discussed love, the true love, UNCONDITIONAL LOVE. We spoke about FORGIVENESS. From the abstract, we went back to her situation, her own personal condition. I suggested to her that she could end her suffering if she so desired.

How, she asked, determined to put an end to her pain. I told her that first she should put away all images of her husband. All things that belonged to him, all traces of him. That included removing his books, his favorite chair, his pictures. By so doing, she would put into action the riddance for herself of reflective memory I mentioned she should change her apartment, by rearranging the furniture, repainting the walls and redecorating her environment. This was the first step in loosening the hold of the disquieting thoughts and negative emotions.

Janet did these things. She cleaned out almost everything that had belonged to her previous life, to her life with her husband. She redecorated the entire apartment. As she did so, her outlook on life started to change, for the better. She had a sense that maybe this process was actually going to work. Her consciousness started to shift, a positive feeling taking the place of the negative emotions in which she had floundered.

With that shift in consciousness, Janet also began to realize that the other woman had nothing to do with taking her husband away. And she recognized that she could no longer blame the other woman for her cancer. Be releasing the hold of the negative emotions upon her, she found she could forgive the other woman.

When she called me, she mentioned the cancer had stopped hurting. She said she hardly felt any pain at all. On Janet's next visit, we spoke again about love, unconditional love. Her belief was becoming stronger, and she was now ready for the big test. Could she work out the remaining psychological blocks,

UFOs: Key To Inner Perfection

the resistance to letting go, of completely surrendering and embracing the unconditional to someone she thought she loved?

With the recognition that the other woman was not responsible for taking her husband away she began to send LOVE to the other woman. At first, she had resistance, for the negative emotions and destructive thoughts were battling for their survival. But the moment she could send that woman love in total honesty she experienced a strange fluttering in her side. Weeks before, the cancer had stopped hurting. Now to her very great surprise, she sensed that not only had the cancer stopped growing and spreading, but that it was actually shrinking. It was a bizarre feeling for her, as if someone had let the air out of a balloon.

Yet, as this phenomena occurred, she realized that LOVE, unconditional love, was healing her cancer, healing herself. Janet progressed in her consciousness. Not only was she able to forgive and send love to the other woman, she was also able to get beyond the pain and hurt she felt from her husband's actions. Instead, she projected love and forgiveness to her husband, expecting nothing in return, but honestly feeling that she could rejoice in his new success.

Weeks later, she reported that her cancer was gone. Not just shrinking, but gone, completely. When she went back for a visit with her medical doctor, he was astounded. Whereas before, when he had pronounced a death sentence on her, this time he gave her a clean bill of health. The cancer was gone.

Janet's case in but one example of many where the power of forgiveness and love can turn our lives around, even when it seems that there may be no hope, no possibility. To follow up on Janet's life conditions, her whole life has changed for the better. She realized that her neediness had emotionally created her problems. And with that awareness, the self-revelation, her life became brighter. People started to call her again. She was offered a new job. She became involved in another relationship and married the man. They moved to upstate New York. She had made her peace with her first husband, who had married the other woman and moved to California. And she and her first husband are now good friends.

For me, to be part of the process, as a channel for the healing, is a glory and a blessing. It always serves to reinforce and reconfirm my admiration for the master JESUS. For JESUS was truly one of the greatest healers to walk this earth. We have heard of his miracles, of his abilities to heal.

Never did JESUS see a person as deformed. He always saw them whole, in divine perfection, as his FATHER has created them—PERFECT.

To JESUS, there was only imperfect thought. With his mind enveloped in the CHRIST consciousness, he was aware of the causation for any physical infirmities. By visualizing a person as he knew he was, perfect, made in the image of the

UFOs: Key To Inner Perfection

FATHER—that energy created a wholeness and the imperfection in that person vanished.

Just as Janet's faith in LOVE healed her, so too will your own personal faith heal you. You are the one who must do it. It won't be done for you. You must put your faith into action. Two of the precepts of faith in action are FORGIVENESS and UNCONDITIONAL LOVE. Forgiveness erases causation.

No one said it would be easy. Neither does it have to be that hard. The more you practice, like a muscle toned by use, the more you will be able to put your faith into action. As you do, your perception will become clearer. You will be able to see the process and your causation in life conditions, in the way Janet and I walked through her reflections, going from the symptoms back to the causation. By touching base with the reasons behind her taking on cancer, we could correct the emotions and psychic implant from that causal event. just as Janet released herself from the hold of negative emotions and truly healed herself, you can do the same.

Dependency and possessiveness are concurrent curses in our relationships. They are major lessons we all have to learn in relatedness. One of the areas of relatedness that is especially difficult, because it is so subtle and therefore potentially deceptive, is family. Many of our relationships are by choice— our marriage partner, our business partner, our friends. And we can choose to end those relationships. Although it may not always be easy to extricate ourselves from the relationships by choice, we can still do so. But with family. . . . well . . . .

They say blood is thicker than water. So is quicksand. FAMILY relationships can be especially difficult because they are born from dependency. If they are parent-child relationships, that is especially true. For the child was dependent upon his parents while he was a baby. And often parents become dependent upon their children in their later years. This dependency is also part of the early conditioning within the family structure: parent-child, sibling-sibling, parent-sibling.

All sorts of rivalries may be allowed within defined parameters, but a strong sense of obligation is also built-in to family relations. By that early conditioning, we are taught to accept from someone within the family what we might never accept from someone in a relationship of choice. And why? "Because it is family"

In the name of family we often meet some of our greatest tests. One of mine came through my brother. As a child, I looked up to my older brother. I wanted to be like him, even to the point of following him and enlisting in the NAVY when I was nearly of age.

After serving his enlistment time in the Navy my brother reenlisted in the Marine Corps. During World War II, he traveled the world. He became a dedi-

UFOs: Key To Inner Perfection

cated career man, the epitome of the "esprit de corps" associated with that branch of the Armed Services. When the war ended, my brother reenlisted. He came back to the States and became a D. I. (drill instructor) at various marine training camps.

His career was unfolding. He received a number of merit commendations. Not only was his career flourishing, his personal life was also opening up. Between World War II and the Korean conflict, he got married and started a family. He had a son and a daughter. During this period, I did not have a lot of contact with him. I was married at the time, and had my own life to contend with. But he was my brother, and I was still very proud of him. When the Korean War broke out, my brother was sent into combat. Secretly he always likes to have a cause to work for and through. And this was it. He saw a lot of action in Korea, as did many of his comrades, and was himself wounded by shrapnel in his legs.

He received the Purple Heart and other awards. Combat was a way of life for my brother. He had but one thought: The duty of the military: kill or be killed. Therefore, when the Korean war ended and he left the service briefly he was like a fish out of water. The massive nervous tensions that had been within him, tensions he was able to release through combat duty increased without an outlet.

He and his family moved all around the country. His family wanted roots, a stable life. He wanted adventure. My brother became frustrated and started to drink more and more. He reentered the service. He was a master sergeant in the Marine Corps when the Vietnam involvement began. He was sent into action. His main love was fulfilled. For a time the combat within himself was relieved by the physical combat in war. That war ended for him as well.

He came back to the States. He was lean, tanned and eager. He had made it through that Southeast Asian hell. He had survived. On his return, my brother was stationed at Parris Island, South Carolina, where he trained recruits. This lasted for a while, until he lost interest. He left the service, with a chest full of ribbons. He was ready for the world. But was the world ready for him? He believed that all doors would open to a veteran who had served his country

It did not happen that way. My brother became frustrated, confused. He and his wife were constantly arguing. As days became weeks, then months, with no opportunities opening up to him, my brother sank lower and lower into the turmoil of his own inner world. His insecurities, his fears, his frustrations started to eat at him. The combat was engaged, the war within himself.

One of the greatest travesties of the Armed Services, especially for those who have seen combat, is the lack of deprogramming from service life when the veteran reenters civilian life. We have seen it depicted in the posttraumatic syn-

UFOs: Key To Inner Perfection

dromes of many recent veterans, who are unable to cope, and to move beyond that experience of hell. So it was for my brother.

After many years in combat, he just did not know how to live in a noncombat situation. He had never been debriefed, de-programmed, readjusted. Combat increased in his home life: The arguments with his wife, his inability to deal effectively with his children. Questions of what he could do for a living gnawed at him. The doors of opportunity had not opened. His potential employment picture was reduced to being a security guard, or a cop in a small town. Maybe an insurance salesman, or any kind of salesman. He did not know. What he did know was that the possibilities contrasted starkly with his combat image, the fantasies of self-aggrandizement, the delusions of grandeur.

Inertia ensued. My brother was unable to move on. He was in a paralytic state of STOP, NO-GO. His wife divorced him. He started to drink again. The more he drank, the more negative he became. He began to lie and cheat. He lost every job he tried. He became addicted to the bottle. Unconsciously our mother supported his habit. He would ask her for money telling her he needed the funds to travel for a job. In truth, the money was paying for his drinking habit. He started to steal. My brother traveled around, and tapped into our mother's friends. He would go to their houses and knock on their doors. He would say he had a truck full of antiques broken down on the highway and could they lend him money to make the necessary repairs. He would tell them he would mail them a check.

This went on for a period of time. He sank deeper into the booze. He found himself down in the Bowery in New York City, a bum, reliving his past from the bottom of a bottle. One cold winter day when it was sleeting outside, there was a knock at my door. I opened the door to see my brother in shirt sleeves, soaking wet, and filthy dirty. He smelled of booze, urine and waste. It shook me to my core to see my brother like that. Remember, this was the brother I looked up to, revered, and wanted to be like when l was a child. But he was not there. Before me stood a man who had given in to his fears, weaknesses and insecurities. He begged to come in. I was angry with him for using our mother to feed his addiction. But at that moment l could not make a judgement. He was cold and hungry; he begged to come in. He was crying. I barred the entrance with my body. I told him he could not enter. I told him to straighten himself out, and turn himself in. And then I slammed the door in his face. On my brother.

I screamed inside myself with pain and rage that I should have to do this...to my brother. The brother I loved. I sat and cried for hours. I pleaded with GOD, praying that l had done the right thing.

Immediately I was plagued by guilt and fear that something would happen to my brother on account of my actions. I RISKED the fear of his death, to do the

UFOs: Key To Inner Perfection

thing I thought right. I knew that Alcoholics Anonymous insists you close the door on a loved one's face. For they believe the shock may help bring the alcoholic loved one to some semblance of normalcy and the desire to get himself straight. I knew all this, because I had counseled others for their own personal problems, for their own loved ones. But this was my brother, and the test was for me, not another.

My brother did turn himself in. He sought help at Serenity House in Connecticut. He left many times, but he always returned. He realized he needed help. It takes massive courage to work through the turmoil of personal conflict. My brother made it. Today, my brother has his life together. He is married again and has a good relationship with his children. He has grown tremendously, his consciousness expanding, and he is still growing.

What an experience that man put himself through. What pain. And yet, the lessons he learned have contributed to his ever-expanding consciousness. He is my brother, and I love him. Can you? Can you love your brother, your sister, a stranger on the street? CAN YOU LOVE?

Indeed, you can love. And I mean truly love, without the conditions, without the expectations. You can do it. You probably have done so in the past. Remember when you "fell" in love? Perhaps the other person seemed to come from out of nowhere. But he appeared in your life. And you loved him with all of your heart and soul. If you have experienced such relatedness, you can well appreciate the power of the love force. For when you are in love, you feel as though you could conquer the world. No task is beyond your reach. Why? Because you are energized. You are in rapport with life itself. And as a result, you become more creative, more vital, more joyful. Life takes on a golden hue for you. Does it still? It can, you know.

UFOs: Key To Inner Perfection

COMMUNITY

Man lives in groups. He joins together into communities. We have all heard the saying that no man is an island unto himself. We live in interaction with others. We live in society. What is society? Basically society is the living materialized thought form of the collective consciousness. Society reflects the state of mankind. Together, you and I and all the others in our community create the patterns and standards of our society And as such, society is not static, but rather in constant flux in accord with our thought processes and our actions.

Look at society today and you see the state of mankind. Although each of us is here to evolve ourselves, to grow and develop beyond our present capabilities, we do so within the parameters of relationships and community. However, just as we discussed in self-mastery through relatedness, we should recognize that society has effects upon our self-mastery as well.

In society we see the power of group dynamics in operation. Conditioning by peer pressure often leads to a blind acceptance of the conventions and standards of society. We assume it is easier to go along. The line of least resistance. Of course, by doing so we may be stunting our own growth and evolution. It is not easy to swim against the current, especially in our day and age. The reinforcement of the collective consciousness is not only experienced by our own personal interaction with the world. In this era of the communications revolution, the mass consciousness is being broadcast twenty-four hours every day out onto the air waves on all forms of energy frequencies. To be in this world but not of it is a difficult task. In our present time, it seems harder because of the constant bombardment of the collective psyche's thought forms, magnified and enhanced by global communications systems.

Turn on your television any time. That wizard's wonder of magic and imagination has been reduced to a glorification of immediate ego gratification. Although gross characterizations, so many of our television programs revolve around the following emotions: Greed, fear, lust, anger, hate, violence. How many television programs concentrate on, even to the point of extolling, the negative emotions?

UFOs: Key To Inner Perfection

Where are the programs of faith and uplifting, the shows that entertain and enlighten? There are some, only a few. The television industry programs largely to the negative emotions. And the consequence? A reinforcement of the negative in the collective consciousness upon each individual viewer and, on occasion, with dire results. We have probably all heard or read about some of the tragedies that have followed certain television showings.

With the power of suggestion enforced by thousands of minds focusing upon that dramatized action on the television screen, individuals have acted out the bizarre behavior they have seen on television. In our legal system now the debate rages over the question whether a temporary insanity defense can be claimed due to the influence of a television program. When we, as individuals, get to the point of realizing that the negative emotions of the collective consciousness are only a hindrance to our own self growth and development, that is a time of critical choice. It is a crossroads in our lives. For it is a time when we not only question society's attitudes, but also wonder whether those attitudes are in harmony with our own internal feelings, that growing sense of true individual expression within ourselves.

At that time of critical choice, many people decide not to go forward. There is too much resistance. It is too radical to change. Instead, these people opt for the ways and mores of the herd consciousness once again. They figure it is easier to go along. It may appear to be, but in the long run it is not. That sense of growing individuality within you may be buried effectively but it can never be snuffed out. There will be another time, another crossroad.

For those who decide to go against the grain, it is not easy. It demands all the fortitude and will power of a true gladiator, off to do battle with the dragons of societal conditioning ingrained in your consciousness. It takes great courage to stand up for your convictions when they contrast so fundamentally with society's notions. It takes great stamina. You may be ridiculed, you may be alienated. Why? Because you have become a threat, a threat to the herd consciousness.

Part of the herd consciousness is getting while the getting is good. Born from individuals' lack of self-awareness, society reflects our individual attempts to hoard, accumulate and get as much for ourselves as we can in as short a period of time. It is known as maximum return. In optimizing potential for maximum return, society tends to cut corners. Morality gives way to amorality and then immorality. Aberrant behavior becomes justified because everybody does it, and if you do not, then you are just plain stupid.

In maximizing return, there is often the tendency on the part of society to focus solely on the immediate effect and to ignore or neglect the long-range consequences. We see it today where societies have abused their resources and laid

UFOs: Key To Inner Perfection

waste to their environments. All in the name of forward progress. Some progress! We are takers, not givers. We have lost the balance in life.

The North American Indian talks of man being the guardian of the earth, as being the caretaker. That wisdom has gone unappreciated. As the white man settled west across the North American continent, Indians were herded into reservations. The white man celebrated his victory in gaining the land the Indians had lost. However, what the white man never understood, and still does not understand, is that man cannot own the land. He is here to take care of it.

Some caretakers we have become. We have taken from the earth, without giving back in return. Except our toxic wastes, our decimation of the countryside. And the consequences? Mankind is at a crossroad. He has poisoned his waters, polluted his skies. He has turned a paradise on earth to a noxious wasteland. Instead of being in rapport with life's natural cycles and the abundance given to us on this earth, we have pillaged and raped our home, our planet earth.

With our consciousness based upon fear and a unrelieved greed, we have created for ourself: LACK. Many of our brothers and sisters are hungry; millions dying from famine. We are quickly diminishing our fresh water resources. We have created for ourselves all the problems derived from our misguided actions. If we continue in this same vein, the outcome seems inevitable. The end is near. Or is it?

Inevitability smacks of an inability to change. Man has the opportunity to change at any point. Certainly the problems won't immediately go away. We have reaped from what we have sown. But we can find solutions.

You may disagree. You may seem to feel that the factors impacting societal conditions today are overwhelming, beyond corrective action. They are not. It is only a question of man changing his consciousness, altering his perspective. And how will society effect this? First of all, BY YOU, BY ME.

By changing gears in your outlook, by your own growth made stronger by having to go against conventional opinion, you and I, and the others who are devoted to the unfolding of our spirit while in matter will indeed have an impact. Like the pebble dropped into a pond, our every action has a rippling effect, the reach of which we cannot fully appreciate, or perhaps presently cannot understand. No matter. What is important is your faith, and implementing that faith into action, by realizing your spirit in matter, and manifesting your spirit in action.

It is not easy. Nobody said it would be. Or if they did, they were not telling the truth. Part of the collective consciousness in society is the accepted belief and attitude. One of the cornerstones of this belief is religion. Not the kernel of truth that each religious teaching has as its foundation. Rather, religion as a structured

UFOs: Key To Inner Perfection

orthodoxy as an institution of prescribed rights and wrongs. Many people assume that by growing spiritually you become more religious. Not so. Unfortunately in our day and age religion no longer truly ministers to the human spirit, nor truly comforts the human soul. Today religion has become an institution, seeking to increase its financial position and spread its political power base. We see religion now ever more involved in the secular world, in temporal existence, turning its back on its real purpose of providing guideposts to the spirit along the way.

Just think how religion has been used in the past. It has done much to blind the individual's growth, to thwart the unfolding of true individual creative expression. Instead, it reinforces the collective consciousness to the detriment of the self-developing individual. How has religion done this? By emphasizing our fears, our guilt, our sense of unworthiness and separation. Religion holds out carrots with the threat of sticks, but the promised carrot is an elusive quest that religion holds out beyond our present reach.

How many religions concern themselves with the future? With the salvation coming not now, not in the present, but in some hereafter. It is often necessary for religion to promulgate future salvation, for it provides the dependency needed for the continued faith of its adherents. Otherwise, today's religions would serve no purpose. They would not have the hold they do, keeping so many of us captive to our fears and guilt.

We will talk later about true religious teachings. For the moment, however, consider what l have said. What buttons have I pressed? Are you silently fuming from the words you have just read? Are you angrily swearing epithets at me for some imagined sacrilege? Or can you see the truth of what l say? Our journey through life is entangled by temptations and tests that are ever so subtle. Sometimes, we get lost. That is OK. It is all part of our progress.

I mentioned religion in this context for you to consider how even the most apparently safe and nurturing shelters may not always be safe harbors in a friendly port. There is a saying that life does not get easier, it gets clearer. That clarity of mind, clarity of purpose, comes to us through our increased awareness. The more aware we become, the subtler are the tests. It is all part of the process of honing ourselves so that like a diamond we can reflect the true light through our being flawlessly

While fear has been used to win our belief in various religious systems, or more to the fact, religious organizations, its converse emotion has been just as effective in societal conditioning. GREED has been one of the strongest motivating influences for the lives of many fellow travelers.

A FOCUS ON LACK GENERATES FEAR. TO COMPENSATE FOR FEAR, WE

UFOs: Key To Inner Perfection

REACT WITH GREED. The bull and the bear of economic conditions. Roots nourished by our sense of our individual selves: a lack, something missing, within ourselves. The very first questioning of real purpose or meaning in a individual's life begins the slow, often cumbersome, journey on a path fraught with dragons and lairs along the way. We stand foursquare against conventional opinion, the accepted knowledge. It is like spitting into the wind.

But what's interesting is that no matter how strong the resistance, the growing individual will also sense an increase in resilience, a developing inner strength born from a growing peace in pursuing the quest of self-discovery and enlightenment.

UFOs: Key To Inner Perfection

WE NEVER GET MORE THAN WE CAN HANDLE

Believe it! You may not want to, but you will have to give that one up too. For to think otherwise sets you up for defeat before you even begin. It is a real limitation, a real blockage tied to an acceptance of present security no matter how grim the conditions, because of the unwillingness to "risk" change.

And what's the alternative? In our society running on empty, a lack of true self-respect and awareness, creates constant caroming between those two heavies: Fear and greed. Those two cornerstones to our HELL ON EARTH. How many of us have imagined what it would be like to be financially wealthy? We imagine how all our problems would be solved. We would be on easy street. Of course, it is a beautiful fantasy but unfortunately one that is out of sync with reality People with money have no fewer problems than those without. The problems are different. The fears do not go away. Sometimes people are driven to acquire great wealth by their sense of lack. They believe, as we are led to believe by our image makers, that by gaining vast amounts of money they will relieve their fear and their sense of lack.

It does not always work that way. For some people are driven to accumulate vast sums of money then fear that what they have been able to hoard will somehow be taken from them. In reaction, they bury it. In bank vaults, in interest-bearing bonds, in some avenue to maintain, perhaps even safely increase their worth. Material worth, that is. But often, these very same people are those who live in poverty. Maybe not a material poverty but certainly a spiritual poverty All that they have accumulated, all that they have gained, is like some hollow victory the taste of bitter ashes.

Everything in life is in a state of motion, constant movement. To gain material goods and then to hoard them from a sense of fear is not in sync with the material function of recycling. Think about it. Think about it in terms of the natural, virtually automatic, function we perform.

In breathing, we breathe in and we breathe out. If we do not we die. In nourishing our bodies, we ingest food. But we also perform the natural function of eliminating the wastes from our food intake. If we do not, we get constipated. And we become sick.

So too with money. For money is energy—green energy, if you will. If we keep that energy in a state of inertia by hoarding it, we too become ill. Money creates a false sense of power. If man does not know how to handle money it will destroy him. How many examples are there of those who have suddenly gained great wealth only to have it make them much worse off than they were before? In recent years, with the increasing popularity of lotteries and get-rich-quick schemes, we have seen the examples repeated over and over. There is a saying that money is the root of all evil. I disagree. The problem is not with the green energy but rather man's use or, more appropriately misuse of that energy.

One arena in which this becomes chillingly evident is when a man of wealth is nearing his death. Since he cannot take it with him when he goes, a greediness suddenly erupts among the man's relatives and close associates. It is not rare to see people of good character and quality transformed into scheming, conniving types, who plan and plot how they will get a share of the money.

The intrigues in families that occur regarding legacies and inheritances are mind-boggling. It can made people sick for a schizophrenic depression is likely to occur. The schizophrenia being between a real LOVE for the one who is nearing death and a total GREED for their money. Some bounty, some reward.

The LOVE for money, the total concentration on material accumulation, eventually leads to devastation. To repeat, money is not bad. It is energy. How we use that energy how we make use of money is the determining factor whether it is good or bad. If you have money keep it in the flow. Remember, whatever you give out comes back to you tenfold.

There are so many things to learn. So many things to relearn. And the time to relearn them is now. For the twentieth century is a period filled with enormous change to both man and his home, the planet earth. With these changes come great testings indeed. Never before has man's scientific knowledge and technological advances catapulted mankind to the brink of self-annihilation.

Certainly our understandings and discoveries have been remarkable. We have the ability to split the atom, to get beneath matter into subatomic forces. But what have we done with this knowledge? We have created missiles and weapons, to the extent that we can now blow our earth apart many times over. From fear, from our own sense of lack, we have used our knowledge not for the betterment of mankind, or for the improvement of quality of life on earth. Rather, our recent discoveries have become for us like a Pandora's box, unleashing destructive ca-

UFOs: Key To Inner Perfection

pabilities and the potential for man's extinction.

But why?

Because we have drawn upon our rational, reasoning mind, a state of consciousness focused solely on matter. Because we have negated the intuitive, higher mind, we have lost sight of spiritual and social sciences. This unbalanced state of mind in the collective consciousness is the cause for the turmoil and chaos to come. The handwriting is already on the wall. We see it in the graffiti scrawled imperiously on public buildings, sacred monuments, beautiful edifices. Take a ride on a New York City subway train. Almost every car is marred by the graffiti of someone seeking to leave their mark, by crying out their individuality. It is often a pathetic display but one that is part of the natural evolution.

For we have reached a state of overpopulation. The collective consciousness has fallen out of sync with the natural process of procreation. Today we breed with no thought regarding outcome. Instead of creating a child from love, children are brought forth from our mere animal instinct of having sex. And so, a child is born. A child that may not truly be wanted, or respected for his own personality or his own evolution.

What's likely to occur is that the child has no way of expressing itself within the family structure, a structure that in our day and age is increasingly deteriorating. With no outlet for creative self-expression, with no respect from parental figures, the young soul goes forth and scratches his name, logo, or sentiments across public walls.

History has a way of repeating itself. Until the lessons are learned, society will go through similar patterns in its cycles. One of the most obvious, of course, is the pattern of war and peace. It is as though because man has not found real peace within himself, he cannot live peacefully with his neighbors. War breaks out, and the emotions of heat and negativity spend themselves. Peace then follows, with a blind hope that the previous war was the one to end all wars.

Until the next one. And so it goes. But is it inevitable for man, for society to be in constant conflict? No. It does not have to be that way. Certainly there are similar cycles, and similar phases within those cycles. But mankind's response to social cycles can spell the difference between aggression through war and a catalyst to transform the collective consciousness. In the past, mankind has chosen war. What will mankind do in the future?

That decision, that choice, resides within each one of us. For we as society; by our individual examples and deeds we can truly effect great changes within the collective. After all, change is a continual part of the process. And conscious change allows for a realignment in sync with nature, with natural law We will discuss some of these natural laws subsequently. And we will also give techniques by which each of us can better our own lives and thereby serve as catalysts for the changes in the life of the collective.

While it may not be easy to go against the collective consciousness, it is indeed a natural part of an individual's evolution. For society's belief and attitudes regarding life and the living have fallen completely out of sync with true reality. Mankind has developed his lower mind, the computer mind with its wonderful capabilities. In so doing, however, mankind has locked himself into an experiential world filtered through the analytical, reasoning mind.

We think things through. But in our thinking process we rarely question the abstracts, or premises, behind our review and consideration of life experience. Because we are conditioned by society we accept the underlying standards as being true. They are not.

In developing the lower mind, man separated himself from that intuitive link to the supra-consciousness, that connection with GOD and natural law. As in all cycles, so too with this one. In this century man has rediscovered his higher mind. On an individual effort, people are starting to seek reconnection to that aspect of mind. There is a quiet yearning afoot, the natural yearning in an individual's self-development and awareness.

It is stronger during this period in man's evolution and provides the seeker with some solace in the swim against the tide of conventional wisdom. There will be times when we may err and lose our way. We too will fall into the traps and pitfalls of the collective patterns created by society. We will find ourselves doing things because of society's influence. The impact of group dynamics.

It is OK. It is all part of the process. It may be necessary to get sucked into societal patterns and pitfalls every now and then. To judge our actions as mistakes or errors is to condemn without full understanding. Besides, our potential liability to make transgressions through the power of the collective consciousness keeps us humble, and spiritual arrogance is an inevitable test along the path. Secondly that very transgression increases our awareness, hones our vigilance along the quest.

And that quest? Our purpose? The realization of our selves and the true expression of our individual creativity through unconditional love. By your actions, you will be known. And your example, your being, will impact society and influence the collective conditions. Ridding ourselves of the programmed patterns inculcated by the limitations of societal conditioning is one of the tests in our self-development, in our growth. It may be difficult, but it is not impossible. It may seem that way but it is not. You have to be able to believe in magic, in the power of

UFOs: Key To Inner Perfection

change and transformation. Can you? Will you?

During this time in man's evolution when we are seeking to reconnect with the higher mind, all sorts of groups and philosophies have sprung up which promise to provide the means, often an easy way to develop the higher mind. If we are weak within ourselves, we are likely to be seduced by one group or one individual into believing that they can make it easier for us. They promise us the way they provide answers to our questions, and offer us techniques by which we can speed our process of development.

UFOs: Key To Inner Perfection

SEEKER BEWARE

The journey of growth and self-development is an arduous one, and often a lonely one. There are many seductions and temptations along the way. One of those is the false prophets that presently abound. Like a carnival fun-house, groups and individuals today are barking their claims of being the one true answer, the one "true" teaching to lead you to Nirvana, down the glory road to paradise, heaven on earth. All you have to do is join. Some will say that they are sanctioned by the blessed Virgin Mary or that GOD has chosen their group as the one to bring truth to the world.

Seeker be aware. Be aware of those who have rigid structures, wear uniforms or demand uniformity These groups attract people. Some of those they attract are innocents, others emotional cripples who seek to escape their everyday life wanting a miracle to happen. For them, a miracle did happen—they joined a group. Although it may seem extreme to you, many of these present day groups have a certain similarity to the phenomenon that overtook the German nation in the 1930's. Hitler's Third Reich offered to fill a void in the German nation. We are aware of the consequences, but we have forgotten the lessons that were to be learned.

In these so-called "spiritual" groups today many of our individual wants, what we believe to be our "needs", are fulfilled. Similar to Hitler's Third Reich, these present-day groups also fill a certain void, by offering us the temptations of filling our wants. And what are these wants? Among them are such emotions as:

Wanting to have a purpose or meaning in one's life. Many groups purport to be on a mission, and that mission is often the lofty one of saving the world. (How is that for spiritual arrogance?). It is effective, for who isn't tempted by a chosen one to bring truth, light and love to the world?

Wanting a relatedness with other people. Because the purpose of the group is shared by the individuals involved in the group, there is a common shared experience which allows for a mood of sharing one's self with others in the group.

UFOs: Key To Inner Perfection

This attitude is fostered by the group, for it reinforces the individual commitment to the group. Consequently in many groups, there is a certain permissiveness expressed between people. It may be given the name of free love, but often it is the sharing in sex, without the stigma of a one night stand.

Wanting our basic needs to be covered. Food, shelter, even a pittance of income are often provided by a group.

Wanting friends. Wanting knowledge or understanding. Wanting something to do. Whatever the emotion we seek to fulfill, spiritual groups do indeed seek to fill that want, that sense of need. Perhaps the strongest pull toward a group is that it allows us to give up responsibility for our own individual evolution. It is as if by joining a group, we can close the door on all the clutter in our own personal consciousness.

This is not to say that all groups are tarnished or disreputable. Nor does it deny the power of group dynamics that can afford a catalyst for the individuals growth. But, please, realize that the majority of the inner work, that most of our individual readjustment, has to be done by us as individuals, by our selves.

I am not saying you shouldn't joint a group, or shouldn't share in your experience with others. Not at all. What I am asking is that you be aware of the group with the fancy trappings, and the use of words that sound so heavenly. Always investigate the group before you join. Do not be fooled or misled by sham appearance. Really look, before you leap. Do the leaders of the group live up to their teachings? Do they practice what they preach? Are they living their philosophy? Are they able to step down and meet you on a one to one basis? Or do they stay perched upon their throne?

In our century millions are turning to the group experience. Community sharing is certainly good if it is kept to true brotherhood. But, unfortunately in practice it is rarely the case. What tends to occur within groups are that petty jealousies begin to arise. There are those caught in self-aggrandizement who seek power within the group. The power elite confuses the message, adding to the friction, and eventually the group decays.

Some groups thrive on a strong disciplined fear, from their teacher or leader. With a ritual and dogma as structured as the U.S. Marines, these groups I call COSMIC BOOT CAMPS. They are children of the Third Reich. For they draw upon mythologist understanding of natural law a mystique of technique and elaborate ritual to bend the individual will to the group force directed by the leader. However, if that is what the individual needs to experience at this place in time, so be it. To the innocents, I say: SEEKER BEWARE.

There is a great deal of seduction among the groups. They will accost you on the street, on public transportation. They will use whatever means or manner to get you. At an airport, at a railway station, they may come up to you and thrust a book into your hand. They will tell you it is yours, free, a gift with no strings attached. Then they will ask you to donate in the CAUSE OF GOD. Of course, if you accept your free gift and happen to walk away without giving a donation, they are likely to go into a fit of hysteria.

I am not saying these followers of one teacher or another are malicious. On the contrary. Often, these souls are brainwashed individuals who truly believe they are doing the work of their master. They may be a nuisance, they may be intrusive. But they provide another gift. Another test. That test, that gift, is to be able to realize that these followers feel you need the group experience. If you find a group that feels right to you, a group whose teachings and practices you have really investigated, then join. But be aware! Do not lose sight of the purpose in the group experience. And that purpose? To extract from that group, from it's teachings, what you need for your own growth, your own self-development.

Some people join groups for that reason. In fact, a majority do so. However, once inside the group experience, our reason for joining the group, our purpose within the group, becomes confused. We become tempted, seduced by what the group can provide us in filling our wants, satisfying our desires.

Instead of listening to the teacher within, that voice within ourselves that truly knows and understands, we listen instead to the leader of the group. We start to question the rightness of that small voice within ourselves. We assume our insights, our understandings, to be something less than those of the leader or teacher of the group. We forego the role of the active gladiator out to slay our own personal dragons along the quest to self-development. Instead, we become the follower, a passive participant to the force of the group.

Have total faith in the teacher who lies within. Because of our sense of personal lack, due to our desires to relate to others, we sometimes forget the teacher within each one of us. Or if we acknowledge its existence, we question its accuracy and its reliability. Don't.

Accept yourself where you are. See yourself for who you are. Still your mind and listen in silence, so that you can hear the teacher who is within you. In our day and age, when we are constantly bombarded by all sorts of external stimuli, it is hard to quiet the mind and turn inward. It is also essential.

The power of the collective consciousness is stronger in our present time by reason of the media. Societal attitudes and beliefs are reinforced by the power of the media. To a greater or lesser extent, each one of us has been programmed by the massive hypnotic influence of television. The majority of people are ad-

UFOs: Key To Inner Perfection

dicted to the television, especially in our United States. Are you aware that on a per capita basis, the television is on in our homes six hours of every day? One fourth of the entire day about one third of our waking hours, are spent with the television going. Perhaps we use it as background noise. Perhaps we have it on as a companion when we are alone.

The influence of television, the programming it airs, reinforces the massive self-gratification we see today. No one really thinks for himself. He depends on others to tell him what to do. This tendency reinforces the appeal of the group experience. There is a minority which is bucking the tide. There are people who seek to bring about change, to incorporate the spiritual concepts of enlightenment in their daily lives, and awaken the stirring consciousness. Are you one of them? Will you be one of us?

What is the alternative? To willingly go along, as the line of least resistance, with societal mores and actions. To become sucked up into the constant need of possessing more and more. This need is never sated, the thirst for acquisition never quenched. Except when we change our consciousness.

Water will always reach its own level. Like will always attract like. Whatever we worship, we receive. Both in our individual lives, and in the life of the collective. Negativity breeds negativity. Think negative thoughts, and you create negative conditions. Be confused in your thinking, and you will create confusion in your environment.

The chaos and confusion in our world today had a starting point. It did not materialize out of nowhere. Rather, the starting point was born from a consciousness mired in negativity - fear, greed, a focus solely on material goods. This negativity is reflected in all forms of media. Even where there is some claim for objectivity in reporting the facts—just the facts—the subjectivity in thinking intrudes.

Think about it. When you watch a news program on television, how often do you see a "good news" story? If there is one, it is often a human interest feature to which three minutes of coverage is given. Buried at the end of the news broadcast, compared to maximum broadcast time given to the "negative" news, these human interest features become lost in the shuffle.

What do we see on the news? All the things wrong in our society. We see people starving to death in Africa. We see others fighting to their death in Central America. We see terrorist activities causing death in the Middle East. We see the homeless, the destitute, the unemployed in our United States. We see budget crises, prices going up, an economy that rebounds from recession to expansion with the latent threat of a depression around the corner. We see the crime reports with the muggings, the killings, the rapings and kidnappings. We see all sorts of evi-

UFOs: Key To Inner Perfection

dence of mankind moving into a self-destructive mode.

Is it any wonder that the nightly news tends to depress us? Is it any wonder that people who are fed this type of reality night after night, day in-day out, are frightened nearly to death? Not really

Where the question, where the true wondering comes in, is why we attune ourselves to that kind of reality. Perhaps you may say that the awareness of society's plight is necessary in order for it to be corrected. And I would agree with you. However, what I would question is whether we become aware of that reality? Or does that reality suck us into an attitude, a regimen, that is based upon fear?

Look around, and I believe you are likely to agree that too much concentration on the ills of the world can create ills within ourselves. People live in fear today. Have you ever visited someone who lives in New York City? Ring their apartment doorbell, and you wait for the door to be opened. Much of your waiting is likely to be while the person inside unlocks the three or four locks he's got on his door.

Many of us have become prisoners within our own homes. We fear to venture outside. We are afraid to go out into the world. And why? Because we have become programmed by our news media to all the fears and frights of living. Some living, some life. Not only do we become afraid of life, but we take these fears and worries into our bodies, creating the conditions for dis-ease to gesliate, for illness to appear.

Look at our society. For all the wonders of our technology for all our scientific advances, how healthy are we? Perhaps we have eradicated malaria, smallpox, the bubonic plague. But our society is ravaged by other plagues—the cancers that have reached epidemic proportions, the new viruses we know so little about, the self-limiting diseases of our society's sickness. It does not have to be that way. You know it. Otherwise, you would not be reading through this book.

The eradication of the various illnesses that presently dog our society will not come from scientific discoveries. On the contrary ridding society of sickness will come about when we look not merely at the effect, or symptoms, but the causes of the disease. And that cause stems from our conditioning—our individual conditioning, as we discussed earlier in the case of Janet, and societal conditioning.

Break that cycle of pain. You can, if you will. Instead of focusing in on negativity keep you focus on the positive, the uplifting. Rather than watch all the gore and mayhem on the television screen, ingest words of comfort, images of beauty and true love. Do not fill your belly, your mind, or your emotions with junk food. Love yourself, and give to yourself the gifts of nourishing food, enlightening thoughts, delightful emotions. Too hard? No, it really isn't. But you are the one

UFOs: Key To Inner Perfection

who must make the choice.

Are you tired of living in a hell? Of being ensnared by the negativity and fears rampant in today's world? If you are, you will find the strength. No matter how weary you might be, once you make the commitment of turning your life around, you will find a sense of quiet encouragement prodding you on.

That does not mean all the negative conditions in life will go away immediately. However, in reacting to the negativity around you, respond not in kind but with a different approach. Reply with positive thoughts, with unconditional love and with your level of understanding. If you watch the news and see a family's life shattered by a fire that has destroyed their home and robbed them of all their possessions, send those people your prayers. Pray for their recovery for their comfort, and their well-being. In your mind's eye, see these people recovering all that was taken from them. Pray that their tragic experience can be turned to good use by making them more aware, ready to create a new and better future.

So too in warlike conditions. When we watch the news and see the needless slaughter of innocents caught in a dispute over a boundary line, do not throw your hands up in dismay and question whether mankind can avert a global holocaust through nuclear war. Do that and you too are feeding the negative situation.

Recognize that the leaders of a country truly do reflect the consciousness of the people. Realize that the collective is indeed caught up in the morass of material accumulation. Be aware that dark forces have these leaders, and consequently these people, in their grip. And then work to resolve the conflicts.

How? By the power of your mind, the power of your creative visualization. See the country in dispute as being healed, made whole, and resolving the differences that have flared into warlike conflicts. Visualize the people of this country as gaining knowledge from their experience, so that they too can make a better life for themselves and their countrymen. In your prayers, in your reflections, in your moments of creative visualization, send love to the world.

The world is in dire need of it. Your prayers, your love, your creative thoughts will have an impact, and eventually will work their effect. The more you clean up your own act, the more effect you will have upon the world. Wars reflect the inner wars within mankind in his present state. Change that state, and you change the conditions. Make peace within yourself, and you are more likely to see peace within the world.

With leaders like these, you might ask. The leaders of a nation reflect, and reflect incredibly accurately, the state of the people of that nation. All of us, as individuals, are part of the collective, part of society. As such, our responsibilities are not merely to ourselves, but to our brothers and sisters, and to our community

UFOs: Key To Inner Perfection

You can't opt out of being involved. For you are involved. Even if you were to go off to some mountain region, find a shelter for yourself and devote your time and energy merely to your own personal evolution, something would be missing and something would be extending beyond your sheltered life. The thing that would be extending beyond your own personal life style is the ripple effect of the pebble in the pond. By changing your energy patterns, by accelerating your growth, you change the energy patterns on our earth.

Some of the greatest masters who walk the earth are unknown to man. For some of these masters do indeed cloister themselves away to do GOD's work, while they live on the earth plane. These are individuals who have transmuted the base metal of human emotions and have realized the CHRIST-like consciousness. They are individuals who may no longer need the lessons in interactions— the relatedness with others, or the involvement in community.

For most of us, however, retreating from the world is exactly that: retreat. Progress through life is accomplished through meeting our challenges and opportunities and gleaning the lessons to be learned in each one. Two of those avenues are in our personal relationships and in our interactions with society's conditioning. By opting out, you may be copping out.

We are here to realize the spirit in matter. As we will discuss in more detail shortly, the mystery of Golgotha with the crucifixion of JESUS THE CHRIST provided mankind with the victory of spirit over matter. The ascension of that "miracle" is a transcendence each of us is here to perform. First, by realizing the spiritual side of ourselves, and secondly the victory of our spirit over the confines of our material world.

We cannot make that ascension if we retreat from the material world. Rather by involving ourselves in the world, in the community of man, we have the opportunity not only to raise ourselves in consciousness expansion. We have the opportunity to help our brothers and sisters along the way. Our society is out of sync with reality. There is much to be done, much to be relearned along the way. Will you be one of us who is ready to steer society back into harmony? If you choose to do so, choose to do so now. For that is all there is. Right now.

How? From this book, from other guideposts along the way you have an inkling of how to turn your life around. You are beginning to realize that your own growth and development can be done by only one person— and that person is YOU. We have touched upon the individual's responsibility the opportunity for self-mastery through relatedness and from choosing to go against the societal grain. In the next section, we will talk about our earth, our environment, some of society's beliefs that we have accepted as knowledge, and have you consider alternate truth, or what may seem to be possibly disconcerting other realities.

UFOs: Key To Inner Perfection

OUR EARTH, OUR WORLD

Our earth reflects mankind. The conditions on our planet earth reflect the conditions of the collective consciousness of mankind.

This planet on which we live has been called the planet of the cross. For the earth is a testing planet, a space in time where humankind has the opportunity to go through a myriad of experience. In order to grow to learn, to evolve. The crucifixion of JESUS THE CHRIST on the cross at Golgotha was no mistake. It was a lesson, a divine teaching for each one of us. But what have we learned from it?

Unfortunately the majority have learned little. Instead, they wait complacently for the divine savior to return and provide them the way. The second coming is not to be expected in a wave of glory with the heavens opening up and gilded chariots coming down to lead us from our lessons, from our experiences. The second coming is when we, as individuals, realize the lessons of the crucifixion. For the ascension occurs with the victory of spirit over matter. This is the crux of the matter, the ultimate testing for each one of us on our planet earth.

By our individual efforts, we grow toward that victory. And in the process, by our examples, we impact the collective. Like a pebble in the pond, the rippling effects of our lessons are learned. Although we are given a home with all the conveniences imaginable, with resources in abundance: look at what we have done to our earth. We have acted like overgrown children throwing a tantrum. Instead of caring for and nurturing our planet, we continually operate from a destructive mode.

Without any regard to the consequences involved, we have raped our mother earth. We have taken from our earth, with no intention of giving back in return. We act as through the earth itself were but a tangible, inanimate object. A monopoly board on which we play our games, act out our fears and sense of lacks. In the process, we have destroyed sections of our earth that once were abundant with plant life, with vegetation that could feed millions upon millions of our brothers and sisters who do not have enough food to eat.

UFOs: Key To Inner Perfection

We have cut down our trees, our forests, our woodlands. We have fouled our lakes, streams and rivers. We have injected chemicals into the soil, always seeking immediate return for our efforts. Never seeking to give back, except the minimum outlay.

The North American Indians, when confronted by the encroaching settlement of the White Man, never understood the concept of ownership of land. It was a term foreign to their realities. Consequently the White Man "bought" the land by treaty negotiations, or took the land by conquest. For ownership, possession, was a necessity for the White Man's world.

The Indian, on the other hand, understood true reality: MAN IS HERE TO CARE FOR THE LAND, NOT POSSESS IT. Quite some difference, with radically different results. A land of plenty that the Indians had served as guardians for, became a land of optimum use. Man came, he saw and he conquered. In doing so, he sowed seeds which we in our present day and age are now reaping. And the harvest?

Under agribusiness techniques, food production has peaked and the land despoiled. The amount of soil erosion in the world is phenomenal. The topsoil that remains has been sterilized by chemical additives in the form of fertilizers and pesticides. The poisons aimed at increasing the abundance of our land has, in turn, turned against us. Chemicals are seeping into our fresh water supplies, into the underground aquifers that give us our drinking water, our potable water supplies.

Only now years later, are we becoming aware of the effects of our misuse of knowledge, our misapplication of technology The lush forests and wilderness that once were part of our planet earth are no more. Either by stripping away the mountainsides in exploration of minerals, or the clearing of tropical forests to create fragile savannahs on which livestock can graze and roam. Even in the furthest reaches of our earth, man has left his mark. Industrial activity and of our choice in energy sources, we have polluted the atmosphere to such a point that primeval forests, distant preserves far from modern man's direct intrusion, have been affected. Acid rain, our effect upon the atmosphere, creates precipitation so acidic that wilderness lakes have become lifeless, incapable of sustaining life in their once crystal pure waters.

Our earth is going through an accelerating process of desertiflcation where we, humankind, have turned lush areas of our plant into deserts. Turning abundance into lack. But why? Why should we be creating lack from abundance? It all gets back to our selves— the sense of lack each of us feels, the negative emotions we broadcast into our environment, the state of humankind's collective conscious-

UFOs: Key To Inner Perfection

ness. The negativity of our consciousness is destroying our planet, and in the process, our *selves*.

It does not have to be that way no matter what some of the doomsayers might say The doomsayers have their audience, because they are broadcasting fear, an emotion so conditioned within us that it is like a button easily pushed. What the doom- sayers forget, however, is the potential for change. There is always the potential for change, a change in our consciousness and consequently the change in our conditions.

Never forget that. If you do, you are creating a set of limitations that will be very hard to break through. There is a saying—a false one—that the more things change, the more they remain the same.

We have been taught a lot of falsities. As we have discussed before, our education system is not to educate our selves, but rather to condition us to a set of accepted beliefs and attitudes with potentially dire effects, unless we question society's ways. But question them we must. For we must reeducate ourselves to the true reality. Not merely the appearance of reality but the substance behind the image.

We have talked about some of the points for reeducation regarding our individual purpose in life, the opportunities in relatedness, the power of group dynamics. And now we will talk about more of them.

One is a belief regarding the earth itself.

UFOs: Key To Inner Perfection

THE EARTH IS A LIVING ENTITY

The earth is not a monopoly board on which we can act according to our whims, with no consequences from our actions. Man once believed the earth to be flat. The earth is not flat. But neither is it round. At the turn of the twentieth century man became increasingly aware that the earth's surface had changed through times past. Known initially as continental drift, now known as plate tectonics, earth sciences recognize the earth's surface to be a mosaic of plates, which like floating rafts move across the face of the earth, sometimes sliding past one another, sometimes crashing into one another, sometimes one overriding another plate. This scientific discovery advanced our recognition of our planet as the living earth.

Yet, it is a scientific discovery we have not fully integrated into our living. We still believe that we can do to the earth what we will, and without any consequences from our actions. Have you ever listened to the earth? Have you ever stopped a moment to reflect upon our planet and wonder about the cycles our earth mother is going through? If you would, you would hear a cry of anguish, for our earth is close to the brink of dying, thanks to man's unconscious actions.

All the negativity we have heaped upon our planet has affected our earth. Despite the increasing evidence all around us, too few of us really see what we are doing to our earth mother. Too few of us really care. Part of the problem is our sense of limitation. We see the earth as some huge body far beyond our individual impact. But it is not.

Do you remember some of those wonderful myths and legends from when you were a child? One that always fascinated me was the story of Johnny Appleseed and the image of a man, one man, walking across the continent dropping seeds along the way. Perhaps only a myth, maybe only a legend, but in that story is the seed of truth.

You and I influence the conditions on our Earth.

Don't believe the earth is too great, your vision too small, to work wonders on our planet. If you do, it creates a feeling of disconnectedness. And there is already too much of that. We are connected. Connected to one another, to the other species that make their home upon our planet, to the cycles of our earth itself. And the earth is not some isolated planet in the midst of a vacuous void in a lifeless solar system. The earth is connected to the other parts that make up the whole. Our temperature, our seasons, our cycles in agricultural production are all related to our earth's positioning in the solar system, in relationship to the sun, and the other components of this system.

The days in which we live are a phase in our earth's cycle when we are likely to see increased earthquake and volcanic activity changing climate conditions and bizarre weather systems, natural catastrophes that are likely to shake us to the core. If you wish to see the earth's spasms as punishment, that's your choice. However, you could also take a different view. You could recognize that similar to ourselves, with the cleansings and purifications we must go through as we evolve in our own lives, the earth too has a process of purification.

It has happened before. Countless times, the earth has gone through a cleansing period, a transition period during which significant changes take place among the species inhabiting the planet earth. Some are recorded as the flood legends that every religion and culture tells about in their traditions. Others are noted with the shifts concurrent with the phasing out of the dinosaurs, and with the mutations and adaptations that life on the planet goes through.

At times, the earth's changes are gradual. Other times, they are quite dramatic. Sometimes, they are the result solely of the earth's natural cycles. And then there are times when the earth's changes are aggravated by man's influences, man's actions. Many of the forthcoming earth changes are in truth the consequence of mankind's own actions, our misuse of knowledge and the wrong application of our technology Our own actions vis-a-vis our earth are the result of an incorrect perspective.

Few people would accept the concept our earth as a dynamic, living-breathing entity They might accept the idea of a living earth, a planet on whose surface life abounds. But to think of "terra firma" as having a life of its own, that would stretch their imagination.

STRETCH YOUR IMAGINATION-Do not be locked into the accepted wisdom that may be accepted but may not be wise. It is part of the process of relearning, of rethinking, of becoming truly aware.

THE EARTH IS ALIVE

Because we have incorrectly accepted our earth to be "terra firma" and, consequently have thrust our whims and actions into her dynamics, our earth is sick. We have not nurtured the earth. We have asked our earth to nourish us, but we have not given anything back.

You and I can do so. By planting a seed, by tending a garden. By refusing to despoil our environment with our wastes, our garbage. By seeing the earth as alive. One of the glories from our technological advances has been the photographs of our earth taken from our satellites launched deep into space. With the water surface a deep blue, our earth is seen as a magnificent orb, circling through time and the infinity of space.

By our thoughts of our beautiful planet earth, we can seek to make her whole. By our prayers, in our reflections, with our thanks for all that we have been given, we can send healing thoughts to the planet we make our home. There is a belief, a belief prevalent in society today, that we should get while the getting is good. With no regard to the future or to the consequences of our actions, this attitude presumes we are here for only a short time.

UFOs: Key To Inner Perfection

TIME

What is time? Time is a measurement. Some times measure seasons, the seasonal variations of spring-summer-fall-winter. Other times measure days by the rise of the sun, the setting of the sun, and the dawn of a new day. Our clocks measure time. There are sixty seconds to a minute, sixty minutes to an hour, twenty-four hours to a day and 365 1/4 days to the year.

TIME is also a subjective interpretation. Think about it. Have you ever had the experience where time seems slower than usual? Or when time flies by without your knowing where it has gone? Five minutes may drag by so slowly it seems like an hour. Other times, five minutes may pass in the twinkling of a moment. Not very objective, this concept of time.

One of the most curious aspects about this concept of measurement is its use in our own lives. We have had one example with the five minute time interval. Perhaps trivial with no real consequence, but there is another aspect of time that is truly limiting. That time is the idea of a lifetime. Lifetime? The measurement of time between birth and death. So what's the big deal, you might ask.

Only that the interval of measurement for a lifetime is limited by the aspect of measurement itself. Can we measure eternity or infinity? No matter how many mental abstractions we might come up with, no matter the mathematical equations we might derive, there is no true measure of eternity or infinity. Only the measurement of pieces of eternity of parts of infinity.

So too with our measurement of life and death. Although we like to consider mankind as having evolved in understandings to a point of real knowledge, we still make measurements in our own lives. A measurement that is defined from the moment of birth into the physical body of the baby to the point of death for the same physical body—Birth-death.

If we assume that earlier man was less sophisticated than ourselves (a theory prevalent in our society at present), then we must wonder whether in his consciousness, our predecessors stood at the dusk of day and saw in the setting of the

UFOs: Key To Inner Perfection

sun an end to life. For from the light of day man was thrust into darkness at the turn of night. Was that the end? Had man in that one day experienced all of life, to be extinguished with the coming of night? Perhaps, we imagine our predecessors huddling in fear, waiting through the darkness of night, to be devoured or taken by death.

What a surprise, we must think, awaited earlier man when the sun arose the following day and he was still alive. After a while, with the sun's dawning and setting day after day man must have come to a realization that there was no termination to existence concurrent with the sun's setting, plunging earth life into darkness.

So it is with our selves. Despite our great advances in material knowledge and our discoveries about our physical world, we are similar to our imagine predecessors. For until recently we have assumed that this measurement of a lifetime has taken into account the entire life of our being, from the point of our physical birth to the point of termination at physical death. Perhaps we have even scoffed at what we consider to be the superstitious beliefs of our ancestors, who would bury their dead with their various tools and weapons for their journey into an "afterlife."

With our own sophistication, we have ridiculed a belief that man continues on beyond the death of his physical body. And perhaps some of us still do. However, in recent years we have become increasingly aware that physical death does not mean the termination of our being. Rather, it is a transmutation of our essential being from one form into another.

Physical birth is not the be-all. Nor is physical death the end-all. This belief has been commonly called "reincarnation" Various religions from all different cultures talk about such a theory—the theory that man continues on beyond death and comes back to life in physical form at a later "time."

I personally believe in reincarnation. In my own research regarding survival, I have found this theory to be true. By means of hypnotic regression, I have experienced snatches from my past lives. I have been a rich man. I have been a poor man. A beggar man, a thief. I have been a male, and I have been female. I have been heterosexual and homosexual. I have been black, red, yellow, brown and white.

Each of these different experiences has added to my evolution, to my soul's progression. As I experience these many different personalities, these varied environments, I have learned about myself. I have made amends for past actions that were inappropriate, and I have been given opportunities as a result of my past accomplishments. I am personally working through past karma.

UFOs: Key To Inner Perfection

KARMA—The law of cause and effect. What goes around, comes around. As ye sow, so too shall ye reap. As you do unto others, so it will be done to you. For every action, there is a reaction.

This is karma.

Karma is in reality the experiences we are going through at this moment in time in our daily associations with our selves, in relationship with others —friends, loved ones, society—how we react to certain situations, how we resolve conflicts. Our karma and the way in which we work through it largely determines our dynamic interactions with our surroundings, eventually coming to the conclusion that LIFE is our greatest teacher.

By means of my experiences through hypnotic regressions, I came to the belief that there is no pain, no horror associated with dying. It seems like falling off into a gentle sleep and awakening into a much clearer atmosphere. The realization of dying is only for a few moments. There is an experience of being lifted from the physical body, of entering into a tunnel and meeting your deceased loved ones. There is a slight confusion as to where you are. But that confusion lifts.

Having knowledge about life after death is very helpful. It will assist you in your next transition, when you are ready to leave your present physical body behind and continue your journey into the worlds beyond. In describing the transition, let me draw upon the analogy of school. The transition is similar to graduation day when school is over and it is time for summer vacation. As vacation begins, we talk with our school mates. We share our collective experiences of what transpired in class (our lifetime)— what we have learned, what we did not learn; the good times we enjoyed, the hard times we endured. We reflect back on the problems we encountered that created confusion in our growth, in our personal development. Things always seem clearer in retrospect, when we are more detached and not as involved in the momentary experience. We can see those we might have hurt during the school year, those we might have rejected, used or abused. As we look back, we also become more aware of our right actions and those that were not quite so right.

When we are ready to come back into physical life, we decide for ourselves what lessons we need to learn, to master, in order to progress in our soul's journey. Let us assume that in my last transition phase, my last summer vacation, I came to an understanding that I had rejected someone from whom I could have learned a great deal. In reflection, I could see l had caused that person great emotional pain. I felt a strong empathy and compassion for that person I rejected. From this new understanding, I told my collective classmates that I wanted to go back into the next grade (my next life) to learn what it is like to be rejected. And

UFOs: Key To Inner Perfection

so, I chose to come back for the experience.

I then made a decision of what school would provide me the greatest experience of learning rejection. I realized that my next mother and father (my earth parents) would provide me with that kind of experience. They are my next classroom in which to learn.

So I chose my mother and father, knowing full well their race, color, creed and social position. I chose them for the relationship that would provide me with the early programmed experience I would need for the REJECTION lesson. I knew of their marital relationship, how I would be affected by it at a later date.

Before I embark on my new adventure, the next classroom in earthly life, I am shown the whole scenario of my future life. I go to what are known as the Akashic Records, where everything that was, is, and shall be, is recorded (Your super consciousness).

I see the day I will be born, the day I will die. I see everything in between. I see my early relationship with my parents, the early rejection experience. I see my life in school, and the rejection experience. I see my enlistment in the naval service, and the rejection experience of my ego. I see my marriage, and the rejection in personal relations, and I see my divorce. I see the progression of rejection experiences.

However, I also know that the moment I have grown sufficiently, the moment I have truly learned this experience of rejection, I will no longer need those kinds of experiences. I will have gained a wisdom that will lift me from that programmed way of life.

UFOs: Key To Inner Perfection

LIFE IS AN ENDLESS SERIES OF EVENTS, EXPERIENCES AND LESSONS. HOW WE SOLVE THEM IS THE GIFT

Give thanks for the adversaries in your life, and they will indeed turn out to be miraculous gifts. Knowing my future scenario before my present incarnation, I was somewhat prepared for my new adventure. Knowing full well that life is a continuous cycle of classroom/vacation, I was ready to embark for the transition from spirit into the physical. The classroom is to learn, the vacation is to assimilate what we have learned.

Vacation was over for me. I left the spirit world and entered the womb of my mother. Remember I had chosen my mother, who by now was three months into her pregnancy. I became acclimated to the tiny quarters in the fetal position, floating around in symbiotic fluid.

And yet, although my physical body is in the process of taking form within my mother, my consciousness is very much alive. I hear both the inner and outer dialogues of my mother. I hear such things as: "Maybe we can't afford this child," and "maybe I don't want this child."

All these fears, all these beliefs are transferred into the consciousness of the spirit personality in the womb, the child to be. As I lay there, I take on the conditions of my environment, and I absorb. Six months later, after nine months of my mother's pregnancy it is time for my rebirth into this physical world of great learning. As I leave my mother's womb, I am guided out into the material world by the doctor who assists in my physical birth. He slaps me across my backside. I yell in protest, the primal scream of my self-assertion.

As I cry out upon entering the physical world, the doorway to my remembering consciousness closes tight, my memory of all past lives, of all past experiences, vanishes from my consciousness.

I have no recall of my past, nor do I remember what I have asked to learn in this lifetime. I am now in the cold, cruel, physical world, starting as if from scratch.

UFOs: Key To Inner Perfection

At this moment in time, I am very psychic and loving, and physically very dependent. I cling to my mother as my security blanket. My training starts. The programming, the conditioning of my lifetime experiences begins to manifest. I have entered the classroom for another round of learning, of lessons to be mastered.

And so it goes. From physical birth to physical death beyond, through the transition into the spirit world. Then back. There is no end, no finality no termination to life. Physical death is but a transition, a transformation of the soul from its physical bondage into its spiritual life.

Can you believe that? Can you honestly believe in the truth of reincarnation?

Nothing is ever as true for us as that which we have experienced. And the fact of the matter is that many of us have likely experienced evidence of life's continuity indications that physical death is not the end to life's journey. How? By witnessing the process of a loved one's transition. Not the sudden wrenching from life by violent death or sudden death. Rather, the slower process of dying.

If you have ever shared in another's experience of making that transition, then you are likely to be aware that much of his dream state, even waking state, is focused on people he has known who have made the transition before him. His thoughts, his dreams often incorporate deceased relatives or friends.

Although some may say that these dying people are going through delusional states, in reality they are not. For just as there are guides along our way so, too, do our loved ones come back to help us make the transition from the physical state through death into the spirit world.

Until recently, this attitude would have seemed a superstitious belief handed down from "primitive" man. However, research on terminally ill patients has confirmed this fact. And those touched by a near-death experience corroborate this understanding.

If it is difficult for you to accept this fact, that is OK. As I said before, the greatest teacher is our own experience. For myself, I know the truth of what I say. I know it because I have experienced the near-death experience. And it is an experience I would like to share with you.

It happened many years ago. I was having dinner with some friends. It was an elegant affair, candlelight, wine, good food and wonderful company. However, as I took my first bite of food, my mouth and throat began to feel strange. My nose started to run. Minutes went by and my throat became very restricted. I found it difficult to breath. Then my nostrils began to close as well. I could hardly breath.

Suddenly; I was filled with panic. Leaving the dinner table, I headed for the

UFOs: Key To Inner Perfection

bathroom. My body was heating up. Perspiration dripped from my body I felt delirious, and wanted to vomit.

I had to literally fight in order to breath. Yet, the more I fought to breath, the more restricted my throat and nostrils became. I banged my fists against the wall. By this time, my friends were aware of my predicament. They raced into the bathroom. I know they must have asked me a million questions. I heard them, but I could not respond.

Instead, I pointed to my nose and throat. Through primitive sign language, I tried to make them understand I could not breath. They tried to comfort me, but I did not want to be touched. I was fighting for my life. Helping me, my friends took me to the elevator, down to a car and rushed me to the hospital. In the hospital emergency room, the last thing I remember was a nurse telling my friends:

"Would you please get him off the desk, he is knocking the papers to the floor."

I blacked out. Then my vision came back, but it was quite bizarre. I saw myself leaving my physical body in a crumpled heap on the floor. I could see my friends trying to pick me up, interns running to my side. The next thing I knew I was in a long, dark tunnel. At the end of it was a light, a very brilliant light. I was moving rapidly toward the light, and could hear a whooshing noise in my ears.

I felt strange, a weightlessness and I had the subtle realization that I could breath again. My conscious mind's focus was on the light just ahead of me. The light was shimmering, and very intense. As I got closer to it, it became like a misty film. I went through the light, experiencing it as a momentary tingling sensation.

And then the light gave way to the most incredible view The only way to describe this panoramic vista is to liken it to a beautiful summer's day in the country. There was a dazzling illumination before me, the colors unbelievable, some of them beyond the visible in our physical dimension.

I could see people walking in the distance. The horizon was filled with mountains, trees and lakes. I heard sounds of great beauty; sounds beyond description. As I stood there, it was not cold and it was not hot. It was .... PERFECT.

Suddenly I heard a dog bark. I saw a dog racing toward me. But it was not just any dog. It was the dog I once had, a black poodle named "Pepe." I couldn't believe it. An emotional floodgate opened inside me. Tears filled my eyes, Pepe jumped into my arms, started licking my face.

As I held him, he seemed so real, more real than I had ever experienced him before. I could feel him, I could smell him. I could feel his weight and hear his breathing. And I sensed his great joy in being with me again. I cried with happi-

UFOs: Key To Inner Perfection

ness. I had loved this animal while he was alive, and now being with him again, he seemed more real, more loving. I felt my tears being licked away by him.

When I looked up for a moment, I saw a man in his forties. He was standing in front of me, smiling. He looked familiar, but I could not place him. I looked again and recognition clicked. I was amazed.

I realized the man was my stepfather, whom I loved very much. The reason I hadn't recognized him right away was because he looked so different from the way I last saw him in his earth life. He had died at the age of seventy from terminal cancer. At the age of eight, my stepfather had contracted infantile paralysis. It left his body very deformed, necessitating the use of crutches for him to walk. Later, when he was in his sixties, cancer struck. The cancer took its toll on his physical body, which began to shrink and shrivel.

He had suffered greatly with the agony and pain of the cancer. And my last vision of my stepfather had been his lying in his death bed, begging me to bring him a gun so he could shoot himself.

But now before me, he was standing straight and tall. He was not using crutches. There were no deformities. Instead, he appeared to be in a state of perfect health, looking as if he were in his early forties. I was completely overwhelmed.

Again, a surge of emotions filled me with joy. This man, in this new body was my beloved stepfather. I placed my dog on the ground and stepped forward to embrace my stepfather. Suddenly; I heard a strong voice was heard in my consciousness, telling me: "not yet!"

I did not understand. I screamed out: "Why?!"

Then this very strong inner voice said: "What have you learned? And whom have you helped?"

I was dumfounded. The voice seemed to be outside myself, as well as within. Everything stopped for what seemed a moment. I had to think of what was asked of me.

I could answer whom I had helped. But I could not answer what I had learned.

While this was going on, I could feel the presence of my dog moving all around me, tugging playfully at my pants. I was pondering those two questions in my mind, I kept hearing them over and over within my consciousness. As I reached to embrace my stepfather, I looked into his eyes, which were filled with the greatest love. I heard him say to me, "I love you, my son!"

At this moment I shouted out, "I love you, Pop!" He seemed to be only about ten feet from me.

UFOs: Key To Inner Perfection

My vision moved along the horizon and there, standing hand in hand, were my dear grandparents, looking radiant and healthy. They were beautiful, youngish looking, smiling and waving to me. My heart at this time was experiencing emotional joy, a release, a freedom of knowing that we never die, only the old outer shell is discarded.

We remain the same reflection, the SOUL reflection as the physical body once was. Then I heard other barking, and there appeared a few of the other dogs I had once had. There is really no way possible to make you believe what I tell you as truth, unless you have the same experience. As I stood there for what seemed to be an eternity I wanted to embrace and be absorbed and merge. I wanted to stay. The unbelievable sensation of not wanting to come back is so overwhelming. That was the moment I felt myself being pulled away and back. It is like I have gained the knowledge, I have had the experience, I have expressed my emotional feelings to the ultimate. I could not prevent my returning into the tunnel of narrow focus.

It felt like a giant magnet was pulling me. My heart was going in one direction and my physical body in another. I did not even have time to say good bye. Yet I had the most extraordinary feeling that I will see them all again. There is no time and space there! I was now racing backward in time, in the long dark tunnel, the light at the end was fading rapidly. This time the whooshing sound was even greater. My consciousness was being stretched like a giant elastic band ready to snap. When I snapped, I awoke in a subtle state of shock and a light pain in my body. I was now back in my body and the first thing I witnessed and experienced was the hypodermic needle being plunged into my arm.

I heard a voice say: "Welcome back." I never asked who said that nor did I care at the time. It was told to me that I was out for at least 10 minutes (dead). Brain cells begin to die in four minutes!

The cause for this incredible event (experience) was an allergy to pine nuts used in pesto sauce which I ate that night! My experience is similar to those shared in the books of Elisabeth Kubler-Ross, and Dr. Raymond Moody and a whole series of books relating to clinical death, as experienced by many others.

Breathing is the most important thing that a person can do for developing psychic energy and expanding inherent psychic talents. This chart is to be utilized in conjunction with instructions to follow.

UFOs: Key To Inner Perfection

PAST, PRESENT, FUTURE—AN INNER PROCESS

This technique employs a sense of finding oneself, forgiving oneself, and loving oneself. We do suggest some very soft music for the background, such as the tape cassette of ANGEL LOVE! Keep the music soft, so as not to distract your focus. Find the time each day when you will not be disturbed by any outside intrusions, such as family loved ones or friends. Let them know that you want this time to be alone and meditate.

That's all you tell them! Do not share the process you are about to do with them, unless you know they are very sincere. For there is a metaphysical law that states the moment you tell something (SHARE) you weaken it.

My suggestion is to perform this technique in a comfortable chair, sitting in an upright position. Do not do it lying on your back, for you might go to sleep, and lose the process. Make sure the spine is gently relaxed. Loosen all restrictive clothing which might refocus your attention while doing this technique. Place your feet firmly planted on the floor in front of you. DO NOT sit in a cross-legged position for this exercise!

Begin by closing your eyes, your hands palms down upon your knees or thighs, and breathe with a balanced breath. A balanced breath is equal counts in to equal counts out, through the nostrils only. If you can breathe out for the count of seven, breathe in for the count of seven. If you are short of breath you may use a five count or six count.

Remember, breathe in very slowly and out slowly so gently and so delicately that you can hardly feel it or sense it. Then you are doing it correctly Gentle breaths in and gentle breaths out, or even balanced breath. Find yourself becoming centered. Heavier breathing might create a clogged nostril. Remember, gently and slowly.

After about five minutes of this BALANCED BREATHING, you will sense an altered state of consciousness, where your whole body feels relaxed. If you want to help the process, you suggest to yourself that with every breath you take, your body will become more and more relaxed. Deeper and deeper. . .more peaceful and calm. . .very relaxed. After a few of these auto suggestions, your body will respond.

UFOs: Key To Inner Perfection

When you begin to experience yourself on the borderline of complete relaxation, begin the process.

1. VISUALIZE, and if you cannot visualize, then SENSE yourself sitting on a deserted beach just before sunset. It's late spring, the day is beautiful. You hear the occasional cry of the gulls. Your gaze is out over the water and into the horizon. It seems you are deep in contemplation. There's no one on the beach but you. Suddenly you sense the presence of someone near. And from the left hand side you hear a small voice say "Hello." You turn and see a little child. If you are a woman, let the child be a little girl. If you are a man let the child be a little boy

2. The child is about 4 or 5 years old. Its eyes are bright with the joy of finding you. The child comes closer, stands in front of you, and with a big smile, it says "HELLO." Then with a flash of light, you discover that the child standing in front of you, is YOU! You see yourself as that young child, so filled with love and dreams and hopes. You observe the child, knowing full well what it has gone through, and will go through. You know the direction in life it will take, you know the pain it will experience, you know of the hurts and fears it will learn by the mistakes, the joys. You look at the child, so innocent, so guiltless. Your heart opens. Do you feel that you want to help and guide this child, so it doesn't experience what you have experienced? You can't, for that child is you. You can't change history; only be guided by it.

3. The child looks right into your face, directly into your eyes, with a love so powerful...its little arms reach out to you in love.

4. You reach forward to embrace the child... you hold him or her close, feeling that both of you merge one into the other. You love this little child so much, so beautiful, so free, so full of hopes and dreams. You embrace the child within. You hold on to that portion of yourself, embracing and merging until you feel enveloped by love, and sense that you and the child are one. You experience what that child will experience. Yet, you already experienced what that child has experienced, therefore you have a sense of greater compassion, a wider acceptance, and in reality you VERY MUCH love that little child.

5. Just allow all those faint felt feelings to manifest. If you feel you want to cry, do so. These are your feelings! Give yourself enough time to come back into the reality of the now

6. The moment you are again aware that you are sitting on a deserted beach gazing out to sea, you become aware of another presence on your right side. You turn your head and see in the distance a lonely figure coming towards you. REMEMBER, if you're a man, make it a man. If you're a woman, make it a woman! The figure in the distance walks slowly in your direction, yet that person seems famil-

UFOs: Key To Inner Perfection

iar. As the figure comes closer you can see it is very old. The person stops in front of you about ten feet away You stare in amazement, for here in front of you stands YOU at a very old age. You look into your own eyes, and you see the wisdom of the ages. For now you are confronted with your future. You experience what you have mastered. You see and feel the most incredible emotional love. Now you observe the journey you have taken. You see lines of travel etched in your face. Your heart bursts with all the love that you feel for your wonderful future self.

7. You sense the collected experiences that you have mastered, and yet this OLD you seems so unscarred, so unhurt, that you begin to feel an incredible transformation taking over your consciousness.

8. This OLD one extends arms out to you, for that wonderful loving embrace. REMEMBER: This old one is you, coming back from the future. As you embrace, you instantly forgive yourself for this self-imposed limitation you placed upon yourself, for the point of growth where you experienced them. As you pull your older self close, you feel the frailness of its body yet you are enveloped in its love.

ALLOW YOUR FEELINGS TO EXPRESS THEMSELVES

AND TAKE ALL THE TIME NEEDED.

9. Sense yourself completely merged with your older counterpart. When this is truly seated within your present form, sense the wisdom filling your mind. Now you have experienced your past, your present and your future. You have just experienced the SEED pattern for you upon this planet. This is to teach non-judgment, unconditional love, and a sense of being merged with your multidimensional self. Realize, you can always affect and alter your highest potential.

10. As you come back to the reality you sense that you are alone on a deserted beach, but now you are surrounded and bathed in life. ALONE? You are never alone. For a few moments you have captured TIME, to experience potential! After experiencing this process, you can always go in either direction from now on, to assist you in your evolutionary experience with soul progression. You will acknowledge an inner guidance for corrective changes you wish to make, and all destructive habits will vanish. You will be observing YOU for the very first time, as GOD views you constantly...in LOVE and LIGHT.

REMEMBER: The young child and the old you is still there, waiting to embrace you anytime you make this journey! WORK with this process once a week, and within a month, your greatest potential will be realized. A technique is only a technique. But if you master the technique, then you become the technique. Don't expect miracles with the first try. Miracles will manifest automatically by the effort, discipline and the priority you have for CHANGE.

UFOs: Key To Inner Perfection

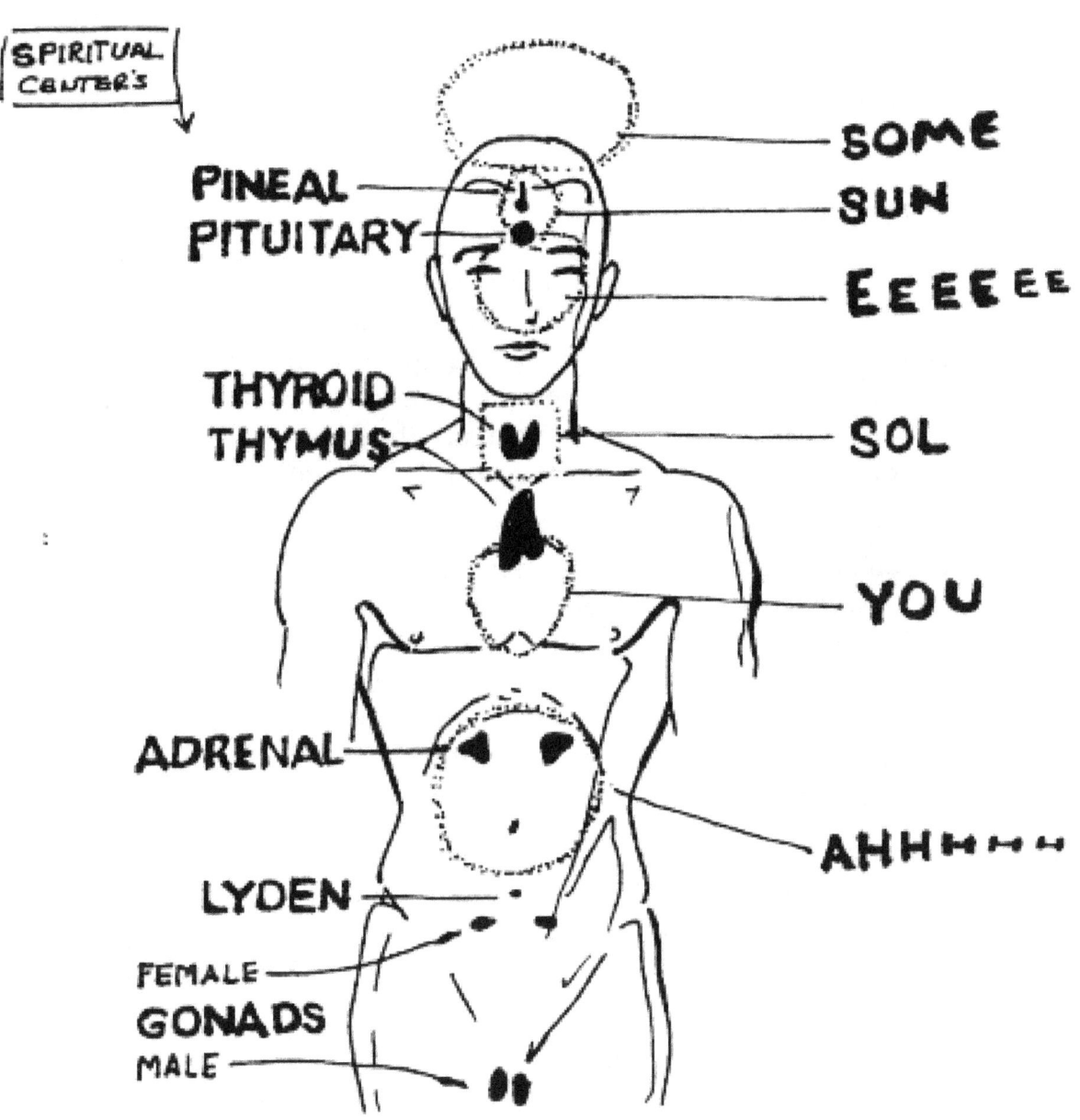

Breathing is the most important thing a person can do for developing psychic energy and expanding inherent psychic talents. This chart is to be used in conjunction with the sonic exercises described in this book.

UFOs: Key To Inner Perfection

DEVELOPING PSYCHIC ENERGY—SONIC BREATHING

Breathing is the most important thing that you can do for developing Psychic Energy (Prana, Ki, Chi, etc.) and expanding your Psychic talents (Greater Awareness). Most of the good breathing techniques we borrow from the Yogis. These practices have been used through the centuries and with remarkable results. The spleen, the appendix, and the heart are the three physical organs which transform the food energy taken into the system, into Psychic energy

These organs act as "TRANSFORMERS" of energy These days, everyone can help himself to a richer, fuller life, to more energy success in their endeavors, and all of their dreams can come true. Psychic energy is in the air we breathe, called "PRANA" or life force. The longer we breathe, the longer we live. Breath controls the body and its functions. It controls our emotions and our way of thinking. Deep breathing and meditation are two of the best things any man, woman or child can do. It brings self-realization, a better understanding of the oneness (YOURSELF) to the oneness of the Infinite (CREATION).

Breathing can retard age, or slow the aging process. The more you practice, the more you will notice that your negative thoughts will be dissolving, and the more you will become positive in almost everything you do. Breathing is FREE, you can have all you want; just learn to use it properly and you will see outstanding results. It will give you a healthier, more creative mind.

When you deplete the emotional energy in the body you deplete the psychic energy (GREATER AWARENESS). That's why you see people growing old before their time. Negative, emotional and distorted thoughts deplete psychic energy. Psychic energy and spiritual energy are one and the same, one leads towards the other. The final goal is that all roads lead to the spiritual!

Through deep breathing, the oxygenation of the blood stream is improved, and every vital organ, endocrinal gland, nervous center, and body tissue receives better nourishment. To breathe correctly is to stay young longer. All you have to do is to look around, look at all the people you know. You will see amazing things:

UFOs: Key To Inner Perfection

the way they walk, look and talk, their personality, the way they dress.

You can tell if they are breathing properly or not. Most of the time they are not. And I'm speaking for 85% of the planet. Most people DO NOT KNOW HOW TO BREATHE PROPERLY!

Rule No. 1: AVOID NEGATIVE THINKING! One of the best books on Psychic Energy is by Joseph Weed. What we plan to do with this book is to change your breathing habits to a more controlled breathing practice. We will use WESTERN techniques which employ breath controlled by the mind. Techniques used by the DRUIDS, the American Indians, Egyptians; for the SONIC BREATHING technique, we thank our extraterrestrial friends. (ALIEN BEING).

First, select a quiet place to practice, at a time of day in which you will not be disturbed. In the Druid technique, the lungs are completely filled and completely emptied. They call it the BALANCED BREATH. Equal counts in to equal counts out. If you can breathe in for the count of seven, let it out for the count of seven.

But when you breathe in, you breathe in so slowly that you can hardly feel it or hear it. Very gently slowly and quietly in and then out, repeating this breathing practice for at least five minutes or longer, per day. If you can spare the time, you will reap the rewards. BALANCED BREATH is indeed magical.

When you inhale, let your stomach come out, inflating it like a balloon. Just feel your lungs getting full. Remember, breathe very slowly with a regular rhythm or count. Sit comfortably in a straight back chair, with the back and spinal column straight, head erect, eyes closed. Your hands should rest palms down on your knees. (KNEES ARE POWERFUL ENERGY CENTERS)

This also keeps the psychic energy retained within your body as it constantly recycles itself within the Physical, Mental, Vital and Emotional bodies.

Breathe through your nostrils only, mouth closed. And as you breathe, concentrate on that spot between your eyebrows, about one inch above the bridge of your nose, better known as the Third Eye. You should subtly experience a pulling sensation from that area of your forehead, and a heat buildup. Begin now with the (BALANCED BREATHING). This technique will enhance and extend your ability to FOCUS, and will also increase your memory to a greater degree. It will also assist in releasing the personal tensions and frustrations we create within ourselves!

Rule No. 2: Try and do all breathing techniques on an empty stomach, and for that matter all techniques should be performed on an empty stomach, to achieve greater results. Remember body and mind go together. It is further suggested by a few of the American Indians that you have a bowel movement before you per-

UFOs: Key To Inner Perfection

form any of these techniques. I find that to be of great value for very obvious reasons. For when the physical body is empty the mind is more alert and aware, intensifying a greater creativity which is expressed in our everyday lives. These techniques are of great value. They have been personally selected to bring you, the reader, the most positive results in quickening and stimulating your own personal growth.

Next, the very powerful and yet very simple RELAXING BREATH. This technique was done in the Temples at Luxor, Abu Simbel, Cairo, and Gizeh, by the early Egyptians, as well as the Druids in England. Most of the American Indian nations expressed this technique among the shamans of the different tribes. It will have the effect upon you, the reader.

Take a deep full breath through both nostrils, inhaling for the count of eight (POWER NUMBER). Hold your breath for the count of six (BALANCING), and then exhale for the count of eight. (POWER NUMBER) = power in receiving and power in giving. The six acts as a bridge and a balancer for both the incoming and outgoing powers. When you inhale and exhale, you breathe in with slow deliberate counts. Follow the above directions, and you will feel yourself becoming very, very relaxed, and a sense of great power manifesting throughout your body Enjoy it!

Feel how calm it makes you feel, with a new sense of awareness that you are on the threshold of new discoveries about yourself. Never force or speed through these exercises. Savor them. Your conscious thinking can be focused upon the light (GOD) or your inner quest upon the path. KEEP the FOCUS on the spiritual!

All the techniques that we have personally selected in this book should be done sitting in a straight back chair or on a stool. Hands palms down upon the knees, head erect, eyes closed. And if you are wearing any restrictive clothing, loosen it, so you will not be disturbed within the process of the technique. Remember, a technique is only a technique. If you put in the time, you will benefit GREATLY! The rewards will be outstanding. Once you have mastered the technique, you BECOME the technique. How much time can you give to your own personal salvation, to your own growth and well being? It's all up to you and to your personal priorities in life.

If you want to learn to play the classical piano, you have to take the lessons. If you do the techniques as a painful hardship or a discipline experience, be aware! When you do the technique because you love it, and sense the joy in renewed health and well being, then you stand to gain the greatest amount of results from it. How you FOCUS your consciousness, tells exactly where you place yourself in your everyday world of affairs, and how you present yourself to others.

UFOs: Key To Inner Perfection

Within this book I have presented my story of my own personal encounter with an alien being. So wonderful was the experience, after the initial shock left, that I am left communicating with a very unusual-looking entity from another dimension or another world. I personally feel that they are right here among us, from other coexisting realities, or dimensions of time-space. The reason we can't get a hold of them, is because they vibrate to a different frequency yet they have the incredible abilities of materialization, in and out of our three dimensional world.

The gifts of that encounter are manifold; the experience was truly awesome in scope, as it led me to a deeper and greater concept of GOD. I can only share my experience of how it affected me and my own personal life. Earlier in this book, I stated that I came from a background of skepticism, like I assume a great majority of the population to be. Yet I always entertained the sense and feeling that there was a greater world beyond, not just this physical planet.

So what I am saying, is that I had an advanced perception of something else, on the other side of our spiritual mountain. I was going to find it. Again, since early childhood I was on the quest for the GRAIL within me. There are thousands of individuals who will read this book, and experience the same things that I have experienced. Yet, each one of us is on a time frame of evolution, and if we feel the urgency and that becomes our priority, the exploration of our spiritual consciousness manifests, and we seek the answers to the unexplained, searching for our own inner truths.

The story of that encounter is within these pages, so all I need relate is to the actual practice of this SONIC BREATHING technique. You will notice on the chart showing the Chakras or the electrical energy centers, so we only work with six. Those of you who have made it a practice to meditate, balance and focus on the energy centers, will notice the absence of the seventh, or what we call the First, which would be located in the sexual region of our anatomy It was stated by this being of a phenomenal intelligence, that if we started with the First chakra, we might get hung up in that energy center. And that these sonic sounds can and will reactivate the glands within the body of man. Medical science might be missing the boat, because their exploration does not go far enough into the other bodies that man lives within. We are talking about the Astral, Etheric, Vital, Psychic, Spiritual, Mental bodies that all men coexist with presently. Man is more than his body. He is a multi- dimensional being. Man is in touch with the universe within as well as without. Every gland in man's body has a responsibility for all the other bodies man finds himself enveloped in. This is becoming common knowledge to millions of individuals.

To me as an investigator and researcher, and a practitioner as well, I find these sonic breathings to be the best that I have encountered in all my travels,

UFOs: Key To Inner Perfection

classes, studies, and practices. I was told that the vibrations these sounds set up within the body affect certain psychic centers. You start in Beta, midway reach Alpha, to find your self in Theta, a very deep relaxed state of consciousness.

You will find that peaceful state to be EUPHORIC!

The first sound ,will be AHHhhhhhhh. What you do with this sound as you will do with all the rest, is to take a deep breath in, and breathe out with sound. After a little practice, you will regulate your voice to come to a comfortable pitch, and you stretch that sound out as far as you can on one breath only This sonic sound affects the solar plexus, about two inches below your rib cage. This whole area, could be considered to be your second brain. Everything, whether it be mental telepathy clairvoyance, or healing, is manifested first within the solar plexus. It is received and sent from this region. Listen to your GUT reaction (SOLAR PLEXUS).

Remember, when you do these sounds, extend the sound as long as you can. Find your own personal level, and sense and feel the vibrations in your solar plexus area. You should also experience a heat buildup as well as a vibration in your solar plexus. You might want to call this exercise SPIRITUAL AEROBICS for your glandular system. The reverberation this sonic gives off, also helps to remove any clinging mucus to the glandular system.

1. (SOUND) AHHhhhhhhh

You're sitting in a straight back chair, feet flat upon the floor, eyes closed, head erect. Hands palms down upon your knees. Take a deep full breath—make the sound (AHHhhhhhhh) till the lungs are completely empty. Pause very briefly (Few seconds). Take another deep, full breath and repeat the exercise. Each sonic is done three times. Pause in between for about 15 seconds, experiencing yourself go deeper and deeper into that wonderful altered state of consciousness. Again you will notice a body heat up, due to the fact that you are exercising your glands sonically for the very first time.

2. (SOUND) Youuuuuuuuuu

This time feel the reverberation within the heart. Physical as well as spiritual. Not only does this sonic strengthen the heart on the physical level, but it opens the spiritual heart to envelop the universe. The spiritual heart (GOD CENTER) is in the right side of your physical heart. Not only is this sonic good for you mentally and physically but very good for the voice as well! Now take a deep full breath...(SOUND) Youuuuuuuuuu, extending the sound until the lungs are empty. Feel the vibration in your spiritual heart. Repeat this sound two more times, experiencing yourself going deeper and deeper, becoming more and more relaxed, and this is so! Pause 15 seconds.

UFOs: Key To Inner Perfection

3. (SOUND) Solllllll (SOL)

This next sonic sound is for expanding your creative center, and also directed towards strengthening your thyroid and thymus glands. You should experience a subtle vibration warming this area of your throat. Now take a full breath. Sollllll until the lungs are completely empty then repeat again twice more. Pause 15 seconds before starting the next series. Sense and feel an expansion in your neck region.

4. (SOUND) Eeeeeeee

This is the special sonic that rejuvenates the psychic glands which are the size of pin heads at the base of your cheek bones. The vibrations from this sonic will affect your senses, your hearing, sight, smelling, tasting. Experience the tingling effect it has upon these areas, and in the weeks ahead, you will be amazed how the perception of your personal reality has changed. Many of the inner psychic talents will begin to manifest themselves. Now take a deep full breath Eeeeeeee till your lungs are empty then repeat it again twice.

5. (SOUND) Sunnnnnn

Concentrate all your attention to that space between your eyebrows, home of the Pineal and Pituitary glands. These vibrations are directed to your Third Eye. These spiritual centers (CHAKRAS) need exercise also, much like your body. To perform this sonic sound (BREATH) place your tongue behind the top front teeth with slight pressure. This technique will intensify your creative talents, for greater awareness, and you will begin to experience your knowing, and an inner joy that will manifest itself as you begin to feel the EARTH CHANGES manifesting themselves upon the planet. Now take a deep full breath Sunnnnnnn. Mental and physical concentration on the sound coming out of your mouth. When you have exhaled (PAUSE)...repeat this sonic exercise twice more., Remember, stretch out that sonic sound as far as possible, and repeat this sonic breath twice more. Then pause for 15 seconds, sensing every sensation you have already built up.

6. (SOUND) SOME Sommmmmmm

This last sound will be SOME. This is done with the lips and mouth closed, so a humming effect is set up. You should be able to experience the vibration in your brain, as if your brain were subtly boiling. Keep your eyes closed throughout these exercises...and try to FOCUS your attention to that area between your eyebrows. In other words, LOOK WITHIN. This final breath is the one that seals you in a vortex of the GOD energy. These sonic breathings are in actuality KEYS for unlocking dimensional doorways to other parallel realms of time/space. You now possess the key. There is nothing to fear. This technique takes you to the highest within yourself, which attracts the outer. Now take a deep full breath

UFOs: Key To Inner Perfection

Sommmmmmm until the lungs are completely empty and then repeat again, twice more.

After you have completed this series of SONIC BREATHINGS, we suggest that you go into your own personal silent space for at least five or ten minutes, and experience what will manifest. Just release any expectations, completely free yourself...and ALLOW it to happen at the level of consciousness where you presently find yourself.

Set aside a certain time each day to do these exercises. And with each day try to extend the sonic sound a little more. You will find yourself becoming more relaxed, increasing your vital energy, looking younger and more healthy. This technique also assists in healing ourselves. The more you do, the better the results. BUT GIVE YOURSELF ENOUGH TIME! As the weeks and months go by you will see and feel definite results. Never overtire yourself.

Breathing, like meditation, is a lifelong study and contained within both are the secrets of the universe and all phenomena. The longer you breathe, the longer you live. If you are interested in bettering yourself, then this technique will open those previously locked doorways, leading to your even greater potential. Breathing is a science...one to be practiced everyday. You will be GREATLY REWARDED! This is the path that leads to SELF DISCOVERY. . .it's exciting!

Since that time in 1972 when I experienced that encounter, I have had some remarkable things happen to me. As it was stated, the secret is in the doing, for how long is up to you. You can't get to six o'clock before I can. If your INTENT is solid and sound, and your personal motivation is pure, the doors to the other dimensional realms will open wide. (KINGDOMS) Communication and love will be experienced.

As one day folds into the next, as one breath blends into the next, as one thought extends itself into the next, as one idea manifests into the next, as one step forward brings us into the next, as one sleep cycle repeats itself into the next, as one meal moves us into the next, as one minute dissolves, another appears.

Repeatable cycles, repeatable movements, repetitions expanded and extended to go beyond, on the constant spiral of perpetual gestation. All part of the evolutionary plan of the GRAND DESIGNER (GOD).

Within the repeatable cycles are new discoveries, new opportunities and a far greater potential. To discover that we are more than our bodies, more than our brains, we are CONSCIOUSNESS beings housed in physical cases for a very short duration of time, made to experience, to learn lessons, as each breath unfolds into another.

UFOs: Key To Inner Perfection

We live upon a planet of SELF DISCOVERIES, a planet of slow primitive soul progression, so it seems. Yet spiritual evolution is forever...and forever is all eternity, never ending, always beginning, always unfolding with greater and greater potential. Yet every individual on this planet is separated by different time frames. A time in which to learn, a time to love, a time to work, a time to grow and to experience. These are the cycles of man's spiritual evolution. As we discover more about ourselves, we begin to GO WITHIN ourselves, unlocking the doorway to true knowledge.

Our awareness explodes with excitement as self-discovery leads us home. Within all of us are the secrets of the UNIVERSE, all knowledge of all things, of all time. What a glorious discovery that we are indeed in the image of the grand designer, the manifester of everything (GOD). What a great joy to find out that everything we have always wanted has always been ours. What sublime bliss to know we are indeed our fathers children, and GOD loves us with an unconditional passion. We are all in preparation for our journey home, victorious and successful in resolving all conflicts that have appeared along the path, to eventually merge with this incredible LOVE!

The techniques in this book will help you explore the higher altitudes of consciousness, so you may see the distant horizons clearer, to see where you have been, where you are at the moment, and your direction into the future. This provides you with clearer sight to see the obstacles which might be blocking your path, and the ability to circumvent them. We cannot force anyone into our belief system, ideas or thoughts. There will always be provided the right time for everyone to make their own personal discoveries about themselves and the world around them. It's time now to FREE ourselves of the restricted judgments and limitations of the collective consciousness, and become individuals who are willing to explore the RISK, the herd consciousness to become truly the GOD I AM!

UFOs: Key To Inner Perfection

AUTOSUGGESTION: VALUABLE TECHNIQUES

To those in the physical five-sense world, autosuggestion is a miraculous phenomenon. You can accomplish astonishing things with it. It can help to remake and rebuild. It can correct habits, can reshape your life for the better, and in general just bring a completely new outlook to your life.

Remember: all suggestion is autosuggestion. Suggestion can be environmental, verbal, or mental. Television is a huge form of suggestion, with its constant form of the same commercials, of buy this, or get that. After a while it begins to sink in, so we find ourselves going out and getting the product. What you are doing is presenting an idea to the mind, directly or indirectly by thought, word, tone, look, or some inner or outer agent.

Autosuggestion, it can be said, is talking to your self or suggesting to your self. Autosuggestion is simple to perform. If done right, it can help bring you your desired goals, and help make those dreams come true; that is, if they are for the good. Anything you do, which is not for the good, will always come back to you, so please keep this in mind. This is a psychic- mental power whose tendency is to transform itself into action.

Anything man can conceive he can achieve. Therefore, all suggestion is autosuggestion. A lot of illnesses are self-inflicted, caused by our own negative thinking, by constant repetition, and by being slightly lazy with our minds, by programming ourselves, like so and so gives me a pain in the neck. Well, sooner than you think, if you say that long enough, you'll get that pain in the neck.

Change your way of thinking to the positive side, through autosuggestion. Autosuggestion will develop new confidence, so much so that you will emerge a new and striking personality. You have learned MIND CONTROL, the method to control and dominate your mind. We have billions of little brain cells in our mind, and we end up using only 7 percent of our brain power. Through autosuggestion, you can achieve your ambitions. Learn to use your own powers and develop them to the highest degree. If you really want to become successful, in any walk of life,

UFOs: Key To Inner Perfection

concentration of the mind, through the power of suggestion, must be understood, and mastered.

Many people are suffering because they have hypnotized themselves into their present, uncomfortable condition. They are victims of unfortunate autosuggestion. Through autosuggestion you can change all that. Concentration, positiveness, and consciousness are also prerequisites. Select your mental attitudes. You can just as well cultivate the positive, constructive kind, as the negative.

Each and every time you practice autosuggestion, you will be successful in bringing on the hypnotic state, and you will be successful in accomplishing anything you wish to achieve. By working with and developing autosuggestion, you begin to understand the workings of the subconscious mind, and understanding it, you will be able to bring it under your conscious control.

This mind-dominance can be achieved by any normal person, with practice. The subconscious mind has absolute control of the functions, conditions, and sensations of the physical body. Today suggestive therapy holds an important place in science, and many wonderful cures are presented at its doors. It can break open your psychic awareness, for a better you. To help yourself, it is only necessary to have faith in yourself through autosuggestion. Make your affirmations with confidence.

Believe that you can accomplish what you desire. Be positive and know that you can, and you will. Rearrange your way of thinking on the positive side, with statements like: I WILL, I CAN, I SHALL, I AM GOING TO, IT CAN BE DONE. Tell yourself that you are getting better and better everyday. The subconscious mind has charge of the sympathetic nervous system, which is "rested" at the base of the spinal cord. It controls the involuntary muscles, organs, and functions of the body The conscious mind has no power to act on these, but the subconscious mind has perfect control of them. It takes command of the entire body in cases of extreme danger like shock, accidents, etc.

Now with autosuggestion, we work in the realm of the subconscious mind. The subconscious mind is a spiritual, creative, separate entity. It can live with the body and also act independently of the body. It never perishes. In other words, the conscious mind cannot exist without the subconscious mind.

Now let us get to the actual practice of autosuggestion, and its techniques. The realm of self hypnosis is a total and complete period of relaxation, a peace of mind so full of contentment that life's problems and worries seem to fade away It is a feeling that you can achieve happiness regardless of your station or position in life. First of all, find a quiet, comfortable place such as your own bed. Or you can fold a blanket and place it upon the floor. Then find a comfortable position

UFOs: Key To Inner Perfection

upon your back, arms by your sides, feet slightly apart. RELAX.

Next, place a bed lamp, or a lamp with a blue, low voltage, 7 1/2 watt light bulb at the head of your bed, or at your head if you're upon the floor. BLUE, by the way is the most soothing color to gaze at. Now gaze directly at the bulb in such a manner that there is a slight strain on your eyes. The light should be directly overhead, and you are peering intently at it.

Let nothing interfere with the steadiness of your gaze. Concentrate fully on the little bulb. It will appear to grow larger and smaller, as though it were breathing. Now, consciously RELAX. Feel your legs growing heavier, feel your arms growing heavier, feel your whole body growing heavier and heavier, deeply relaxing!

All the while, you breathe very slowly through both nostrils, and exhale through the mouth. Keep your gaze fixed upon the blue bulb. Think of nothing but the concentration upon the blue bulb. Detach all other thoughts from your mind. Gradually you will begin to lose all sense of feelings in your body You will feel like lead, as if you were sinking into the mattress or the floor.

It will appear as though you were entering another world. In a short while, you will not be able to move a muscle. Gradually you will pass into the hypnotic trance. There is nothing to fear. It is a very beautiful and relaxing experience. Now, while in this relaxed state, while conscious of your relaxation, you are able to repeat to yourself, once, twice, several times if you wish, what it is you want to accomplish. Make your affirmations positive.

You will, as time passes, and you practice and become expert, develop autosuggestion to so great an extent, that you will completely control your subconscious mind, to the point where it will obey your conscious desires. This is a simple technique that will bring fantastic results. It must be practiced daily. You must also have the desire to want to change yourself for the better.

Remember, that while doing this type of practice, you will have the strong desire to fall asleep. Be conscious of this desire and try to prevent it. That is at least until you reaffirm your affirmations.

Each and every time you practice autosuggestion, you will be successful in accomplishing anything you wish to accomplish. Remember, KEEP AN OPEN MIND! Avoid being dogmatic. There is always something new for you to learn in this world of material things. Learn to help yourself through autosuggestion. There is no danger in this technique. If you fall into a trance, all you will do is have a good refreshing sleep, and wake up more RELAXED than before.

UFOs: Key To Inner Perfection

HOW TO MEDITATE

Life is a rush and flurry and strain of affairs and events. Thoughts and emotions and activities are all a part of this modern life. So now comes the need for periods of real stillness, when you lay aside activity of mind as well as body; a time for you to disassociate yourself at will from the affairs and interests and become still in all your being. You will soon discover a balance in your being that will soften the strain and make your judgment surer.

The result of Meditation will open your Psychic and Spiritual awareness and help you to attune to the cosmic consciousness, both on the Astral and Etheric planes. Invisible forces will begin to work for you. If you go into this realm of Meditation with pure spiritual thoughts and a sincere desire to better yourself, so you can help to better mankind or be of service, then you will receive a great deal from your efforts, and growth will be rapid.

Practice the techniques given here or any of the above mentioned. They are all good, and will aid you in your psychic and spiritual growth. All Meditations should be slowly and deliberately conducted, taking time to experience the steps indicated. The serious student should meditate every day. Meditation often results in a feeling of vibrancy and lightness throughout the day. Clarity of vision comes from regular practice of Meditation.

You will find that true happiness can be attained, but its eternal source is within man and not without. With regular practice you will notice a subtle doorway begin to open and those who learn to pass through that doorway enter a new world of spiritual betterment. You must remember—and this is very important—that if you use these techniques for the BAD (negative), causing harm to others, it will backlash with a devastating effect.

The object of Meditation is to impress the lower consciousness with that of the higher world. There are many good books on the subject of Meditation. If you are interested, INVESTIGATE!

Now let us get to the actual technique: If you are going to Meditate at home,

UFOs: Key To Inner Perfection

bathe first, followed by deep breathing. Proper breathing is very important. Unconfine the body by wearing one light garment which will eliminate one type of physical impression from the consciousness.

You should set aside a certain time of day to Meditate, as well as the place and the duration of Meditation. What are the best hours? We have found that immediately after arising in the morning is best. The second best time will be noon and sunset.

1. Posture is important. Choose a straightback chair. Sit well back in the chair, feet firmly on the floor. Keep the spine erect, not rigid, but relaxed and straight. Head up! Hands resting on the knees, palms facing **upwards**. This should be a completely relaxed position. If you want, you can get into the Lotus position of the Yogis. The reason for not lying down is that you might fall asleep. Keep your eyes closed.

2. Breathing is next. We find that to become very relaxed, you begin with deep full breaths through the nostrils only. This we call a BALANCED BREATH. Equal counts in to equal counts out. If you can breathe in for the count of seven, let it out for the count of seven. Through your nose only. And each time you breathe in, center your concentration on the space between your eyebrows, referred to as the THIRD EYE. Take deep full breaths, filling your lungs with prana (Energy) (Life Force)

3. The next step is to suggest to yourself that you are getting very, very relaxed. Start down at your feet, and slowly work upward. Sense and feel yourself getting very relaxed. Create. My feet are relaxed, very relaxed, my legs are relaxed, very relaxed, and so on up the body. All this under your breath. When you have reached the head area, you should be ready to meditate. The highest point of realization should always be shared, sent out as a force for good. This practice is designed to help you realize that you are not your body but something apart from it, that you wear the body, work with and through it.

4. Next is the object of Meditation. We have our students select an object, a picture, a bit of verse, or a person. See this all in the Mind's eye. Sense and know that it's there. Stare at the object, picture a bit of verse. Then close your eyes and see only that, the object of your concentration. Detach yourself from all outside noises and surroundings. Breathe deeply but gently. CONCENTRATE, CONCENTRATE, CONCENTRATE. See beauty in the object. Set aside a certain period of time for this. What will come to your mind will be a great experience. ENJOY!

5. This is a subtle technique for the beginner. With time and practice, the breathing techniques will be altered and your methods will change. For the more

UFOs: Key To Inner Perfection

you practice the better you become. And you will find that you can Meditate almost anywhere at any time. But again, the best place is a certain room in your apartment or home which you consider a quiet place, a place that shuts out noise and busy surroundings. This Meditation is to be practiced daily. Now let LOVE and PEACE and VITALITY fill your body and make itself felt from head to toe!

UFOs: Key To Inner Perfection

WE CAN ALL BE PERFECT

Perfection is like looking at the picture on the face of a packet of morning glory seeds. You look inside the envelope and you see hundreds of little tiny seeds, laying there looking limp. Yet all we have to do is to plant them in fertile soil with love and light, so they are able to manifest themselves to their fullest potential. . .according to the GRAND DESIGNER.

Again you look at the picture on the face of the packet, there you see this beautiful, brilliant blue morning glory energized by the sun. Its fullest potential expressed, its reflected perfection realized, its intention fulfilled. Some of us find it hard to believe that when we look at the seed and then at the picture, that the seed is already perfection awaiting the moment to become self realized, extending itself toward reaching its greatest potential, bursting forth in its magical color, reflecting back to GOD its gift!

And you say "My GOD, this little seed is going to become that magnificent morning glory!" If we could witness this with time lapse photography that would give us a better opportunity of realizing that there is a seed pattern for everything on this planet, and throughout the universe. Who creates these patterns?

The Grand Designer, the planetary architects, the mind desire of GOD? All of the above and more! Much more. We may not fully understand the mechanics of this incredible process, but in time we will.

There has to be a mind desire to take the formless seed pattern to its fullest potential, to express itself as perfection. Seed patterns alter slightly as TIME, spiritual evolution, unfolds itself into our futures.

The little seed pattern for us human species (HOMO SAPIENS) is a creation so magnificent, the imprint so perfect, that we all have the potential of becoming the living GOD. At least this is the imprint of our becoming, of reaching that potential and eventually being able to express it to the fullest, according to the GRAND DESIGNER. I believe there is a grand designer behind every man and woman on this planet.

UFOs: Key To Inner Perfection

This planet (EARTH), the testing planet, is the classroom to express our potential to its zenith, and then go beyond. We are presented with FREE WILL and FREE CHOICE. Some individuals have no idea what that means. Yet behind the free will and free choice is the Grand Designer. At a very young age, we develop our own ideas of earthly distortions, parental programming, and taking on the conditions of our environment. The seed pattern begins to change its shape.

We are influenced by the human family, and the parameters of our original seed pattern take on grosser form. We present ourselves with limitations and doubt, so we begin to shrink our potential for whatever time frame or life time we might be trapped into at the moment. We will all eventually reach and express our seed pattern in all its superb brilliance.

Do not be saddened by these words, because the seed pattern of what you are meant to become is already with us. It's imprinted within the higher self, the reflective image of GOD manifested in all humankind. As we distort that image of GOD within ourselves, the communication between you and your higher self shrinks and fades from our conscious view. Society's view (MAINSTREAM, Homo Sapiens) is completely distorted, creating a momentary detour in the collective consciousness (LIKE ATTRACTS LIKE).

If all the hands that reach, could touch, what a better world we would have. If all the boundary lines were dissolved there would be peace on this planet! What do I mean by the boundary lines? The racial boundary lines of color, ethnic, male-female, national (NATIONS), rich and poor, religious, political, financial, academic, property, personal boundary lines by choice. There are hundreds more, all created by the false EGO, that separates man from GOD!

When boundary lines are created, the perfection of humankind begins to dissolve, and fade into the background, giving way to a state of precocious insanity where we really begin to think that WE are in charge. WE, meaning the individual I. Even though we seemed to be lost in the wilderness of our own personal struggles, the emotional conflicts of a distorted ego, the higher self waits patiently like an eagle gliding on the thermal currents of life, observing higher atmospheres, until it needs to land to nurture and for nourishment.

Then, when the higher self presents us with a momentary merger, we sense a high of spiritual inspiration, we seem to have more reverence for life all around us, we feel as though we can REALLY FORGIVE our enemies and we want to spread our enthusiasm to every one around us. These are the moments of great testing, when others think you're crazy. You go beyond what others think, because in reality it's none of your business. You sense a heightening of creativity, and a presence of LOVE so strong that it will have a lasting effect upon you, acting as a guidepost to your divine perfection on your pathway of spiritual evolution.

UFOs: Key To Inner Perfection

As we work to realize our foothold on all the emotional conflicts which are in reality those experiences provided by the GRAND DESIGNER, so we may learn the lessons of going beyond the conflicts of where we seem to be trapped!

Living life upon this planet is a series of incredible experiences that are actually assisting us with that eventual merger with our HIGHER SELVES. It's not going to be easy. Often it is indeed very painful. We have to experience many emotional deaths which can be devastating, as it takes our EGO, like a lump of silly putty being squeezed into different shapes, which oft-times resemble our personal thought forms. Where is divine perfection?

It's there waiting patiently to be discovered. The more you surrender to the emotional deaths, the more the closer highest self moves to help you realize that you are doing the right thing. These are the moments when many individuals begin to sense the presence of GOD within. These are the victorious moments when you discover that you are indeed divine perfection, that you can really love yourself, not out of EGO, but because you are one with (GOD). These are those thrilling moments when you feel so elated, and your problems seem to have vanished, that it's good to be alive.

Many may never experience these sensations in this lifetime. Everyone of us is on the planet to gain certain experiences, certain lessons to learn. Each one of us living, breathing, magnificent souls has a different pathway to walk. The way we live places us in different time frames, such as a time to work and experience, a time to love, a time to die, a time to create, a time to release. And what is so amazing is that out of the 8.1 billion individuals who live upon this planet, there are no two alike.

They are separate-individual GODS in the making, making their lives the best they can, gaining the gifts of eventually reaching and successfully merging with their HIGHER SELVES. You don't have to fight it, because it's going to happen to all of us—NOW or LATER!

Man is the only one who carries around the seed of his own perfection, yet it takes the women who receives his seed, to nurture it, to nourish it, and to bring it into life. What a magical moment. Just think for a moment, that everything in the universe is mated pairs trying to find each other, so they may come together to become the one. Your light bulb would not work, unless there was an equal polarity of both the negative and positive currents of electricity

Man is positive in polarity and the female is negative in polarity. And when those two polarities are in balance and become one, lights go on all over the world. That's why in relationships, both man and woman is on the hunt, seeking everywhere for their soul mate, their equal polarity, the other half of their perfection.

UFOs: Key To Inner Perfection

Usually out of need and impatience, we pull in the right polarity but with distorted circuits. Meaning bad relationships. Most of us attract into our lives whatever we may be projecting at the moment!

Man is 70% masculine and 30% feminine, woman is 70% feminine and 30% masculine. So with that in mind, I will suggest that the moment you can release the ego (MACHO IMAGE) and begin to merge and identify with that other percentage, you become in balance with the universe and your higher selves, and the merger with perfection is close at hand. You don't have to wait.

When you look into the mirror simply acknowledge and recognize who you really are. You are perfection seeking divine perfection. You are the GOD, I AM potential. We may not express it, but we are all a little homesick for heaven. When you merge with that other polarity within yourselves, heaven is on your doorstep.

You are more than who you think you are. You are more than your bodies. You temporarily borrow these body cases for a duration of time, to carry the spirit/personality in the physical five senses world, so we may gain the necessary experiences on this plane of existence. We do not own the body we happen to be living in at the moment. We can only occupy it. So, therefore, if you understand that it was given to us in trust, you will not prostitute your body by addictive habits, wrong thinking, and taking it for granted.

The human body is close to divine perfection as the universe itself. The universe follows a path of complete perfection, where humankind does not. We are the highest form of two brain variety creatures, of super animals in the flesh, with the greatest potential to become GODS in the true sense of the word. We have the potential of our picturing that manifestation. There is an inner intelligence that goes beyond that.

How can you tap into your higher self, when you have been programmed that you are a sinner, that you are unworthy, that you don't deserve? All these limitations block our view. All these limitations are only illusions we have created. We must begin to develop a faith within ourselves. No longer do you empower outwardly you empower the GOD within. All wisdom is at home in the higher self.

How do you tap into the higher self when you are so burdened down with your personal disbeliefs? FAITH! It comes from your heart, an inner knowing and believing, where your inner awareness seems to expand from horizon to horizon. It's a feeling of knowing, you don't know how you know—you just know. It's much the same sensation as being overshadowed by a feeling of exaltation, or being caught in a rapture.

Your personal intuition magnified by all personal experiences and millions of past lives present a much greater knowing of right from wrong. If it resonates within your heart, it's true. Dare to think for yourself, going beyond the man-made restrictions of a misguided orthodoxy. Most religions have done so much to instill fear into individuals, blocking their potential. Most religions were created by MAN. GOD has always been GOD, and will always be GOD! Religions will always change. Religion and Politics are both cancerous malignancies upon the FREE THINKER!

Whatever happened to the spiritual brotherhood that we had come to believe the church was providing us with? Today more than any other time in recorded history millions are dissolving their association with the old outdated orthodoxy. Yet today the INQUISITION still exists. The spiritual brotherhood has vanished, making way for the social cults. They are all trips! Follow the inner teacher, the inner guru, the inner master, the inner GOD. Empower yourself as being the living GOD potential.

It's time to resurrect ourselves and realize we have never done anything guilty or sinful. In the eyes of an all-loving FATHER, we are divine perfection, we have all opportunities, we have all gifts for who and where we are at the moment. When we can recognize ourselves for the first time as the GOD, I AM, the cells, molecules and atoms, will accept that command and out-picture themselves, and the physiological features of your body will begin to reorganize itself into the original seed pattern of your intended perfection.

If you're overweight (FAT) you're going to lose weight, and mold into the perfect image that you're meant to be. That's when you merge with your higher self. It's much the same as slipping on a pair of rubber gloves, that conforms to every shape. The rubber glove being in perfect form, slips onto your hand and transforms your hand into its perfection. You merge with your higher self the moment you can identify who you really are in the mirror. That's why the mirror can be your truest friend.

Have a love affair with yourself, not out of EGO, but an acknowledgment to your own inner and outer perfection. If GOD truly dwells within, at least a fragment, then how can you ever see yourself as less? I know many who go to the mirror the first thing in the morning, and stand there transfixed, looking at what the cat dragged in. They search for bloodshot eyes, crows feet at the corners, exposed pore and pimples, and snaggelly teeth. They miss seeing within themselves their own divine perfection.

I will admit that looking into the mirror early in the morning can be a horror story. Therefore you must look beyond the vision, see and acknowledge and recognize it, the more you become. The image in the mirror reflects back exactly the way you think and the way you judge yourself. Whatever you worship, you will become. Think about that the next time you go to the mirror. Change the image

UFOs: Key To Inner Perfection

that you see, see yourself in the image you want to be, and if this resonates in your heart and you begin to feel it, then you will become it!

How can you feel it, how can you tell when you're doing it right? As you look into the looking glass, and say "Mirror, Mirror on the wall, who is the fairest of them all," from the film Snow White and the Seven Dwarfs. It may seem difficult at first, but if you use your creative imagination with skill the image will change. If you feel it from the heart, the image will change constantly!

A simple technique to use while looking into the mirror, is to make an affirmation. An affirmation is the use of a few very powerful words that will keep you in focus and centered as you go beyond your own doubting. You repeat the statement (AFFIRMATION) over and over for about seven times, with a lot of conviction and positive determination. When you look into the mirror, be convinced that you already are divine perfection.

When you pronounce the words verbally (ALOUD) that is for the physical. When you whisper the words, that's for the mental. But when you think of the words, that is for the spiritual. When you think the words and feel flushed with energy surging throughout your body when your head begins to bristle in the back of your neck, and when you feel your skin tingle, that's when your higher self is merged with you. That's when you are doing it right!

You can call it being very fervent with ourselves, being in the rapture of the moment with GOD. That's all it is! This is what works for me. I know that everyone is different, yet we have to have a common meeting ground for inner exploration. I cannot assume that it will affect everyone in the same way. Yet from hundreds of the shared conceptions, it works with a great deal of success.

Within us all is the spark of self realization that leads to self discovery. Everything we've ever wanted to know is within us. The moment we stop empowering the outer, for the inner, that is when all doors unlock themselves and reveal their hidden secrets. Some individuals feel like they are trapped in their bodies. Remember we don't own our bodies, they are only entrusted to us for a duration of time. The body is meant to be utilized maturely.

The physical body is the outer reflection of the inner consciousness. Like all living things, it has to be nurtured, loved, worked so it may enjoy the living dance of evolution. It may seem that the female carries the greatest burden. The man implants the seed within the woman, but it takes the woman to fertilize it, to manifest it into form so it may express itself in full materialization, and outpicture its divine perfection.

The woman is imbued with more intuition and wisdom for her task as the living mother. Man is still the warrior in disguise, yet the moment he gets in touch

UFOs: Key To Inner Perfection

with his feminine aspect, his duality, he merges with his higher self, and eventually into the androgenous state. The androgenous state is when both man and woman merge with themselves, the masculine and feminine aspects of themselves. This will be a much higher state of perfection, where both polarities of the individual are merged equally.

Don't panic, you will have plenty of time to have relationships that will present you with some wonderful conflicts awarding you a chance to experience and grow. Eventually our hot passionate lusting will dissipate itself, making way for a highly creative, tremendously talented, satisfied being, filled with unconditional love for all humankind; a person who treats others as he wants to be treated, an individual so totally focused and centered, so spiritually motivated that he will be of greater benefit to all humankind.

Sound boring? Sound tedious? It all depends upon your point of view. Aiming for perfection is only for those individuals who have the courage to want to change themselves, who want to go beyond the man-made restrictions of our programmed society, who dare to be different, who are so totally unsatisfied with the present conditions on our home planet, that they have released the myth, the anchors of yesterday to risk the fear of losing everything they have to touch the light of the universe. The universe is what is awaiting all of us in future time, a time when we will sail through the heavens and be completely at home. Many feel deeply within their hearts, that this planet is not their home. There lingers deeply within the superconscious the haunting sensation that pulls us heavenward; an inner working that something so magnificent awaits us all.

True perfection dwells in your heart, the point of all feeling. Today more than any other epoch of time, great changes are taking place. The prophecies of old are becoming today's reality. Yesterday is dead—LET IT GO! Move forward to the NOW! This is all we have and know! Tomorrow will take care of itself when it arrives.

The GRAND DESIGNER is perfect.

UFOs: Key To Inner Perfection

ABOUT THE AUTHORS

MARC BRINKERHOFF

In UFOlogical terms, if anyone sees a UFO more than once or claims numerous encounters, they are known as a "repeater." Because they feel the odds of meeting up with an ET even once has to be in the million to one range, most conservative UFO researchers and the various "scientific minded" investigative groups tend to frown on the claims of such individuals. For the most part, they do not take too kindly to the likes of "repeaters," though there are always a few exceptions to any rule.

Marc Brinkerhoff claims to have established an ongoing relationship with aliens, but he also seems to have the uncanny ability to point his camera at the heavens and take photographs of things that have no business being in the sky. Marc's first UFO experience took place when he was just five years old on an athletic field near the Mahopac, NY high school. As best as he can recall, it was around 3 P.M. when he observed a large silvery sphere, "like the metal ball in a

UFOs: Key To Inner Perfection

pin-ball machine. No sound was heard," but he does remember, "receiving a feeling of great love from it."

Since that day, Brinkerhoff contends that extraterrestrials have been contacting him and other humans. Apparently, they are programming us to save the world and the universe from a possible destruction. He sees the aliens as being benevolent, human-like, "Space Brothers," who are here NOT to harm us, but to lead us along the path to spiritual enlightenment and to usher in the New Age.

Marc is also the author of the book, "Your Spirit Animal Helpers" along with Phyllis Giarnes, and the art book, "Marc Brinkerhoff ~ Animal & Fantasy Art" and says that his aim is to capture the noble spirits of all creatures he paints or draws, and in some way bring their soul voices to the world. Much of his inspiration comes from studying Michelangelo, Buonarroti, Raphael and Leonardo da Vinci along with horse and animal artists like George Stubbs, Edwin Landseer, Sam Savitt, Ralph Thompson, Wesley Dennis, Rein Poortvielt and C. W. Anderson.

http://www.intergalacticmission.com/index.html

http://www.marcbrinkerhoff.com/pages/paintings.html

UFOs: Key To Inner Perfection

SHAWN ROBBINS

Shawn Robbins is a paranormal investigator, ghost hunter and psychic who has revealed on the air how people can spot a UFO.

Active for many years in the field, Shawn is a noted psychic and paranormal researcher who has been ranked one of the top ten psychics in the world. For years her predictions were covered in the New Years edition of the National Enquirer. During her career, she has been a special consultant for the New York City Police Department, United States Navy, and numerous leading Corporations.

Shawn Robbins is the author of four best selling books including the new hard back edition of WICCAPEDIA, Sterling Publishers ,now in its second printing. Other best sellers include "Shawn Robbins Prophecies For The End Of Time," "More Prophecies For The Coming Millennium," and "Ahead Of Myself."

She is an expert in the field of mystical, spiritual, and psychic sciences, having lectured extensively on these subjects throughout her career. Shawn was one of the three original psychics in the CIA Stargate program trained to spy on the Soviet Government. Her code name was Madame Zodiac.

UFOs: Key To Inner Perfection

Shawn was one of the original ghost hunters and mediums utilized by famed parapsychologist Hans Holzer in dozens of haunted houses across America. She was also an instructor at Tim Beckley's New York School of Occult Arts and Sciences.

Look for Shawn Robbins On Facebook

https://www.facebook.com/profile.php?id=100008530788284

UFOs: Key To Inner Perfection

TIMOTHY GREEN BECKLEY

Timothy Green Beckley is a UFO & paranormal pioneer. Since an early age his life has more or less revolved around the paranormal. The house he was raised in was thought to be haunted, he underwent out of body experiences at age six, and saw his first of three UFOs when he was ten. The event stunned him so much that he took out every book on the subject that he could find in the library. He wrote to the local media questioning the policy of silence he was convinced was taking place worldwide.

At fourteen, he was already appearing on national radio and TV, proclaiming the existence of the aliens (whom he now believes to be inter-dimensional to some extent and, as another likely possibility, the product of Nazi wartime technology.)

Beckley began his writing/publishing career in his youth. At age 14, he purchased a mimeograph machine and began putting out "The Interplanetary News Service Report." Over the years, he has written over 50 books on everything from rock music to the MJ-12 documents. He has been a stringer for the national tabloids, such as the Enquirer, the Star and the Globe, and the editor of over 30 different magazines (most of which never lasted more than a couple of issues). His longest running effort was the newsstand publication UFO UNIVERSE, which ran for 11 years. Today he is the president of Inner Light/Global Communications.

www.conspiracyjournal.com

www.teslasecretlab.com

UFOs: Key To Inner Perfection

RECOMMENDED WEBSITES

UFO WARMINSTER

Welcome to the UFO-Warminster website.

This web site is intended to be the definitive site for information about the phenomenon that haunted the skies above the small, quiet, rural town of Warminster, in Wiltshire, during the 1960s and 1970s. Its aim it to be encyclopedic rather than analytical, although analytical — and perhaps whimsical — articles will be posted as and when.

We have provided scanned images of Ken Rogers' *Warminster UFO Newsletter*, Peter Paget's *The Fountain Journal* all issues of the newsletter produced by the UFO-Info organisation.

We have also provided a variety of other information about the Warminster mystery.

We can never be sure what caused the events around the town — they might have been the result of UFOs, natural phenomena, the army, mass hysteria, or whatever you personally believe. However, of this we can be sure — for many years the the town was the focal point for *something* interesting.

This site is edited and hosted by Steve Dewey and Kevin Goodman.

Steve Dewey is the co-author, with John Ries, of *In Alien Heat* (Anomalist Books, 2006). This book is a historical and cultural appraisal of the Warminster phenomenon. Steve is skeptical about UFOs and other related phenomena.

Kevin Goodman is the author, with Steve Dewey of *UFO Warminster: Cradle of Contact*. This book chronicles the events Kevin and his friends experienced in the town during the mid-1970s. Kevin has a more open mind on the Warminster mystery.

http://www.ufo-warminster.co.uk/

FACEBOOK GROUPS

WARMINSTER UFO SKYWATCHER
Digital night vision skywatching

In and around the Wessex triangle,and the UFO subject generally.....along with ancient sites and energies and ley lines...and most of all...keeping that flame burning for the Warminster mystery

UFO WARMINSTER COMMUNITY

AN EXCITING WORK OUT OF THE PAGES OF UFO HISTORY

CAN EXTRATERRESTRIALS SHOW US THE SECRETS OF TRUE HAPPINESS? WHAT ARE THE METHODS FOR LIVING IN HARMONY WITH EVERYONE ON THIS PLANET? WHAT ARE THE SPECIFIC COSMIC LAWS EACH OF US NEEDS TO UNDERSTAND IN ORDER TO SURVIVE AND EVENTUALLY FIND THEIR TRUE PLACE ON THE PATH TO PERFECTION?

Wars! Disasters! Personal Hardships - Death!

We have to deal with such devastation on a daily basis while inhabiting our physical bodies whilst living on a very imperfect, materialistic, planet. But is there a better more superior way to an individual utopia?

Is it possible that extraterrestrials have developed an inner cosmic wisdom that when shared with the human race could pave the way to establishing a virtual heaven on earth? Can they look into the true depths of our soul and see our imperfections and direct us along a more positive path in life?

Here are two books-in-one originally published during the Golden Age Of Flying Saucers which reveal the true experiences of UFO contactees Cederic Allingham and Dino Kraspedon and their all-too-fantastic meetings with alien beings from far off worlds.

Their stories are intriguing, controversial and full of awe, but in the end it is up to the reader to decide their validity.

INCLUDES AUTHENTIC PHOTOS OF SPACE SHIPS AND ALIEN BEINGS

Cederic Allingham and Dino Kraspedon are two of the most controversial authors of the Golden Age of Flying Saucers. A British astronomer, Allingham captured a photo of a being from another planet — all be it as he walked back to his ship — as well as a device which looks much like the photos of the space ships that George Adamski snapped a couple of years earlier. Some say that Allingham never really existed though he did speak before a local UFO group before disappearing.

One of the original UFO contactees operating from Brazil, Kraspedon told of meetings with loving beings from outer space with a great knowledge of science and technology which they were willing to share with humankind. Later, Dino was arrested for being a terrorist as his message of peace, love and universal brotherhood, took an alarming turn. This book is an exact report of these early UFO manuscripts with an extensive update by Beckley and Casteel, two well known researchers.

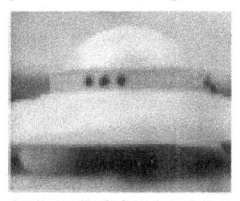

( ) SPECIAL OFFER: Published to sell at $27.00

SPECIAL PRICE TO OUR READERS IS ONLY $22.00 + $5 S/H
Order Flying Saucers From Mars and My Contact With Flying Saucers
TWO BOOKS IN ONE VOLUME!

(Just ask for Flying Saucer Contact Book and we will know what you mean).

**Timothy Beckley • Box 753
New Brunswick, NJ 08903
PayPal Orders - MRUFO8@hotmail.com**

Also available. The most important UFO film of all time. UFO! Approx 90 minutes. Circa 1956. Real movies released with Pentagon approval! - Add $20 to order ($42 total plus $5 S/H)

EXPOSING THE UFO FEAR FACTOR!

DANGER LURKS ALONGSIDE OF US IN THE DARK! THE ULTRA-TERRESTRIALS TAKE ON A VARIETY OF HORRIFYING SHAPES AND TERRIFYING FORMS! THEY HAVE ATTEMPTED TO TAKE CONTROL OF OUR THOUGHTS AND POSSESS OUR SOULS AND BODIES!

Here are authentic accounts from the "Twilight Zone" of UFOlogy! Stories of encounters with the supposedly friendly "all-too-cute" ETs are NOT always the norm and represent only one side of the coin. Little Elliot may have befriended Steven Spielberg's cozy, cuddly alien, but all too often our almond-eyed visitors have been known to abduct, dice and slice and put us through a universe of utter torment.

Not only can the Ultra-Terrestrials be damned ornery but they have the power to interfere with both our physical and mental states and put dread into our hearts. Thus the term "UFO Fear Factor."

They can often wreak havoc on an entire household following what might seem like a benign close encounter but which ends up going well beyond a cosmic one-night stand. The Ultra-Terrestrials possess various characteristics in common with spirits from the dark corridors of demonology and have been known to produce the same sort of phenomena at UFO landing sites as you would find in a haunted house or at a séance.

* Witness grows 5 inches following close encounter! Hair of observer changes color overnight! * West Virginia man abducted by weird "vegetable"-like Ultra-Terrestrials. * Valuable objects vanish upon arrival of strange shadow beings in New Jersey home. * The mystery of the "Crawling Stumps" in Oregon. * Giants bully youngsters in Brazilian UFO terror attack. * "Fireballs" cause massive blackout. * A man named "Fred" (a pseudonym) recalls under hypnosis a horrifying sexual experience involving a half human/half animal creature. * Dr. Karla Turner, who passed away from breast cancer after she started reporting on the negative aspects of the UFO abduction phenomenon, noted: "A surprising number of abductees suffer from serious illnesses they didn't have before their encounters. These have led to surgery, debilitation, and even death from causes the doctors can't identify."

Some abductees experience a degeneration of their mental, social and spiritual well being. Obsessive behavior frequently erupts, such as drug abuse, alcoholism, overeating and promiscuity. Strange obsessions develop and cause the disruption of normal life and the destruction of personal relationships. * Noted author/researcher Brad Steiger offers evidence that many individuals hear the guttural voices of Ultra-terrestrials commanding them to perform demonic deeds. Such was the case of a self-declared prophet of a new religion linked to the slain bodies of a family of five—all victims of human sacrifice thought to be necessary to persuade the "forces" to present the Ohio-based cult with a magical golden sword. * Some of the human implications of what the Ultraterrestrial "invasion" represents are so potentially disturbing and disruptive that well-known talk show personality/investigator Peter Robbins declares that he has no doubt that there are "those" who are capable of just about anything in their efforts to keep the subject from us, including possibly being involved in the untimely deaths of certain truth seekers whose lives have been decidedly "glamorously" entangled with the Unknown.

UFOS -THE DARK SIDE • SUGGESTED READING

( ) **ROUND TRIP TO HELL IN A FLYING SAUCER**
UFO Parasites - Alien Soul Suckers - Invaders From Demonic Realms by Cecil Michael, Tim Beckley, Nick Redern—Does Satan drive a flying saucer? Are demons abducting humans and performing sadistic rituals?
305 pages—large format—ISBN-13: 978-1606110911—$21.95

( ) **UFOS – WICKED THIS WAY COMES** by Tim Beckley, Peter Robbins, Tim Swartz, Scott Corrales—The Ultra-Terrestrials possess various characteristics in common with spirits from the dark corridors of demonology and have been known to produce the same sort of phenomena at UFO landing sites as you would find in a haunted house or at a seance.
268 pages—large format—ISBN-13: 978-1606111581—$21.95

( ) **EVIL EMPIRE OF THE ETS AND ULTRA-TERESTRIALS** by Tim Beckley, Dr Karla Turner, Brad and Sherry Steiger, Sean Casteel—Witnesses tell tales of unbelievable aggression: "The creatures were hostile and went into attack modes several times, putting up dense fogs. One time when they stopped; It was like a backwards tornado coming from the mouth of the leader of the ships. It was like a ray that he was sending down a funnel. He did it five times, then he left…"
286 pages—large format—ISBN-13: 978-1606111154—$21.95

( ) **CURSE OF THE MEN IN BLACK: RETURN OF UFO TERRORISTS** by Timothy Green Beckley with John Stuart—One by one they have given up their research - perhaps even their lives! — forced to go underground because of threats from the shadowy beings. Are these individuals government agents gone a muck or sinister aliens?
—Large format—ISBN-13: 978-1606110867—$21.95

( ) **TRILOGY OF THE UNKNOWN** by Michael X Barton, with Timothy Beckley—A telepathic message from what were supposed to be benevolent Nordic-type aliens turned out to put the author in great jeopardy when he was shot at by "dark forces." Cat and mouse game with Nazi UFOs, underground races and aliens who want us to keep off the moon.
Large format — 172 page—ISBN-13: 978-1606111079—$19.95

SUPER SPECIAL -ALL 5 BOOKS THIS PAGE— $89.95
(MAIL ORDER CUSTOMERS)
Timothy Green Beckley • Box 753 • New Brunswick, NJ 08903
PayPal: MRUFO8@hotmail.com

UFOs: Key To Inner Perfection

UFOs: Key To Inner Perfection

www.ingramcontent.com/pod-product-compliance
Lightning Source LLC
Chambersburg PA
CBHW081916170426
43200CB00014B/2749